A POWERFUL MIND

A Powerful Mind

THE SELF-EDUCATION ——— *of* ——— GEORGE WASHINGTON

Adrienne M. Harrison

Potomac Books
An imprint of the University of Nebraska Press

© 2015 by the Board of Regents of
the University of Nebraska
All rights reserved. Potomac Books is an imprint
of the University of Nebraska Press.
Manufactured in the United States of America. ♾

Library of Congress Cataloging-in-Publication Data
Harrison, Adrienne M., 1979–
A powerful mind: the self-education of George
Washington / Adrienne M. Harrison.
pages   cm
Includes bibliographical references and index.
ISBN 978-1-61234-725-7 (cloth: alk. paper)
ISBN 978-1-61234-789-9 (epub)
ISBN 978-1-61234-790-5 (mobi)
ISBN 978-1-61234-791-2 (pdf)
1. Washington, George, 1732–1799 — Knowledge
and learning. 2. Presidents — Education — United
States — History — 18th century.
3. Generals — Education — United
States — History — 18th century. 4.
Presidents — United States — Biography. 5.
Generals — United States — Biography. I. Title.
E312.17.H33 2015   973.4'1092 — dc23
[B]   2015013336

Set in Arno by M. Scheer.
Designed by N. Putens.

For my parents

*Having no opportunity to improve
from example, let us read.*

GEORGE WASHINGTON, 1755

CONTENTS

George Washington and I go back a while. My obsession with every-thing related to Washington's life and world began years ago when as a child I was captivated by the 1984 miniseries *George Washington*, which was sponsored by the General Motors Corporation and starred Barry Bostwick and Patty Duke. I'm sure my parents quickly came to regret their choice of programs to record on their shiny new VCR because I was instantly hooked and soon watched the six-hour series over and over again, nearly wearing out the tapes in the process. My parents probably assumed at the time that this newfound interest would pass, much as any fad that captures the attention of a five-year-old. Little did they know that George Washington would remain at the center of my scholarly interests from kindergarten through graduate school and beyond.

When I was young, the stories of Washington's dangerous exploits in the wilderness and on the battlefield were the most captivating. The details about how Washington survived a plunge into an icy river only to then escape a would-be assassin while returning from his first-ever military mission, how he had four horses shot from under him dur-ing Braddock's defeat, and how he personally led his army across the Delaware River one fateful Christmas morning — all were endlessly fascinating and made him seem larger than life. As I grew older, my interests and questions about Washington continued to evolve. Over time I became more interested in how he rose to such prominence in his lifetime and how his popularity endured long after his death. When

I was a cadet at the U.S. Military Academy at West Point, my senior thesis centered on Washington's tour of the southern states in 1791 and argued that he used the tour to shore up faith in the federal government and demonstrate his tacit support of Alexander Hamilton's funding and assumption plan. I was, however, not done with Washington after I earned my bachelor's degree. My thesis experience left me with several lingering questions that I kept in the back of my mind as I packed my books away and headed off to begin my career as an army officer.

There was no doubt that my classmates and I, commissioned in 2002, were destined for service in Afghanistan and, as was to become evident in early 2003, Iraq. I served three tours in Iraq and all in successive leadership positions: platoon leader, company executive officer, and finally company commander. During those long, seemingly endless days in combat, my fellow soldiers and I each did what we could to maintain a sense of normalcy in our lives by devoting the odds and ends of free time we had to hobbies that passed the time and kept us connected to our homes halfway around the world. Some people became gym rats and spent hours lifting weights. Others, like my platoon sergeant, were enthralled by the latest advent in entertainment technology at the time — television shows made available on DVD — and devoted hour after hour to watching everything they could get their hands on from *Buffy the Vampire Slayer* to *The Sopranos*. As for me, I did spend some time in the gym and watched DVDs along with the tiny snippets of news that were beamed to us courtesy of the American Forces Network, but I spent the bulk of my free time reading, thanks to my considerate friends and family who sent history books to me. I also placed orders with Amazon, one of a few merchants that shipped to our overseas army post office addresses.

The combination of my continued interest in reading history and my real-life experiences of leading troops, many of whom were older and had spent considerably more time in the army than I had, in a seemingly endless conflict led me to reconsider those old questions about the nature of Washington's success and subsequent fame that had stuck with me since completing my undergraduate thesis. As I learned how to plan and make decisions based on constantly changing intelligence while doing my best to earn my soldiers' respect and keep them motivated during a war that nearly everyone in the media had deemed hopeless and unwinnable, I thought about how Washington executed the same basic leadership tasks in his career, although obviously the times and the context were hugely different. In the middle of Baghdad the enormity of Washington's leadership challenges hit me from a totally different perspective than I had ever previously considered, for the art of leadership is a relative constant; only the circumstances change over time. Faced with my own contemporary challenges, I thought about the tremendous handicap that crippled Washington — that is, his lack of formal education and military training (apart from a few fencing lessons) — before he assumed an enormous military responsibility when he was my age. I therefore became enthralled all over again by the question of just how Washington did it. This book sheds new light on the subject.

Given that I have spent the majority of my life studying Washington, I freely admit that I have a deep and abiding respect for him despite his faults. His natural talent for leadership was remarkable, and he had a keen understanding of how to perform in a manner that magnified his strengths while simultaneously camouflaging his weaknesses. Over the course of his long career in the public light, Washington had more failures than successes, yet he inspired loyalty from those around him and retained his hold on power even in the face of mounting criticism. Moreover, he mastered the art of relinquishing authority, thus ensuring that the institutions he helped to establish would endure after he was gone. All of that said, Washington had a volatile temper and was incredibly thin skinned. Many of his contemporaries thought his natural aloofness signaled a wooden or even an icy personality. He lacked self-confidence and obsessively sought approval from those around him. Ambition drove him in all of his pursuits, and he was aggressive in matters of business. In other words, Washington was flawed. The real

Washington, whom historians have relentlessly pursued since he rose to international prominence after America gained its independence, had his positive and negative character traits, much as we might rationally expect. In the nineteenth century, historians and biographers, buying into the idea of Manifest Destiny, tended to portray Washington as a demigod and duly gave him pride of place in the pantheon of American heroes. Over time, however, the experience of two world wars, the emergence of the United States as a superpower that nonetheless experienced serious a setback in the Cold War with the loss of Vietnam, and the social upheaval wrought by the civil rights movement collectively reshaped the lenses by which more modern historians viewed the early American past. The result was an emphasis on interpreting history from the perspective of the populace, sparking a wave of revisionism that tended to minimize the role of the founding fathers, including that of Washington.

When embarking on this project, my goal was (and still is) to strike a balance between the old poles and unveil a hidden dimension of Washington in a manner that has never been done before, but that perfect balance has sometimes proved difficult to find. In graduate school, my dissertation adviser, Paul Clemens, admonished me to tone down what, in his opinion, was my tendency to describe Washington in an overtly celebratory manner. Trying to be a good student I did my best to heed his advice and thought I did a good job of trimming adjectives. Alas, at my dissertation defense as soon as he congratulated me on becoming Dr. Harrison, he immediately added that the slant was still there. At first, I was deflated, for I thought I had done my due diligence in hacking away at my own writing. Any writer can attest that one of the hardest tasks for an author is to cull the words that he or she has so painstakingly composed. Upon further reflection, however, I realized that my adviser's criticism was not a bad thing, because it meant that he was still engaging me in a scholarly conversation. He did not criticize my evidence, just the position I took on it. If my readers find a pro-Washington bias in the pages that follow, I offer no apology because it is the job of the historian to interpret evidence and make arguments. Those who disagree with my arguments are, as was my adviser, free to debate the issues. If that happens, I view this book as a success, for lively discussions are the avenue by which history remains relevant.

I have accumulated many debts while completing this project. First I must thank the members of my doctoral dissertation committee — Paul Clemens, Ann Fabian, Jan Lewis, and Ted Crackel — for indulging my interest in Washington and for being generous with their time and attention. I am further indebted to the members of the Rutgers University History Department, including Seth Koven, Alastair Bellany, Jennifer Jones, Phyllis Mack, Rudy Bell, Virginia Yans, Paul Israel, Peter Silver, and Camilla Townsend. Each pushed me to open my mind and look at history from vantage points I had never previously considered, and my abilities as a scholar and educator were greatly enhanced under their influence. Also I wish to thank Katie Lee, my friend and fellow graduate student in early American history, for all of the discussions concerning our respective dissertation topics that enriched both my thoughts and my writing.

This project was completed during my tenure as an assistant professor in the Department of History at the U.S. Military Academy, and I owe enormous gratitude to the faculty there. In particular, I wish to thank Brig. Gen. Lance Betros (Ret.) for giving a former cadet the chance to return to the department as a colleague. I also wish to thank my bosses Col. James (Ty) Seidule, Col. Gian Gentile (Ret.), Col. Gail Yoshitani, and Col. Gregory Daddis for their support and encouragement. Additionally I wish to thank Robert McDonald, who was once my undergraduate adviser, then my colleague, and always my friend, for his willingness to make useful recommendations and to listen to me develop my arguments. It seems that even now, I have not yet ceased to be his student. I also need to thank my friends and officemates Maj. Dwight Mears and Maj. Katherine Opie. Dwight's relentless pace of scholarship was both an inspiration and a challenge to emulate. Katie patiently listened to me talk about Washington within the confines of our office and during my course lectures, and she was even willing to travel with me to local historic sites, never wavering in her encouragement. Katie and I designed our electives on the age of exploration and colonial America together and fostered in our students a love of the early modern world that Washington inherited and reshaped. The conversations we had about these courses changed the way that I think and write about Washington's life and legacy and made me a better scholar. Furthermore, Maj. Andy Forney, Rasheed Hosein, Nick Sambaluk, John Stapleton, Dan Franke, Ray Hrinko, and Sam Watson all listened to me repeatedly talk about this project and were constant in their support, as were the members of the American History Division and the faculty cohort with which I entered the academy. I also owe an enormous debt of gratitude to the editorial committee at the University of Nebraska Press; to my acquisitions editor, Kristen Elias Rowley; and to the entire editorial department for shepherding my manuscript through the academic publishing process.

Finally I would like to thank my parents, family, and friends who have listened to me talk about George Washington for decades. My parents took me to historic sites when I was a child and endured my endless curiosity and tireless chatter about subjects they probably had little interest in at the time. In many ways, I must not have been an easy child to raise, and I'm grateful for all support. My mother even went so far as to make me a George Washington Halloween costume, and to this day she is always ready to jump in the car for a trip to Williamsburg, Mount Vernon, or whatever other historic destination that I want to visit. She has always been the ultimate cheerleader, and there are not enough words to express my gratitude for her degree of dedication. To everyone here and to those I did not mention by name but nonetheless treasure, thank you.

A POWERFUL MIND

Introduction

In 1812, or nearly thirteen years after George Washington's death, an aging and bitter John Adams dashed off a letter to his friend and Washington critic Benjamin Rush. "Washington was not a scholar," he told Rush. "That he was too illiterate, too unlearned, unread for his station and reputation is equally past dispute."[1] It is not difficult to imagine the irascible Adams hunched over his desk in Quincy, surrounded by the library that he had accumulated over a lifetime of scholarly pursuits. At age seventy-seven, his eyes were failing. He fumed over Washington's annoyingly enduring legacy as America's first "sainted" president. In Adams's estimation, Washington was hardly the self-made hero; on the contrary, Adams would argue that he had made George Washington's reputation by nominating him to become the commander in chief of the Continental Army in 1775. Washington then achieved lasting fame by looking the part on horseback, pulling off a good act that carefully masked the fact that he was intellectually not qualified for the positions he occupied. Washington had admirable qualities to be sure, and in better moods Adams could see them. He admired Washington and respected him, particularly his "noble and disinterested" character, which led Adams to conclude that there was "something charming ... in the conduct of Washington."[2] However, Adams's pride in his own scholarly prowess combined with a healthy disdain for those who thwarted his ambitions often colored his judgment. As such, his harsh criticism of Washington must be read bearing in mind that Adams was still sulking over the decline of his own reputation and his failure to win a second presidential term. Nevertheless, his uncharitable assessment has run through the scholarship on Washington almost from the time the ink dried on Adams's letter. It is important to note, however, that Adams and the other critics who scoffed at Washington's so-called illiteracy were unaware that he had engaged in a lifelong program of self-directed reading that was specifically designed to provide him with the useful knowledge he needed to perform each of his occupations.

Fortunately for Washington, even the harshest critics who cited Adams's slight against Washington's intellectual standing spared Washington's overall legacy from the decline that some of the other most prominent founding fathers endured. A famous example is Thomas Jefferson, whose star rose thanks to his brilliance as America's most enlightened founder but fell following the revelation that the rumors that he had had a relationship with his slave Sally Hemings were true.[3] Benjamin Franklin's overall reputation, his intellectual prowess notwithstanding, was similarly tarnished by evidence that he was a womanizer who enjoyed getting cozy with young ladies, even those who were married to other men.[4] John Adams was tainted both in life and death with charges of vanity, mostly because his confidence in his own intellectual abilities tended to negatively impact his relationships with others.[5] Washington, however, has mostly managed to escape the scrutiny of revisionist historians and critics unscathed. Try as they might, no flaws they unearthed, not even Adams's charge of illiteracy, were enough to unseat Washington from his place in the American memory.

Why is this true? Is it really possible that only one of the founding fathers was that perfect while the others were simply human? Even those who do not think too highly of Washington's abilities and decry the manner in which Americans have deified him have a hard time finding any real evidence of character flaws other than his having a wooden personality and elitist manner. It seems that whatever the full extent of Washington's flaws were, he did a pretty good job of hiding them from historians' probes. Washington's act of working assiduously to conceal his imperfections from the public gaze while presenting a carefully crafted image has been widely studied and goes a long way to explain the degree of lasting fame that he was able to achieve. Over the course of his lifetime, Washington mastered the art of performance. He excelled at reading his audiences and had a natural talent for knowing exactly how to behave in order to attain their approbation. He achieved greatness by acting great, but it is not the whole story behind the success of Washington's self-fashioning.

Washington's physical graces may have helped him capture the attention of the right people over the years, but once placed in positions of responsibility, he had to deliver. This one point must be distinctly understood: over time Washington developed a perfectionist mentality that drove him in all of his pursuits. He was thoroughly a man of the eighteenth-century world wherein a gentleman's honor hinged on his ability to succeed. To make it in Virginia society, Washington had to excel in building wealth and cultivating a reputation through public service. Achieving these goals required a certain amount of useful knowledge, and Washington pursued it throughout his life.

Born the third son of a middling planter in colonial Virginia, Washington dreamed of climbing to the top of provincial society. His father planned on the boy being educated in England to equip him for moving up in society; however, those plans were aborted with his father's death when Washington was only eleven. Deprived of the educational opportunities afforded to his older half-brothers, the adolescent Washington suddenly realized the scale of the disadvantage he faced. He did have the chance to attend some local schools as a youth, and he had his older half-brothers to mentor him and introduce him to influential men who would become patrons to the upwardly mobile young man. Washington's mentors picked up where the schoolmasters left off, introducing him to the books and subjects he would need to have a working knowledge of to make his way in the world. This period of early intellectual development following his father's death is when he began to read with a purpose.

Many historians and biographers, including those who have explored the extent of Washington's self-fashioning, have largely overlooked his diligent reading. The overall trend in previous scholarship ranged between two extreme positions: either Washington was born with an inherent greatness that of course precipitated his meteoric rise or he had limited talents and owed his rise more to chance and the goodwill of others who were willing to see more in him than actually existed. David Humphreys wrote the first biography of Washington with his cooperation and editing; it was sparse on detail but overburdened with hero worship. Mason Locke Weems made the next significant effort to boost Washington's mythology with a hardly factual biography in which Weems famously proclaimed that as a boy Washington could not lie about chopping down his father's cherry tree. In the mid-nineteenth century, Jared Sparks, Washington Irving, James Paulding, and Joel Headley each wrote more factual yet still reverent biographies of Washington and argued the case for his inherent greatness. In the post–Civil War years when the historiographical trend turned more toward realism, biographers such as Henry Cabot Lodge, Woodrow Wilson, and Paul Leicester Ford attempted to chip away at the romanticized facade and make Washington human again. Still none of them could seem to unearth any significant humanizing flaws that would diminish his standing. In the 1920s Rupert Hughes and William Woodward tried to portray Washington the man rather than the myth, but they were heavily criticized for going too far and finding more flaws than Washington actually possessed.

Fortunately for Washington scholarship, the publication of John C. Fitzpatrick's more comprehensive edition of Washington's papers enabled biographers in the second half of the twentieth century to base their work on a more concrete footing. Some of the best-known recent biographers include Douglas Southall Freeman, James Thomas Flexner, Barry Schwartz, and Ron Chernow.[6] For these biographers, Fitzpatrick's and the later editions of Washington's papers published by the University of Virginia have built up the evidentiary base significantly, but the old analytical trends still persist in albeit more subtle ways. Each of the more recent biographies portrays Washington as almost completely uninterested in anything to do with scholarly pursuits. While Freeman pays considerable tribute to Washington's positive character traits — such as his self-discipline, honor, willpower, dedication, integrity, and so forth — he also argues that "although his words usually were the mirror of his mind and his nature was disclosed daily in the transaction of business, none of his comrades . . . could believe that he actually was as simple as he proved to be."[7] Furthermore, the tone of Freeman's treatment of Washington suggests that he was born with some of these traits and was successful through diligence. Freeman pays almost no attention to Washington's education and none to his reading or his library.[8] Freeman's research made a significant impact. His work became the standard on which most of the biographies since have been based including Flexner's four-volume series published in the between 1965 and 1972, Willard Sterne Randall's one-volume biography published in 1998, and most recently Chernow's one-volume biography published in 2010. Schwartz's *George Washington: The Making of an American Symbol* is not a traditional biography but rather a study of Washington's elevation to virtual American sainthood. Schwartz definitely hints on more than one occasion that Washington may not have merited his exalted status.

All of these biographers correctly assert that Washington had considerable physical gifts that enabled him to stand out on a dance floor, as well as look good in uniform and powerful on horseback. But he also possessed a good mind that remained focused on the goals he set for himself. While it is true that he was not the most brilliant or imaginative thinker of his generation, he was far more intellectual than either historians or his contemporaries, such as Adams, recognized. One particular example is the study of agriculture, the great passion of Washington's life. As this book illustrates, Washington read and studied the latest farming and horticultural treatises and experimented with them at Mount Vernon in order to revolutionize and expand his modest tobacco plantation into a diverse agricultural empire over the course of forty years. So why have both the scholars who praise Washington's greatness and those who argue for a less exalted interpretation largely missed his intellectual dimension? They overlooked it because Washington did a very good job at hiding it. He was forever conscious of what he called his defective education and went to great lengths to disguise it. He did read, but that reading was a solitary pursuit. There are few concrete examples of Washington borrowing books from friends and neighbors as Franklin did in his youth. Washington seldom recommended books to others the way that Jefferson and Adams did. He made very few literary allusions in his writings and speeches. Plenty of anecdotal evidence, however, tells of Washington leading the hunt and dancing the night away in the grandest ballrooms of the land. Therefore, on the surface it appeared that Washington had little interest in reading. Again this conclusion is incorrect, and one obvious resource refutes the assumptions it was based on — the sizable private library Washington amassed at Mount Vernon over the course of his lifetime.

Nearly every scholar who examined Washington largely overlooked this enormous window into his mind. To date few have studied the library at Mount Vernon. The first to do so was Appleton P. C. Griffin, who developed an annotated catalog of those of Washington's books that the Boston Athenaeum bought in the 1870s and 1880s. Griffin examined each of the three hundred volumes in the athenaeum and painstakingly traced the remaining six hundred volumes that had mostly been sold at auctions across the nation. Included in the catalog is the annotated version of the estate inventory made following Washington's death in 1799, the only known complete list. Griffin's work is the primary reference that historians have used when referring to Washington and his books. Although it is a good resource, it does not shed much light on how Washington read those books or if he read them at all. Another example is the slim volume *The Library at Mount Vernon* by Frances Laverne Carroll and Mary Meacham, published for the Mount Vernon Ladies Association in 1977. It includes the inventory taken of the library at Mount Vernon in 1783 but exhibits just as much interest in the furnishings of the room as in its books.

The appendix to Paul K. Longmore's book *The Invention of George Washington* contains the best study of Washington's reading. Longmore's book traces the interaction between Washington's career and his public image from his debut in the Seven Years' War through the onset of the Revolution and to July 1776. Longmore shows how Washington went from being an upstart militia officer to becoming the "Father of his Country" by connecting his image with the political ideology and cultural values of his time. What Longmore effectively demonstrates is that Washington was more politically shrewd than commonly thought and more closely in touch with the views of his contemporaries than many gave him credit for. He was the ultimate political leader who constantly sought to be perceived as embodying the highest ideals of his society.[9]

In covering Washington's career in public service from his blundering beginnings to his becoming a national symbol, Longmore tries to leave no aspect of the self-fashioning effort unexplored. He portrays Washington as someone who managed to strike the perfect balance between selfishness and public mindedness, between egotism and patriotism. That balance drove his pursuit of fame, yet it fostered an overwhelmingly positive public perception of his character. Longmore argues that it was not Washington's admirers who created this image of infallibility; it was Washington himself. By seeking to embody all of society's norms, he became increasingly adept at hiding his flaws, rendering a public image of himself as the consummate man of his age and ideally suited to lead a people he knew so well. While it is all true, Longmore does not really examine where Washington sought his guidance when giving his masterful performance over the course of more than forty years. He may have had a talent for leadership and good intuition, but surely he must have had examples that he drew on.

In the appendix titled "The Foundations of Useful Knowledge," Longmore explores what intellectual sources Washington consulted and specifically addresses Washington's reading habits and the contents of his personal library. Longmore argues that Washington was a practical reader who devoted more time, thought, and attention to reading than historians have traditionally given him credit for. But Longmore's presentation is laden with problems. First, the brief essay is largely based more on compilations of the inventories of Mount Vernon's holdings than on references to Washington's reading found in his correspondence. Longmore does not make a concerted effort to determine what Washington actually read; instead, he makes broad assumptions that are based largely on a comparison of the book inventories made over time along with Washington's expense accounts. Also although he claims to advance the argument that Washington was more of a reader than anyone had previously thought, Longmore devotes a considerable portion of the essay to the opposing argument by quoting Washington's remark that following the presidency he was too busy in his daily routine at Mount Vernon to make time for reading. Longmore further leaps to conclusions and discusses Washington's assumed disinterest in religion based on the contents of the library, noting that he did not own all of the most popular religious books in Virginia and that no Bible was on the 1783 inventory list. This assumption is problematic given that Washington did purchase a considerable number of religious works and that Lund Washington, who actually compiled the 1783 list, noted at that time it was incomplete.[10] Besides the issues inherent in Longmore's assumptions, another factor detracts from his argument about the importance of Washington's reading: he does not even devote a full chapter in his book to it. With this construction, it does not appear that Longmore considered reading to be as central a component of Washington's self-fashioning project as the book's appendix alone suggests.

Longmore's treatment of Washington's reading is what makes this project possible. While on the surface I agree with Longmore's argument that Washington was a practical reader, I find fault with his methodology and assumptions. By picking up where Longmore left off and delving more deeply into the questions of what Washington actually did read and why, it is possible to properly argue that reading was a key component behind Washington's success. How Washington exceeded all expectations to become the father of his country is now a richer story.

This volume is not a conventional biography, for such work has been repeated too many times after Humphreys's publication of the first one in 1789. This book instead explores the questions of where Washington read, what he read, why he pursued a lifelong habit of reading only certain subjects, and how he used the knowledge he gained from his reading. Answering these questions makes it possible to then renew the argument that Washington was a deliberate reader, always seeking to expand his knowledge base in ways that would help him accomplish specific goals. A thorough examination of Washington's reading also sheds new light on the creation of his American identity. He is the quintessential American success story. He eschewed the fashionable classical education that was the foundation of a European style of mind in favor of a more practical approach to learning that included only those subjects that had an immediate application. This course is what intellectually separated Washington from many of his contemporaries. Washington had no patience for the idea of acquiring knowledge simply for the sake of it. For him the popular phrase "useful knowledge" was to be applied in a literal sense only. Whereas Jefferson found the study of Italian, Latin, Greek, French, and Hebrew absolutely essential in order to read works of literature in their original form, Washington instead threw himself into studying the latest agricultural advances so he could free himself from the nightmare that was the tobacco market.

Washington's defective education combined with the widely known fact that he never learned to read and write in any language other than English in part led to Adams's charges of his being illiterate. Indeed, these self-diagnosed "defects" make Washington's rise and lasting fame seem astounding. Furthermore, that fame cast Washington as the father figure for a people who went from being colonials who admired nearly all things European to becoming citizens of a new type of nation who came to believe that they were setting the trend for an increasingly modern Europe to follow. As such this book affords the opportunity to understand Washington's ideas about the types of reading that would shape his personal development and how he used the knowledge he gained from reading and from his own experiences to envision a new American future that would be more independent in every way from Great Britain and the rest of Europe. Although he was not the first to become a full-fledged revolutionary, once he did make that evolution he far outstripped most of his peers in seeing past the rebellion to begin conceiving ideas about nation building. Therefore, to develop a core understanding of reading's significance to Washington, it is essential to understand what he read, where he read, and why he read certain things and not others.

With that in mind, chapter 1 delves into Washington's background to determine why he was so self-conscious about his limited education. When his father's death aborted his formal education, it had an indelible impact on the boy's life. As the young Washington made his way in the world, he had dreamed of a career in the British army but was thwarted because of his colonial birth and woeful lack of a classical education and money. These impediments burned the already thin-skinned Washington to such a degree that he began mentally to break with Great Britain long before the Revolution was even an idea. This intellectual shift caused him to focus his reading on the subjects that would make him a financial, political, and social success in a Virginian sense.

Having thus established why Washington gravitated toward certain kinds of reading material, his collection itself can then be explored in a richer context. Chapter 2 examines the works Washington read and collected during the early phase of his life in Virginia before the outbreak of the American Revolution and his appointment as commander in chief of the Continental Army. Washington purchased most of the books he collected in this early period, so it therefore presents an interesting opportunity to understand Washington's priorities in selecting reading material during this formative phase of his intellectual development. This chapter lays the foundation for the overall argument that Washington was a very serious reader by making direct connections between what he was reading and what he was doing in both his public and private pursuits. The need to make the connection between Washington's choice of reading and the different positions he occupied is grounded by the argument made in Kevin Sharpe's *Reading Revolutions*. In his chapter "Reading in Early Modern England," Sharpe writes, "A close examination of texts could reveal one of the curiously neglected strands of the political tapestry: the relationship between the word and the exercise of power."[11] Moreover, "the process of reading is more complex than a simple acceptance or rejection of a unified meaning produced by an author or text, and that reading is a cultural as well as personal action, and indeed that, even in our own lives, is specific to moments and places."[12] Although Sharpe's argument is based on his study of Sir William Drake, a university-trained academic in Stuart England, it can be applied to Washington because the relationship between texts, politics, and power in seventeenth-century England still pertained in the eighteenth-century world. Much of Washington's life revolved around his ability to both hold and exercise power. Whether it was mastering the agricultural science so that he could maximize the output of his plantations and thus control his financial future, commanding military units at various levels, or serving in political offices, Washington was consumed with the need to gain, use, and then surrender power appropriately in order to cement his legacy. It therefore makes perfect sense to heed Sharpe's thesis to appreciate that all of Washington's reading was politicized. Understanding what he read in the context of what was taking place in his life reveals his true attitude toward the printed word and the knowledge that he gained from it.

Chapter 3 examines Washington's reading during his time as a delegate to the Continental Congresses and his tenure as commander in chief of the Continental Army. This chapter is at the core of the argument advanced in this book, for it explores the period in which Washington was catapulted onto the world stage in a central leadership role. Although he did attract high-level attention on both sides of the

Atlantic for his exploits during the Seven Years' War, it was short lived, and he was largely a peripheral character, at least as far as the British were concerned. The American Revolution, however, placed Washington in a unique and extremely difficult position. He was charged with achieving a victory over the most powerful military force on earth to secure a new nation. As such he found himself having to build an army and gain recognition of its military capacity while simultaneously proving to be a general officer worthy of the rank. For the Revolution to succeed, that recognition would have to come from both sides — from his fellow Americans and his British adversaries. This seemingly overwhelming task, even more than the presidency, would prove to be the greatest challenge of Washington's career. He quickly found that he was out of his depth and that his army was not up to the task. This chapter shows how Washington's conspicuously limited military education actually forced him to transform his thinking to embrace a new strategy that flew in the face of eighteenth-century military convention. He eventually understood that he did not have to win all the battles in order to win the war. He simply needed to survive. That Washington retained his position at the head of the victorious American army led to his receiving more laurels than any of his revolutionary contemporaries earned. This unparalleled degree of fame ultimately would not allow him to remain a private citizen for long despite his dramatic, Cincinnatus-like act of ceremoniously returning his commission to a packed session of Congress and then galloping as fast as his horse could carry him to his home at Mount Vernon.[13]

With Washington's rise placed in context, chapter 4 explores Washington's reading from the end of the American Revolution to his retirement from public life at the end of his second presidential term. The significance of Washington's presidency is profound, but his position was in several ways far less precarious than it had been during the Revolution. At the point of his election, Washington's fame was at its zenith. He was keenly aware that his presence was the greatest contribution he could make to the newly instituted federal government.

Although it appears simple, his involvement was anything but because he found that he was going to set the precedents for all who would succeed him. As the nation's first chief executive, he had to strike the right balance in his public performances between the familiar monarchical past and the demands of a new republican future. This balancing act called for both delicacy and precision, and he had few examples to guide him. Washington therefore had to pay particular attention to the coverage he and his administration received in the print media, including newspapers, pamphlets, and published political sermons, for it revealed how the American people regarded his performance. This chapter draws the curtain back on Washington's presidential performance in order to underscore exactly how carefully orchestrated his every move actually was.

The image of Washington as president offered in chapter 4 sets the stage for chapter 5, which examines the period covering Washington's retirement from public life in 1796 to his death in 1799. During these twilight years, Washington was primarily concerned with building his legacy. This chapter shows that with the additions made to his collection during this period, he intended the library should contain not only the volumes from which he gleaned useful knowledge over the course of his lifetime but also all of the documents that would be necessary to establish a clear record of his accomplishments for posterity. Here he was concerned with collecting copies of legislative and judicial records, the latest writings about the Revolution and American history, and a considerable number of periodicals. It is also interesting to note that during this time Washington collaborated with his first biographer, David Humphreys, a fact that underscores the criticality of shoring up his legacy as he felt his life drawing to a close.

The final question that remains to be explored regards where Washington read. A large part of the reason why historians have hitherto neglected this subject is that the anecdotal evidence of Washington engaged in reading is scant. He was obsessively private about reading, going so far as to build his library in his home so that it is sequestered from the rest of the house. That Washington was the owner-builder raises tantalizing questions about the design decisions he made to ensure that his library was a safe haven of sorts, a place where he could read and think away from the prying eyes both of the scores of visitors who passed through his doors and of the many children who called Mount Vernon home over the years. Moreover, the manner in which the room was furnished also yields some important insight into how he approached reading as an activity.

Painting an accurate picture of Washington's reading is not without its challenges. For while much is known about his life, any project that attempts to get into Washington's mind requires a certain number of assumptions to fill in the methodological framework that is staked on a certain number of facts. First, when Washington died, his executors made an inventory of the property in his estate in accordance with Virginia law. In the process nearly all the contents in Mount Vernon at the time, including those items that did not belong to Washington personally, were incorporated in the resulting catalog. In terms of the library, the estate inventory listed books that clearly belonged to Martha Washington; her deceased son, John Parke Custis; Bushrod Washington; and other family members who over various periods had resided or were residing at Mount Vernon at the time of Washington's death. It is therefore incorrect to state that Washington's collection consisted of more than nine hundred volumes. While a majority of the books — such as Humphrey Bland's *Treatise on Military Discipline*, Henri-Louis Duhamel du Monceau's *Husbandry*, and Tobias George Smollett's *History of England* — were his, not all of them were.

Second, the blunt truth is that Washington was not a widely read scholar; he lacked formal academic training and limited his reading to works with an immediate, practical application. If he needed to read, he did; however, if he was too busy to read, he did not seem to lament it. Moreover, he simply did not foster a love of learning for the mere sake of it. As such Washington did not seem to approach every piece of writing with the same sense of needing to master it. For example, John

Adams's diary from his days as a law apprentice is littered with entries detailing his rereading of legal texts. On October 5, 1758, he recorded, "I have read Gilbert's 1st Section, of feuds this evening, but am not master of it." The following day his entry read, "Am now reading over again Gilberts section of feudal tenures." Adams continued to reread it the next day, the day after that, and the day after that. On October 9 he exclaimed, "Read in Gilberts Tenures. I must and will make that Book familiar to me." On October 10, Adams boasted that "I read him slowly, but I gain Ideas and Knowledge as I go along." By October 12 he wrote, "This volume will take me a fortnight, but I will master it." He kept at it until he had.[14] By contrast Washington's diary never mentions his reading. Moreover, with a few notable exceptions that are discussed in the following chapters, Washington did not leave very much in the way of marginalia, nor did he leave many pages of reading notes that would be ever so helpful in delineating just how he mentally processed the material that he read. While this lack of notes may indicate varying degrees of interest on Washington's part, it may also simply reflect that he was never taught a scholarly method for reading during his limited formal education and that he did not make note taking a long-standing habit on his own. That said, those texts that do have accompanying reading notes are easily assumed to be more significant to Washington than those that do not. Simply because no marginal or reading notes are in a given work, as in the example of Bland's *Treatise*, however, does not mean that Washington neglected to read it.

Conversely it would be problematic to take the overall dearth of reading notes as license to assume that if Washington had a book in his library, he must have read it. The simple fact that Washington had in his collection multiple works in foreign languages clearly underscores the dangers of making such an assumption because he could not speak, read, or write in any language other than English. Additionally many items in Washington's collection, especially those acquired in the latter part of his life, were gifts. Both ambitious authors and individuals looking to curry favor sent various pieces of writing to Washington. As these gifts were unsolicited and Washington's responses did not always indicate whether he did anything beyond glancing at the titles, it would be sheer folly to assume too much.

Washington did make a habit of writing his name and placing his bookplate in every work he purchased and put in the collection. These marks of ownership are both useful for delineating which books on the final estate inventory were his and which ones he was more likely to have read or at the very least perused. His acquisitions can be corroborated by examining his expense accounts and correspondence with his agents over the course of his lifetime. Therefore, if an item in the collection bore no mark of Washington's ownership or if there was no concrete evidence in any form to indicate that he did read it, then that item was disregarded for the purposes of this book. Determining which works were secured by Washington thus allowed for another critical assumption: if Washington purchased a book for himself, it was because he intended to read it. Given that he designed the library at Mount Vernon solely for his use and did not open it to either guests or even other members of the household, nothing in the room was intended to be a showpiece. Although he designed the rest of the mansion to overawe his visitors, it would have been inconsistent with his character to construct an ostentatious library filled with fine but unread books for the sake of impressing others. Washington never presented himself as a scholar in any way, shape, or form to others, so it simply did not make sense when looking at his library purchases to assume that he acquired them to show off in the same way he did with his bold paint colors, fine carriages, and fancy clothes.

Therefore, the books and other printed materials from the collection that are discussed in this volume were carefully selected to steer clear of the aforementioned fallacies. The majority of the selected works can be proved to have been purchased and read by Washington. Washington is reasonably assumed to have read the rest of them because they bear evidence that he handled and cared about them enough to make clear his ownership and because they fit well within the context of his intellectual needs at the time when he acquired them. This carefully constructed analytical framework reveals that Washington was a man who almost never read for pleasure. He read for the sake of gaining the knowledge needed to accomplish whatever task he faced at a given time and to maintain the reputation that he worked a lifetime to cultivate. Washington read works on agriculture, history, religion, law, government, military science, and current affairs; this program left little room for belles lettres, philosophy, and poetry.

Washington was a practical reader. He clearly valued useful knowledge that made many of his tasks easier.[15] He was and still is the quintessential American success story because he applied his mind to achieving success. He was relentless in pursuing his goals, and his reading is an applied demonstration of it.

This book reveals Washington's mind at work. Painfully aware that he was underprepared for nearly every occupation he undertook, Washington turned to reading as a means by which to learn and to avoid having to rely on others too heavily. It is true that as he matured, he developed a network of carefully chosen advisers and aides whose services were indispensable; however, Washington never depended wholly on them in making his decisions, even in the most precarious situations. Washington's self-directed reading over the course of his life led to a series of intellectual revolutions that saw him evolve from a provincial Virginian steeped in a keen sense of Britishness into one of the pioneers of a newly emerging American identity. More than any of his contemporaries, he became the embodiment of the American Revolution; thus, no one else could have served as the new nation's first chief executive. For far too long, historians, biographers, and commentators have either celebrated his status as one of history's great men or condemned it as unwarranted without sufficiently examining the method behind Washington's success. This book sheds important light on how he realized his achievements. Far from either being born inherently great or being the product of good fortune, Washington was a man driven to rise to new heights. Reading was very much at the heart of his efforts.

CHAPTER ONE

Pursuing Useful Knowledge

The sun was just beginning to peek through Ferry Farm's windows at the dawn of a new day, but thirteen-year-old George Washington was already up and hard at work at a small table by the bedroom window. As his younger brothers Samuel and John Augustine still lay sleeping nearby and the first of the sun's rays stretched through the neatly curtained windows and across the small table, the future father of his country busily copied word for word a translation of an old guidebook for princely behavior that a French Jesuit priest wrote called *The Rules of Civility*. Such a project was no small undertaking for the boy, but little by little he was determined to press on to the end; so he kept scratching at the paper with his quill, careful to keep his ink-stained fingers off the paper. By the time he was finished, young Washington's manuscript consisted of 110 rules for how to properly conduct himself as a respectable member of society. He took pride in his work, for he would rely on these maxims to guide him throughout a long career in the public light.[1]

Washington's youthful act of copying out this antiquated French courtesy manual is almost as well known as Parson Weems's wholly invented cherry tree episode. Parents and teachers of young students have also used the real episode of the teenage Washington working at his desk as an example to study hard and/or as an admonition to behave properly; however, few have spent any time trying to work out why exactly Washington worked so hard. Some chalk it up as an early testament of Washington's future greatness, an example of the sober, ambitious adolescent grooming himself for the spectacularly public life he was destined to lead. Others perhaps take a dimmer view of this episode and see it as an example of Washington's obsessive need for self-control and as a sad attempt by a less than intelligent and socially awkward youth to act normally in the presence of his betters in the desperate hope of attracting the attention of powerful patrons. The reality between these extreme interpretations is somewhere in the middle. Washington was ambitious and, yes, even a little desperate to transcend the social station he was born into. However, his solitary act of copying a courtesy manual word for word into a commonplace book offers an insight into how seriously he took the act of reading, studying, and internalizing the material that he considered to contain useful knowledge. This chapter examines why he developed a taste for reading material that yielded practical knowledge that he could use immediately. To answer this question, it is necessary to probe Washington's biography and explore where his rigid mentality came from by penetrating the heart of his lifelong self-fashioning project and revealing how his unique pursuit of useful knowledge helped him refine his sense of self.

Washington's Childhood and Early Life

When Washington was eleven years old, his father, Augustine, died and left his widow, Mary Ball Washington, the single parent to six young children.[2] Whatever emotional toll his father's death took on the young Washington has been lost to history. Washington apparently remembered little of his father, scarcely referring to him in his later writings, and there is no evidence that testifies to how the young boy grieved. The significance of Augustine Washington's death, however, can still be considered profound for three reasons. First, Washington lost his father at a particular stage of adolescence when he needed his father's guiding hand to steer him to maturity. Second, as Augustine's widow never remarried, it meant that Washington and his siblings were raised by a single mother; so the children needed a positive male role model to introduce them into the patriarchal society of the time. Finally, and most critical, the death of Augustine Washington aborted all plans to further his sons' formal educations.

With Augustine Washington's death in context, it is therefore possible to trace the origins of George's self-fashioning back to his mother. Mary Ball Washington set about the task of rearing her children with an intensity uncommon in eighteenth-century women; she sought to instill in her children deference and well-regulated restraint.[3] Toward the end of his life, long after his fame had reached beyond American shores, Washington is said to have remarked, "All I am I owe to my mother. I attribute all my success in life to the moral, intellectual and physical education I received from her."[4] Those who knew her described Mary Ball Washington as a force of nature; her trademark stiff personality and iron will were traits that her famous son inherited. A relative and childhood friend of George's recalled: "I was often there with George, his playmate, schoolmate, and young man's companion. Of the mother I was ten times more afraid than I ever was of my own parents. She awed me. . . . I could not behold that remarkable woman without feelings it is impossible to describe. Whoever has seen that awe-inspiring air and manner so characteristic in the Father of his Country, will remember the matron as she appeared when the presiding genius of her well-ordered household, commanding and being obeyed."[5]

One particular area that Mary Ball Washington maintained command over was her eldest son's education. Washington was educated at local schools and for a brief period by a private tutor while he was living in the home of his older half-brother Lawrence. The time spent under the direction of this tutor was the closest that the young Washington would ever come to a classical education, for he was schooled in the "principles of grammar, the theory of reasoning, on speaking, the science of numbers, the elements of geometry, and the highest branches of mathematics, the art of mensuration, composing together with the rudiments of geography, history, and the studies which are not improperly termed 'the humanities.'"[6] Furthermore, he received instruction "in the graceful accomplishments of dancing, fencing, riding, and performing the military exercises," in all of which he gained conspicuous proficiency in a remarkably short time.[7] A university education, however, was financially out of the question, and with little hesitation, Mary Ball Washington squelched Lawrence's plans to train her son for an officer's career in the Royal Navy.[8]

To supplement her children's educations, Mary Ball Washington read aloud to them from the Bible and from several anthologies of sermons on a daily basis.[9] Most if not all of these books would go to George, who retained them in his private library for the rest of his life.[10] These daily catechisms were meant to inspire piety in the Washington children and to underscore the central place religious texts occupied in an orthodox, moral life. Mary Ball Washington was equally spartan with regard to her treatment of her children's accomplishments. Throughout her long life, she made a habit of deriding her eldest son's achievements, never appearing to exhibit the least bit of parental pride.[11] The contradictory versions of the highly embellished stories of Washington's relationship with his mother as told by the likes of the Marquis de Lafayette and Parson Weems were fabrications designed to obfuscate the imperfections in Washington's personal history in favor of an idealized image of Mary Ball Washington and were advanced at a time when the concept of republican motherhood was shaping women's roles in the new nation. Mary Ball Washington's parenting style was to leave an indelible mark on her eldest son, who throughout his life was incredibly thin skinned and painfully fearful of criticism.[12]

Washington's Early Reading

Thus with his mother's discipline to guide him, the youthful Washington devoted considerable time in his daily routine to reading and self-improvement, and in so doing he cultivated what would become a lifelong habit of seeking out instructional books first and, to a secondary degree, books for pleasure, such as travel narratives and literature.[13] One of his earliest notes in his childhood commonplace books recorded that he read "the reign of King John and in the *Spectator* read to No. 143."[14]

These schoolboy commonplace books offer a few glimpses of what Washington the student was like. Although they are small and limited in scope, these notebooks reveal fleeting glimpses into the workings of one of the most difficult to penetrate minds in American history. The most important message embedded in his early writings is not their content, which reflects the typical lessons children across the colonies were learning; rather, it is the artistry and care with which he committed these lessons and notes to the pages. Just as he would demonstrate on a much larger and grander scale with Mount Vernon as an adult, the young Washington enjoyed connecting beauty and utility.[15] The neatness of Washington's early reading notes signifies a serious approach to his studies that is reflective of the discipline his mother instilled in him.

From childhood Washington harbored ambitions to circulate in the most elite social circles and serve in the highest levels of the military and government, so he set out early to acquire the requisite knowledge to achieve those goals. Not only did he copy the *Rules of Civility*, but capitalizing on his natural mathematical ability, Washington also taught himself how to conduct land surveys using his father's instruments and books borrowed from William Fairfax.[16] Learning how to conduct land surveys paid several important dividends to Washington. First, he developed an appreciation, and indeed a hunger, for land. Acquiring profitable real estate would be one of his lifelong passions. Second, he gained the skills necessary to earn a living, which was essential for an ambitious youth with little inheritance and no benefactor. Next, once he established himself as a reputable surveyor, he was able to reach out to some of the wealthy landowners of Virginia who could use his services and in the process could become his patrons. Finally, he learned patience and perseverance in reconnoitering land by spending days at a time in the wilderness, experiences that greatly hardened his constitution and prepared him for the military life he wanted so badly to lead.[17]

Without his father to guide him, the upwardly mobile Washington earnestly sought to gain the attention of a surrogate who could usher him into Virginia society. Through Lawrence and, even more important, Lawrence's in-laws, the Fairfaxes, Washington slipped into the mix of provincial Virginian high society. His imposing physical size made him hard to miss in crowded ballrooms. He was graceful, especially on the dance floor, and he quite literally danced his way into the attentions of the rich and powerful. Because of his natural shyness, lack of formal education, and perpetual fear of ridicule, however, he shied away from learned conversations, observed much, and preferred to speak only when he was sure of himself.[18]

Just as the ambitious young man was beginning to make his way into the world of Tidewater society, he was dealt another crushing blow: Lawrence died in 1752 after a long and painful struggle with tuberculosis. Lawrence's death was no doubt harder for the younger Washington to bear than the death of their father, for not only was Washington older and better able to grasp the ways in which death affected the lives of those left behind but also Lawrence had been his younger brother's savior, hero, and mentor throughout his formative teen years. In his will Lawrence bequeathed to his heartbroken younger brother three lots in Fredericksburg and the remote hope that if he were to outlive Lawrence's widow, Anne, and infant daughter (as long as she died without issue), he would inherit the clear title to Mount Vernon and the lands connected to it.[19] This bequest was small comfort to Washington, who felt both the emotional and practical loss of a beloved older brother and mentor. Although he could take comfort that Lawrence's father-in-law, William Fairfax, would step into the role of benefactor and Lawrence's brother-in-law George William Fairfax would breach the emotional gap as a reliable best friend, Washington surely knew that it was time that he seriously made a name for himself in the world. He lobbied for and received a commission as an adjutant in the Virginia Regiment, one of Lawrence's old posts, and he became a member of a newly organized Masonic Lodge in Fredericksburg, rising quickly to Master Mason. Additionally he continued to conduct land surveys, accumulating handsome profits.[20]

Washington First Enters Public Life

Now twenty-one years old, Washington finally began climbing the daunting social ladder, one rung at a time. He still needed an opportunity to impress the powerful men of Virginia who had noticed him only long enough to commission him. After all, military officers who earned no laurels typically failed to achieve lasting fame, for Virginia society was teeming with men who styled themselves as colonels. Washington had his opportunity to make a name for himself when the French invaded the Ohio Territory, lands that Virginia's Ohio Company traditionally claimed for the British crown. In October 1753 George II ordered the Virginians to construct forts along the Ohio River and to send an emissary to determine if the French were in fact trespassing on British soil. If they were, the men were to drive them out by force of arms.[21] The prospect of traveling from Williamsburg to the French fort near what is now Pittsburgh in the winter was nothing short of frightening in the three-mile-per-hour world in which Washington lived, but with what would become a typical disregard for physical danger, he leaped at the chance to deliver his king's ultimatum. Robert Dinwiddie, Virginia's lieutenant governor, chose Washington probably because no one else stepped up to volunteer for such a dangerous mission; however, really no one was more qualified than Washington was. All those years of surveying experience taught him valuable lessons about how to navigate difficult terrain and survive in the wilderness, and he was physically very strong. The journey was harrowing, and Washington escaped death on at least two occasions. On the return leg of the trip, an Indian guide turned on him and fired a musket at near-point-blank range but missed. The unscathed Washington wisely opted not to hunt his attacker down and instead pushed ahead at a blistering pace to avoid any further attacks by other hostile Indians. As he and his guide, Christopher Gist, tried to cross a rushing river on a hastily built raft, Washington fell in and almost froze to death.[22] Washington survived, however, and his mission was successful on a number of levels. On an immediate, practical level, Washington successfully made the British government's ultimatum clear to the French command present in the disputed territory. On a strategic level, after Washington's safe return to Williamsburg he confirmed the assumptions that the British and colonial governments were making about French intensions: they were certainly planning to stay, thus making war probable. With the murky situation cleared up, the would-be belligerents no longer had to guess what the other was thinking.

On a personal level, this mission made Washington famous. He kept a detailed record of his journey — complete with rich descriptions of the lands that he crossed, the French fortifications he visited, and all the details of his narrow escapes — and gave the record to Dinwiddie upon returning to Williamsburg. Dinwiddie immediately had it published in both Virginia and London to advertise the severity of the crisis on the frontier, and in so doing he made Washington a celebrity. Washington was given a day to prepare and submit the manuscript, and he evidently felt pressured. Although not uncommon for authors at that time, he made a point to write the advertisement for the book himself. He apologized "for the numberless Imperfections of it" and emphasized that he had "no leisure to consult of a new and proper form to offer it in, or to correct or amend the diction of the old, neither was I apprised . . . that it ever would be published."[23] The text of the journal offers evidence that Washington did not intend for it to be published. Many of the entries appear hastily written while others read like minutes of a meeting. Moreover, he makes frequent use of abbreviations, and the sentence structure is halting. Despite Washington's apparent fears that his work would be ridiculed for its amateurish prose, the book was widely read, frequently reprinted on both sides of the Atlantic, and often quoted.[24] At the age of twenty-two, the young man whose prospects had previously been uncertain was an internationally published author and was newly promoted to lieutenant colonel and second in command of the Virginia Regiment.

Washington was completely unprepared and unqualified for this promotion. For example, British officers who occupied comparable ranks and positions had spent decades in the army before reaching that level. During their course of service, they would have been expected to maintain their studies of the military arts through reading both classic and new texts on the science of warfare, histories of well-known campaigns, and biographies of great commanders. British officers had an overwhelming preference for Continental books as opposed to English ones. Additionally most British officers preferred reading those Continental books in their original languages; therefore, it was expected that they were able to read in multiple languages, with French, Italian, and German being the most important. At a minimum, however, a mastery of French was virtually required for all senior officers.[25] Evidence suggests that Washington read *Julius Caesar's Commentaries* and a life of Alexander the Great on recommendation from William Fairfax; however, that was the limit of Washington's military education to date.[26] His limited formal education never included French lessons. It would prove to be a significant factor as Washington's upcoming mission unfolded.

By mid-March 1754 reports from the Ohio Country were filtering into Williamsburg that the French were about to make a hostile move. Dinwiddie soon tasked Washington with building up Virginia's defenses on the frontier in anticipation of a possible French invasion. What followed was a blunder from top to bottom. On April 2, 1754, Washington set out for the wilderness with 160 soldiers who were as inexperienced as he was. His convoy moved slowly as the men also had to forge the road they were traveling. Three weeks later, Washington received intelligence that the French had attacked a small combined force of British soldiers and their Indian allies while they were constructing a fort on the forks of the Ohio River named Fort Duquesne. The news that a numerically superior French force was bearing down on them trickled through the ranks of Washington's men, devastating morale. Many threatened to desert. Washington was unfazed. He responded to the unfolding situation with a "glowing zeal."[27] He was so confident in his abilities and his position as commander that he dashed off briskly phrased letters to

Lieutenant Governor James Hamilton of Pennsylvania and Governor Horatio Sharpe of Maryland, urging them to send reinforcements. Still in his attempt to be diplomatic in the face of his utter brashness, Washington included a half apology to Sharpe: "I ought first to have begged pardon of your excellency for this liberty of writing, as I am not happy enough to be ranked among those of your acquaintance." Then trying to spur the governors to act through patriotism, he continued his appeal, stating that the present crisis "should rouse from the lethargy we have fallen into the heroic spirit of every free-born Englishman to assert the rights and privileges of our king."[28] Despite the clumsy nature of these early attempts at fostering good civil-military relations, Washington was evidently successful because the governors complied.[29] Washington's continued audacity, which led to the series of unfortunate events in the coming days, was of course attributable to his youth, inexperience, and lack of education. He seemed to lose sight of the fact that in addition to his demonstrated abilities during that initial mission to the French, he also owed his promotion to his connections. In short, Washington allowed his ego to drive his actions, and it would lead catastrophically to poor decision making in the days and weeks to come.

Washington and the Seven Years' War

The unfortunate events that followed sparked the Seven Years' War. On May 28, 1754, Washington's old guide, Christopher Gist, reported that he saw a small party of French soldiers heading to Washington's position and less than five miles away. Washington hastily dispatched Capt. Peter Hogg, one of his subordinates, with seventy-five men to intercept the French party between the meadows and the Monongahela River. An intelligence update from his Indian ally, Tanacharison the Half King, however, alerted Washington that he had sent his men in the wrong direction. He decided that he had to act. Taking forty-seven men on a night march through a driving rain, Washington rendezvoused with Half King early the following morning, and the two leaders decided to attack the French jointly.[30] Indian scouts led Washington's force to the French location, and as Washington described in his diary:

> We formed ourselves for an Engagement, marching one after the other in the *Indian* manner: We were advanced pretty near to them, as we thought, when they discovered us; whereupon I ordered my company to fire; mine was supported by that of Mr. *Wag[gonn]er's*, and my Company and his received the whole Fire of the *French*, during the greatest Part of the Action, which only lasted a Quarter of an Hour, before the enemy was routed.
>
> We killed Mr. *de Jumonville*, the commander of that Party, as also nine others; we wounded one, and made Twenty-one Prisoners, among whom were M. *la Force*, M. *Drouillon*, and two Cadets. The *Indians* scalped the Dead, and took away the most Part of their Arms.[31]

Washington repeated this account almost word for word in his official report to Dinwiddie on May 29. In giving this version of the events, however, Washington omitted several key details that brought him dangerously close to rendering a false report. Washington neglected to include the specific details surrounding Ens. Joseph Coulon de Jumonville's actual death. Jumonville was wounded in the brief exchange of fire, but he remained conscious and tried to explain to Washington that he was on a diplomatic rather than a hostile mission. The problem was that Washington didn't speak French, and apparently he did not have a capable interpreter with him. As Washington struggled in vain to understand what Jumonville was trying to tell him, Half King stepped forward and drove a hatchet into Jumonville's skull, splitting it open, and then proceeded to wash his hands in the brains of his victim. At that point the rest of the Indians swooped down on the French wounded, scalping them and stripping them of their arms. The horrified Washington simply stood there, unable to stop the frenzied attack for what must have seemed to him to be an eternity. When he did regain his composure, he ordered his men to take the twenty-one survivors as prisoners — Washington would vehemently insist to Dinwiddie that they were spies — and began the march back to his tiny garrison in the Great Meadows.[32]

Washington must have been haunted by the atrocity. It was his first real taste of battle, and under his command the attack disintegrated into a murderous bloodbath. In addition he must have been worried about how the French would respond when word reached them. There was also the possibility that others would offer accounts that differed from his. The French survivors insisted that they were a part of a diplomatic mission and that the British force had attacked them without provocation. One of Washington's men, an illiterate Irish immigrant named John Shaw, provided a sworn statement after the fact that filled in some of the missing details from Washington's account. Shaw indicated that it was during a cease-fire that the wounded Jumonville spoke to Washington and the real massacre began.[33] It is primarily from Shaw's statement that we can gain the closest understanding of what actually happened in that glen. This incident is telling in a couple of ways. First, Washington had failed to control his men. Also, it was the first, but not the last, time that his "defective" education severely handicapped him. That he could not speak or read French led to confusion and arguably created that critical, tense moment when he was unable to comprehend what Jumonville said and Half King butchered him.

The situation in the Great Meadows rapidly deteriorated for Washington and his men. After the incident in Jumonville's glen, the Virginians retreated to construct a crude set of defensive works named Fort Necessity. Washington knew to expect a French reprisal once word of Jumonville's death spread. He must have been relieved to see the remainder of the Virginia Regiment come down the rude road into the meadow, only to be shocked with the news that his commander Col. Joshua Fry was not with them. He had suffered a fatal fall from his horse; therefore, Washington had been promoted again. He was now a full colonel and commander of the entire expedition. A couple of weeks later, a company of British regulars under the command of Capt. James Mackay arrived from South Carolina to reinforce Washington. Mackay behaved politely to Washington but declined to garrison his men with the Virginians. The British made their own camp, much to Washington's consternation. While he was obsessing over this British affront to his rank, Washington's Indian allies were about to desert him. It seemed that Half King was losing his will to fight the French. Washington's best efforts at diplomacy failed. The Indians all left. Washington felt vulnerable, but nevertheless he pushed his men forward into the woods to try and maintain the initiative against the French force he knew would be coming.[34]

The French were indeed approaching. A vastly superior force under the command of Capt. Louis Coulon de Villiers, Jumonville's older brother, was bearing down on Washington's force and hounding the men back to Fort Necessity. When the haggard Virginians returned to the ramshackle fort, it offered little comfort. The supplies were depleted, the tents were ruined, and a heavy rain reduced the ground to a sea of mud. The tiny fort suddenly looked exposed and dangerously weak. That Washington even selected this site for a defensive position reveals his lack of military education. Washington intended the fort to offer protection against a frontal assault; however, he didn't seem to notice at first that it was surrounded by high ground and that the wood line was within musket range. He also made the mistake of neglecting to clear his sectors of fire. An advancing enemy could simply hide in the woods and easily pick off the defenders. If Washington had been schooled in military science, he would have read the books by British fortifications expert Charles Bisset, including *The Theory and Construction of Fortification,* as well as Jean-François Bernard's *Remarks on the Modern Fortification.* These books on conducting defensive campaigns make clear that fortifications are strongest when they occupy high ground and when the defenders have taken the time to clear anything that obscured the views of the surrounding areas and avenues of approach. Failure to plan according to these guidelines nearly always turned the defensive works into a trap for the defenders.[35]

When the French and their Indian allies arrived, Washington and Mackay did their best to make a stand, but while the unseasoned Virginians fled behind cover, the French maintained the initiative. Soon "the most tremendous rain that be conceived" came down, and the exposed Virginians could not keep their gunpowder dry. By evening, there were a hundred total casualties, thirty of whom had been killed.[36] What saved Washington and the Virginians from total annihilation was that Captain de Villiers did not know whether the British were about to be reinforced; so instead of pressing the attack to completion, he sought Washington's sword.[37]

When Villiers sent an emissary to negotiate with Washington's representatives, the Virginians lost all discipline, broke into the rum supply, and proceeded to get drunk. Washington's chief negotiator, Jacob Van Braam, went back and forth between Villiers and Washington, finally delivering to the French word that the British were ready to capitulate. Villiers dictated his terms to an aide with poor penmanship, and by the time Van Braam slogged back to Washington's tent, the document was wet, the ink running all over. In the flickering candlelight, Washington, Mackay, and their officers struggled to read the terms. What further complicated the reading of the waterlogged parchment was that no one present, except Van Braam, could read French with any real degree of proficiency. Relying on his inaccurate translation, which bordered on the dishonest, Washington and Mackay missed some key phrases in the preamble — "venger L'assasin" and "l'assasinat du Sur de Jumonville."[38] In missing these key incriminating phrases, Washington and Mackay agreed that the terms of the surrender seemed generous. The British survivors were allowed to surrender with full military honors, marching out of the fort with their colors flying and drums beating.[39] Washington and Mackay failed to understand, however, that the crucial phrases in the preamble referring to the assassination of Jumonville gave the French a legal cause to declare war on Great Britain. The confession that Washington and Mackay unknowingly signed was the French commander's main object; he had no interest in taking prisoners or flags.[40]

In the aftermath of the defeat, Washington failed to grasp the full implications of the surrender document. He did, however, have some supporters. None of his officers condemned him in their respective reports. Captain Mackay also notably stood by Washington (probably to salvage his own reputation, for he had cosigned the articles of capitulation). Even Dinwiddie was loyal. When Washington delivered his official report on July 17, 1754, the House of Burgesses passed a resolution thanking him for his efforts and expressing condolences for his losses. However, despite the initial show of support, Dinwiddie, in deciding to wait for further British reinforcements, reorganized the Virginia Regiment back into its constituent companies and offered Washington command of one of them but with a demotion of rank from colonel to captain. Washington, who already felt unappreciated, resigned his commission in humiliation.

Washington, however, was not to remain a civilian for long. When he resigned, he hinted to William Fitzhugh, "I have the consolation itself, of knowing that I have opened the way when the smallness of our numbers exposed us to the attacks of a Superior Enemy; That I have hitherto stood the heat and brunt of the Day, and escaped untouched, in time of extreme danger; and I have the Thanks of my Country, for the Services I have rendered it." He further remained certain that his "inclinations were strongly bent to arms."[41] Although Washington's first foray into the reality of combat command had been abysmal, he outwardly lost none of his original thirst for a military life. Furthermore, Washington's command at Great Meadows underscores the impact that his lack of education and training had on this pivotal historical moment. He couldn't speak or read French, nor did he think it prudent to ensure that he had a competent translator with him. He made numerous tactical errors in judgment, letting bravado as opposed to reason drive his decision making. Youthful false confidence aside, however, Washington learned some valuable lessons about the art of war on the frontier that would serve him well in the future. As would become his lifelong custom, Washington set out from this point forward to never make the same mistake twice.

Washington jumped at a new opportunity to serve when he heard of the arrival of Gen. Edward Braddock, who was to lead a new expedition to recapture Fort Duquesne. Washington congratulated the general on his safe arrival in the colonies but then wisely allowed his powerful patrons to talk to Braddock on his behalf. Before long Washington was offered a position on the general's staff. Washington's status on the staff says a great deal about what Braddock thought about colonial administration; Washington was told to report directly to the general, thereby avoiding a repeat of all the annoying clashes Washington as a provincial officer had with regular officers of inferior rank.[42] Braddock seemed to value Washington for his hard-earned situational awareness and welcomed his advice. One of the lessons that Washington learned from his previous forays into the wilderness was to travel light. He advised Braddock to use pack mules as opposed to wagons for logistical support wherever possible. Additionally Washington further recommended that Braddock divide his army and send a lighter, faster force that would be more adept at encountering an enemy in the woods. Despite the notorious contempt that Braddock had for colonials, he liked Washington and promised to help his young protégé find preferment in His Majesty's regular forces.[43]

Although Washington still clashed with other officers and didn't always get his own way with Braddock, his confidence still must have been buoyed when Braddock became his newest benefactor. The comfort was to be short lived. During the campaign of 1755, a combined Franco-Indian force attacked Braddock's army. Panic spread through the British lines as a near-invisible enemy began cutting men down where they stood in their ranks. Washington urged Braddock to allow him to reorganize the Virginians into an irregular formation and to beat the enemy back, but Braddock refused. The British in their tight formations and scarlet uniforms proved easy targets for the hidden enemy. Braddock soon fell from his saddle, mortally wounded, and his officers fell around him. Washington, however, remained unscathed. Despite having two horses shot from under him and four bullets pierce his clothes, Washington remained calm under fire and brought as much order as possible from the chaos. He organized the retreat and supervised the removal of the dying Braddock from the field. Furthermore, when Braddock succumbed to his wound three days later, Washington presided over his burial in the middle of the road so as to prevent hostile Indians from finding his grave and defiling his body.[44] Also buried with Braddock was Washington's only real chance at a royal commission.

In the aftermath of Braddock's defeat, the worst in eighteenth-century British history, the blame fell squarely on the dead general. Braddock's inability to heed Washington's advice to take cover seemed in arrogant disregard for the lives of the men under his command. Virginia's ruling class, meanwhile, lavished praise on Washington. Furthermore, word of the young colonel's deeds spread outside of Virginia's borders to the greater Anglo-American world. From the Carolinas to England, Washington's heroic tale was repeated in the press, and the accolades poured in.[45]

Washington's Reading and His Virginia Regiment

Shortly after Braddock's defeat, Dinwiddie enlarged the Virginia Regiment and offered Washington the command. He accepted at the end of August 1759 and began building the regiment from the ground up. Here we first catch a glimpse of the commander that Washington would become less than twenty years later. Washington had to do almost everything single-handedly, from designing uniforms to conducting drills based on the latest British drill manuals and punishing disobedient soldiers. With specific regard to training, Washington was responsible for training not only raw recruits but also officers. Washington pushed his officers to study, particularly the latest in British military texts such as Humphrey Bland's *A Treatise of Military Discipline*. Washington wrote that "having no opportunity to improve from example, let us read"; for he recognized it was not possible for an ambitious officer to obtain the requisite expertise "without application, nor any merit or applause to be achieved without certain knowledge thereof."[46] Bland's *Treatise* was the fundamental textbook for all British officers. Known throughout the army as "the bible," the 360-page manual spelled out everything a new officer needed to know about how to form and operate a regiment both in garrison and in the field. Bland outlined what an officer's duties were and what officers could reasonably expect from their subordinates. Bland's work is a field manual, a practical guide for new officers that dictated in step-by-step fashion everything that should be done on a daily basis in order to keep the army functioning under any circumstances. Bland also included leadership advice, specifically in the sections that discussed battlefield orders. In chapter 9, "General Rules for Battalions of Foot, When They Engage in the Line," Bland stated: "It being a General Remark, that the Private Soldiers, when they are to go upon Action, form their Notions of the Danger from the outward Appearance of their Officers; and according to their Looks apprehend the Undertaking to be more or less difficult. . . . In order therefore to dissipate their Fears, and fortify their Courage, the Officers should assume a serene and cheerful Air; and in delivering their Orders to, and in their common Discourse with, the Men, they should address themselves to them in an affable and affectionate manner."[47] What is interesting about this particular passage from Bland's *Treatise* is that it seems to fit with the lessons Washington learned from the *Rules of Civility* about the need to maintain self-control. By reading Bland, Washington was able to put into practice in his military life some of the same lessons he had learned to use in his civilian life. These mutually reinforcing guidelines shaped Washington's conduct and eventually contributed to the growth of his mythology.

Colonel Washington's immersion into the study of the military arts is the first significant example we have of his pursuing a specifically designed course of study to help gain the requisite knowledge to handle the station he occupied at that moment. Furthermore, in these early years of Washington's career in the Virginia Regiment, when he was in relentless pursuit of a regular commission, that he made a considerable effort to study military theory in concert with the trends emerging from the British military enlightenment speaks to Washington's sense of his own Britishness.

Throughout the eighteenth century, Britain underwent a military renaissance. As stated earlier, books were central to preparing officers to serve, particularly in the combat arms such as the artillery and engineers, and to teaching them the tactics to lead an army both on the battlefield and in peacetime. British officials used books to set standards for the army, including defining service obligations for those receiving commissions. Eighteenth-century officers increasingly consulted books to expand their knowledge of the military arts through reading about the latest developments on war and encouraged their fellow officers to become professional students of warfare. Those officers who aspired to high commands tended to read and recommend to others a wide array of books on the art of war or what would later become known as grand strategy. One such example is the Duke of Albemarle's *Observations upon Military and Political Affairs*. The Duke of Albemarle fought in the English Civil Wars and was one of the principle advocates for the restoration of Charles II. His book opines on civil-military relations at the highest level and therefore appealed to readers who actively sought high-level leadership positions.[48] Another example is Niccolò Machiavelli's *Libro della Arte della Guerra*, which is a study of the usefulness of war to a state and what a state's war aims should be in theoretical terms.[49] A third example is Vicomte de Turenne's *Military Memoirs and Maxims of Marshal Turenne*. Although Turenne's work was largely autobiographical, he offered many strategic-level insights about how to effectively wage a war; thus the book really falls more under the heading of the military arts than a memoir. He was considered one of the foremost military minds of the age, and British officers regarded him among their favorite authorities.[50] Histories, biographies, and memoirs of famous commanders were all particularly popular, as well as the latest texts on artillery and engineering, works on classical Greece and Rome, and Continental European books on the art of war.[51] Several examples of the field or technical manuals that were the most popular included Guillaume Le Blond's *A Treatise of Artillery, or of the Arms and Machines Used in War*, Sébastien Le Prestre de Vauban's *The New Method of Fortification, as Practiced by Monsieur de Vauban ... to Which Is Now Added a Treatise of Military Orders, and the Art of Gunnery*, and John Cruso's *Militarie Instructions for the Cavallrie*.[52] Some of the favored biographical subjects included Oliver Cromwell, Louis XIV, the Duke of Marlborough, Julius Caesar, Alexander the Great, Charles VII of Sweden, and Gustavus Adolphus.[53] Given the British officers' overwhelming interest in reading and discussing military books, it is reasonable to assume that Washington became aware of this trend during the course of his service. With this in mind, the ambitious colonel Washington's military reading and his advice to his subordinate officers make perfect sense. Unfortunately Washington would have little opportunity to read anything beyond Bland's *Treatise* given his situation in command of the Virginia Regiment on the frontier.

This experience would provide him with lessons that he would need twenty years later; however, in the near term, Washington's miraculous work to turn a ragged handful of recruits into a respectable regiment of obedient soldiers did not merit the attention of those in the British military establishment who had the ability to grant preferment for royal commissions. The rest of Washington's career with the Virginia Regiment was undistinguished in terms of battlefield glory. In 1758 he led two regiments in Brig. Gen. John Forbes's final expedition against Fort Duquesne, but he did not directly contribute to the fort's ultimate recapture.[54]

While Washington clearly demonstrated some of the qualities that are now so synonymous with his later career in the War for Independence, in 1755 nothing about his words or deeds indicated that he could be the future leader of a revolution. Washington, like the majority of his colonial contemporaries, was proud to be British. He tried to build a pedigree worthy of that British identity so that he might achieve fame and glory in the scarlet tunic of His Majesty's regulars. Indeed, a close reading of Washington's correspondence from his career in the Virginia Regiment is almost painful. This young, ambitious Washington comes across as an artless office seeker with little to actually recommend him beyond a couple of narrow escapes. At times when he should have been more preoccupied with his soldiers' welfare, he instead petulantly whined to those in power about the officers' pay inequity. Although Washington had a certain capacity for flattery, especially when it came to dealing with his superiors, he also had no problem with bluntly blaming them for his every failure. Such acts of tactless insubordination did little to ingratiate him with the likes of Dinwiddie, Governor William Shirley of Massachusetts, and Brigadier General Forbes. Furthermore, he relentlessly pestered his superiors in Virginia for leave to seek out those in the British establishment who had the ability to grant his wish for preferment. Each time Washington appealed to the great and powerful in the British civil-military administration, however, he was denied.

Washington Meets Lord Loudoun: The Dream of a British Uniform Is Crushed

The most significant of these repeated British rejections is Washington's interview with the recently appointed commander in chief for North America, John Campbell, Earl of Loudoun. In the period leading up to Washington's meeting with Loudoun, he had grown increasingly frustrated with the string of rebuffs from various British officials. Over time Washington became convinced that Dinwiddie was the root cause of the problem. In Washington's mind, Dinwiddie consistently refused to listen to his strategic advice and instead made contradictory decisions, repeatedly fell short with supply requests, and would not heed Washington's frequent calls for equal pay for the officers. Washington's supporters in Williamsburg went further and convinced him that Dinwiddie was maneuvering against him and hoping to replace him with one of Dinwiddie's Scottish cronies.[55] Although Dinwiddie was actually patient with his ambitious commander, Washington did not recognize it and instead persistently requested leave to meet with those in the British establishment in North America who had more authority than Dinwiddie could boast. Having previously met with only partial success while dealing with Governor Shirley on a matter of rank, Washington shifted his attention to winning over Lord Loudoun.

As leverage for dealing with Loudoun, Washington did have from Governor Shirley an endorsement recommending him as second in command for any future offensive into the Ohio Country. He also had another endorsement from Dinwiddie, recommending him for a royal commission. They gave Washington the confidence to send a petition signed by the members of the regiment to Loudoun asking for patronage. This petition apparently fell on yet another deaf ear. Loudoun announced no new offensive into the Ohio, nor did he pay any heed to the idea that the Virginia Regiment warranted regular commissions. Instead, Loudoun announced the recruitment of more American soldiers who would be led by imported British officers. Upon hearing these latest pieces of bad news, Washington became ever more convinced that the British harbored irrational biases against the colonials. From this point forward, Washington's relationships with those in political power increasingly soured. He clashed with Dinwiddie repeatedly over frontier defensive strategies. Washington and his allies collaborated in order to defeat the governor's measures that they believed ran contrary to the colony's interests. Their actions would prove to be the opening salvos in the long struggle for colonial control between provincial leaders and members of the British administration.[56]

In the face of mounting frustration and challenges to his command and his reputation, Washington decided that he needed to make his case to Loudoun directly. Dinwiddie, acting on instructions from Loudoun, ordered Washington to abandon his frontier forts in favor of reinforcing Fort Cumberland in Maryland. Although Washington obeyed the order, he made sure everyone knew that it was contrary to his advice. Again it represented another example of British imperial authorities going against the expert opinions offered by the colony's rightful leaders.[57] By December 1756 Washington began writing a series of letters requesting, indeed almost begging, for leave in order to travel to Loudoun's location and plead his case. After nearly two months of requests, the now exasperated Dinwiddie relented, adding, "I cannot conceive what Service You can be of in going there . . . however, as You seem so earnest to go I now give you Leave."[58]

As Dinwiddie hinted, Washington was in for yet another disappointment. The dissatisfaction Washington felt at this juncture was tinged with a new level of bitterness, for he had taken pains to ensure that Loudoun knew he was not just any provincial office seeker. Washington prepared a lengthy report on Virginia's military situation that laid out the multitude of problems that existed with supply, discipline, and desertion. Furthermore, he recommended an all-out assault on Fort Duquesne as the only way to mitigate the threat on the frontier.[59] Washington had a dual intent in compiling this rather frank assessment — to convince Loudoun that taking Fort Duquesne should remain the British strategic objective and to show off his expertise, thereby lending credence to his request for preferment for not only his officers but more important for himself. This personal and overwhelming desire for a British commission is apparent in his somewhat artlessly included appeal for Loudoun's patronage: "Altho' I have not had the honor to be known to Your Lordship: Yet, Your Lordship's Name was familiar to my Ear, on account of the Important Services performed to his Majesty in other parts of the World — don't think My Lord I am going to flatter. I have exalted the Sentiments of Your Lordships Character, and revere Your Rank. . . . [M]y nature is honest and Free from Guile." Further down, he came more to his personal objective: "In regard to myself, I must beg leave to say, Had His Excellency General Braddock survived his unfortunate Defeat, I should have met with preferment equal to my Wishes: I had His Promise to that purpose, and I believe that Gentleman was too sincere and generous to make unmeaning offers, where none were ask'd. General Shirley was not unkind in His Promises — but — He is gone to England."[60] Loudoun apparently received the report, but he had other ideas about Great Britain's future on the North American front.

Washington arrived in Philadelphia to meet Loudoun on February 21, 1757; however, Loudoun did not arrive until March 14. Washington had to wait. As he had demonstrated before, though, patience was not one of his virtues. Already suspicious that a significant amount of anticolonial bias was inherent among the great and powerful in Britain's civil-military administration, Washington's opinion rapidly hardened during his wait for Loudoun. Outraged, he wrote to Dinwiddie that "we cant conceive, that being Americans should deprive us of the benefits of British subjects; nor lessen our claim to preferment: and that we are very certain, that no Body of regular Troops ever before Servd 3 Bloody Campaigns without attracting Royal Notice." Rebuffing the British claim that the Virginians were only defending their own property, Washington asserted, "We are defending the Kings Dominions, and altho the Inhabitants of G[rea]t Britain are removed from (this) Danger, they are yet, equally with Us, concernd and Interested in the Fate of the Country, and there can be no Sufficient reason why we, who spend our blood and Treasure in Defence of the Country are not entitled to equal prefermt."[61]

When Washington finally met Loudoun, his hopes of impressing the commander in chief were dashed, for Loudoun received him with the cold civility of an aristocrat to a social inferior. He was not the least bit interested in hearing Washington's strategic overview, nor could Washington convince him to pay any attention to the list of grievances that he had previously outlined on the regiment's behalf. Washington seemed to have traveled all the way to Philadelphia to receive orders and nothing more. Loudoun only made one concession to Washington's position and agreed that Maryland, not Virginia, should have to garrison Fort Cumberland. He neither called for an expedition against Fort Duquesne in 1757 nor mentioned royal commissions. Washington was thus treated as an incompetent provincial capable only of executing orders rather than commanding in his own right.[62] All of Washington's youthful dreams of wearing the scarlet tunic were reduced to ashes once and for all.

Washington returned to his regiment, and in anger, he resumed clashing with other officers over strategy for 1758. He drew rebukes from General Forbes and other regular officers, but in Virginia, he was still held in high regard. He did manage to achieve a brevet rank of brigadier general on the final expedition to Fort Duquesne, but by the time General Forbes's British force arrived, the French had abandoned and burned the fort. Washington was never able to exact revenge for the stinging loss of Fort Necessity. Moreover, his career in the Virginia Regiment was over.[63]

Washington's encounter with Loudoun signified an important moment in his life: he realized his dreams of becoming a British officer would never come to pass. All of his hard-earned, valuable experience could not earn him a place in the British army, whose officer corps was demarcated by bloodlines. He saw that the British administration, which his half-brother and the Fairfaxes for so long had taught him to admire, had serious flaws.

Washington Turns His Attentions to Civilian Life

That Washington did not immediately resign his commission after the ill-fated meeting with Loudoun underscores that his transformation into an American was not yet complete. He simply accepted that it was better to be a Virginian in the British Empire than any other alternative. He therefore turned his attention to doing his duty to his country, Virginia, and shifted his focus to becoming a leader in that provincial society, which did actually appreciate his achievements.

That said, Washington abandoned his study of the military arts that he had begun some four years earlier, for that reading no longer served a practical purpose for him. He instead devoted his energies in the coming years to increasing his wealth and status in Virginia society. Even before he left the Virginia Regiment, Washington was elected to the House of Burgesses and became active in politics while still serving in the militia. In 1758 Francis Fauquier replaced Dinwiddie, and Washington wasted no time in attempting to curry favor with the new lieutenant governor, writing that he was "anxious to earn the honor of kissing your [Fauquier's] hand."[64] Although by that time Washington had earned the respect of his fellow Virginians for his military service and he was getting better at diplomacy, he could not rely on those attributes alone to sustain himself in high society.

To successfully mix in the best social circles, Washington had to learn more about the science of agriculture, history, politics, and religion, for he had to balance being a planter, a member of the House of Burgesses, and a parish vestryman. After he returned to Mount Vernon and began assembling a library, those subjects that had the practical purpose of advancing his social stature dominated his burgeoning collection.

That Washington's transformation into an American was gradual points to the nature of his decision-making process. Thomas Jefferson would later write that Washington's mind was "slow in operation, being aided little by invention or imagination, but sure in conclusion."[65] The question is, why did Washington develop such a slow, deliberate decision-making process? His early military career indicated his propensity for rashness, so why did he have such a gradual shift in mentalities? Part of the transformation can be ascribed to maturity; as he aged, he lost some of that youthful impetuosity. Maturity, however, can only account for part of Washington's mental shift. To fully understand Washington's mental world, it is necessary to place him in context with other future revolutionaries.

Washington came of age in a colonial society dominated by intense royalists. Virginians and indeed nearly all colonists in British America considered themselves fortunate to be ruled by Protestant kings and queens who stood for liberty in the face of their oppressive Catholic enemies. Colonists looked to British history to cultivate this extreme degree of approbation for the empire they were a part of.[66] Washington was no doubt similarly schooled over the years in how best to appreciate the British constitution, the legacy of the Glorious Revolution, and the monarchy itself by his teachers and mentors during his formative years.[67] In fact, the evidence to support this argument is embedded in Washington's angry letter to Dinwiddie after his interview with Loudoun; it recorded Washington's outrage at the realization that colonists were not afforded the same rights as British subjects. Washington, as were all his future revolutionary compatriots, was raised to believe that he shared the same British identity as those raised in England. It was therefore a harsh moment when the colonists realized that their long-cherished assumption was wrong, as Washington's example illustrates. A majority of colonists in the 1750s and 1760s, however, still argued that it was better to be a British subject than any other sort. Caught up in the increasing Anglicization of Virginia politics and the celebratory atmosphere following Britain's final triumph over the French in 1763, the development of Washington's American identity slowed.[68]

Still Washington began to think differently than his colonial contemporaries. By the mid-eighteenth century, many of Virginia's planter elite expanded their reading interests as they increased the size of their private libraries. This practice was in stark contrast to that of their seventeenth-century forebearers, who maintained smaller, utilitarian libraries that consisted of mostly religious, historical, agricultural, and medical books, with perhaps a few volumes on English common law.[69] Less than a hundred years later, when the members of Virginia's ruling class were secure on their plantations and were no longer preoccupied with mere survival in an infant colony, they had the time and the means to broaden their reading to include more languages and subjects. Over time privileged boys were taught to read in Latin, Greek, French, and Hebrew. Libraries began to include more works of literature, natural philosophy, and mathematics along with the staples on religion, history, law, and medicine.[70] Additionally Williamsburg eventually developed a small academic world with the faculty and students of the College of William and Mary and a growing population of lawyers who had to travel to the town to apply for admission to the bar and try their cases. Furthermore, the arrival of Francis Fauquier as lieutenant governor provided an opportunity for members of the gentry who were not trained scholars or attorneys to participate in intellectual conversations on a range of topics. Fauquier fashioned himself as the quintessential enlightened aristocrat. He epitomized everything that young, wealthy Virginians such as Washington and Jefferson aspired to be: classically educated, carefully trained in cultivated social graces, and interested in broadening his understanding of scientific curiosities. Fauquier was a fellow of the Royal Society, and he regularly reported to England on the latest scientific experiments conducted in his colony. He also enjoyed music, genteel company, and intellectual conversations. He quickly recognized Jefferson's intellectual gifts when they met while Jefferson was still a student at the College of William and Mary. Fauquier included Jefferson along with Jefferson's law tutor, the eminent legal practitioner George Wythe, in his inner circle. Jefferson later remarked that during his numerous dinners with Fauquier, he "heard more good sense, more rational and philosophical conversation, than in all my life besides."[71]

Interestingly despite Washington's eagerness to kiss hands and curry favor with the new lieutenant governor, he apparently did not attempt to increase his learning in order to ingratiate himself with Fauquier. Whereas Jefferson had the benefit of a college education, legal training, and exceptional intellectual gifts and the Fairfax men had the advantages of blood ties to the English aristocracy and had been educated in England, Washington's military fame, continued dedication to public service in the House of Burgesses and the parish, and his dancing skills enabled him to effectively associate with the new governor. That said, at this stage in Washington's emerging political career, trying to acquire even a rudimentary classical education by reading everything he could as quickly as possible would probably not have gained him any additional political favor. Instead, Washington chose to focus his reading on agriculture, politics, and religion, the three subjects that were necessary to enhance both his fortune and his political career.

Washington Contrasted with Benjamin Franklin, Another Self-Educated Founder

The significance of Washington's change in mentality resonates more when he is placed in context with that of another founding father, Benjamin Franklin. Although not a Virginian, Franklin offers an interesting contrast to Washington as his formal education came to an early end and he had to make his own fortune and reputation without the benefit of an inheritance. Like Washington, Franklin's initial transformation into an American can be traced to a single moment of humiliation at the hands of a British official. Unlike Washington, however, Franklin did not abandon the pursuit of cultivating a European mind upon embracing his Americanness.

Twenty-six years Washington's senior, Franklin was born in Boston in 1706, the fifteenth of seventeen children of Josiah Franklin, a tallow chandler. Although Franklin's father decided early on that Benjamin was destined for the clergy, the cost of the requisite education was too expensive, and he pulled the boy from Boston Latin and sent him to a less expensive school that taught basic writing and arithmetic. At the age of ten, almost the same age at which Washington's formal education ended, Franklin was pulled from school altogether in order to learn a trade. He was apprenticed to his older brother James, a printer, and learned the business rapidly. Working in the printing business afforded him access to those in the book trade. Franklin fostered an appetite for learning by maintaining good relationships with Boston's bookshop owners, who let him borrow books. Franklin used his natural talents to capitalize on the kindness extended to him in order to establish and build his reputation. He used his brother's newspaper to publish his first writings, and later when he struck out on his own and moved to Philadelphia, his abilities and ambition caught the attention of wealthier printers who were influential in getting him established on his own. The teenage Franklin's ability to win over influential men to serve as patrons is somewhat akin to what Washington did as a young surveyor. Washington used his natural gifts for mathematics and his father's surveying instruments to learn a trade that not only would allow him to earn wages but also would introduce him to influential men. Franklin used his intellect, wit, and writing ability, as well as the skills he learned in his brother's printing shop, to attract the support of men who could help him advance.[72]

Despite Franklin's humble origins and the fact that he was building his fortune as a tradesman rather than through a rich inheritance, he did let it not stop him from pursuing more gentlemanly, intellectual activities. He continued reading as much and as often as he could, broadening his reading to include works in French, Spanish, Latin, and Italian. Together with other ambitious tradesmen and professional men in Philadelphia, he founded the Junto and a subscription library. As a city-dwelling tradesman, establishing an intellectual club like the Junto and gaining entry into other somewhat exclusive members-only societies such as the Freemasons were the best ways for Franklin to transcend his middling social status. Furthermore, he worked through these organizations and used his newspapers to suggest civic improvements for Philadelphia. Franklin's efforts to foster cultural and public works improvements in his city went a long way toward improving his social standing as he likewise increased his fortunes through his businesses. However, in order to become a gentleman and a leader of Philadelphia society, Franklin needed to leave the shop floor and devote himself entirely toward intellectual pursuits. He was able to do so by the 1740s after building his printing business into a successful media empire. Franklin's social rise differs from Washington's. In the planter-dominated South, land ownership, tobacco profits, and military glory could pave an ambitious man's way into the most exclusive social circles. In Philadelphia, the bustling, up-and-coming cultural center of British America, a gentleman was demarcated by different characteristics. Fortunately for Franklin, he was perfectly suited to join in the growing colonial fascination with the Enlightenment that was already flourishing throughout the upper classes of both Britain and

France.[73] Although he tried to continue fostering his folksy image as a hardworking, leather apron man long after his retirement, Franklin aspired to more worldly occupations.

In 1744 while building on the Junto, Franklin launched the American Philosophical Society. He conducted scientific experiments, most notably with electricity. This work was all possible because Franklin was confident enough in his talents to explore beyond the confines of the profession in which he was trained. His lack of an extensive formal education up through the university level did not hinder him in the same way that it did the less self-assured Washington. Franklin was indeed comfortable at the vanguard of American scientific exploration.[74]

That Franklin and wealthy colonists throughout British America strived to broaden their intellectual interests demonstrates how much they were in touch with the latest fashionable trends in the English aristocracy, for in England a parallel movement of increasing intellectual curiosity was taking place.[75] Again that these twin developments occurred on both sides of the Atlantic is a testament to the colonists' belief that they shared an identity with their English brethren. Both Lieutenant Governor Fauquier in Virginia and Franklin in Philadelphia actively worked to establish a scientific dialogue across the Atlantic. Through Peter Collinson, the Library Company of Philadelphia's agent in London, Franklin was able to obtain new instruments for scientific experiments, and Collinson made sure that Franklin's theories on electricity were presented to the Royal Society in 1750. Excerpts from Franklin's theories were then printed in London in *The Gentleman's Magazine* and subsequently translated into French, and they caused a sensation in the court of Louis XV. Additionally the Royal Society awarded Franklin gold medals and made him a member in honor of his achievements, rare accolades for an American colonial with no official pedigree, either hereditary or academic, to recommend him. At home Harvard and Yale awarded him honorary master's degrees.[76] Franklin had become internationally acclaimed, all without the aid of actual university study.

Science may have opened the path to Europe for Franklin; however, his Anglicization reached its zenith when he was appointed the colonial agent for Pennsylvania. He traveled to London in 1757, where he remained for years with only a brief sojourn to the colonies in his official capacity as postmaster general in 1763. In 1762 he was awarded an honorary doctor of laws from both Oxford and Edinburgh and was hereafter known to the world as Doctor Franklin. In 1766 he visited Göttingen University and was presented at the French court. Six years later Franklin was elected Associé étranger of the French Academy.[77]

During his long residence in London, Franklin was as ardent a royalist as any other Englishman. He campaigned vigorously for a royal charter for Pennsylvania and sought out men in the British administration with the power to grant him preferment and was somewhat successful. For a time he was the trusted source on all things American for a ministry struggling with how to reform its imperial administration under the weight of a staggering debt from the Seven Years' War. In fact, Franklin's testimony before the House of Commons was instrumental in getting the Stamp Act repealed. Franklin did an excellent job of presenting the American case to Parliament on February 13, 1766. He patiently answered the 174 questions leveled at him by members of Lord Rockingham's ministry, striking down all the arguments for virtual representation. He only made one mistake that would come back to haunt him: Franklin stated flatly that the American colonists recognized Parliament's right to levy external taxes, such as tariffs and export duties. His testimony, the longest public oration he would ever give, had the desired effect both in Britain, which repealed the act, and in America, where Franklin's reputation soared. He was made commissioner for Georgia, New Jersey, and Massachusetts.[78] The printer and self-taught scientist had become a statesman.

As an office seeker, Franklin in the early 1760s acted not altogether differently from Washington in the 1750s. Both ambitious men eagerly sought preferment from within the British imperial administration, and in their eagerness each overlooked or excused the flaws they saw both in the system and in the individual bureaucrats they encountered. Additionally just as Washington's evolving Americanness was a drawn-out process that accelerated only in the wake of repeated failures and crystallized at the supreme moment of rejection in his encounter with Loudon, Franklin's own transformation into an American was protracted and somewhat reluctant. Throughout the 1760s even as Franklin clashed with Lord Hillsborough and was denied much of the advancement that he sought, he was still slow to catch up with the anti-British sentiment that many of his fellow Americans had developed. Even after the Boston Massacre on March 5, 1770, Franklin's loyalty to the crown did not yet waver; instead, he advocated a new relationship with stronger ties between the king and the colonies without any subservience to Parliament. For Franklin to transform his national identity, he also had to experience an Americanizing moment. That point would occur during his spectacularly public humiliation at the hands of Solicitor General Alexander Wedderburn in the Cockpit.

By 1772 Franklin's British nemesis, Lord Hillsborough, had resigned as head of the American Department and was replaced with Lord Dartmouth, one of Franklin's close associates and a known American sympathizer. Franklin was as optimistic about the future as he had ever been, boasting that Dartmouth had "express'd some personal Regard for me."[79] Indeed, it seemed that it would be easier from this point for Franklin to both transact imperial business on behalf of the colonies that he was representing and to further his personal ambitions as well. During this year Franklin took the opportunity to try to diffuse the tensions between Britain and the colonies once and for all. He wanted to make it clear to his Massachusetts associates who had borne the brunt of British occupation that it was not the British ministry that was to blame for rising tensions; rather a few cunning colonial officials — namely, Governor Thomas Hutchinson — were the source of their countrymen's miseries. Franklin did so by sending some radical leaders in Massachusetts a packet containing letters written by Hutchinson to a small group of influential men, including a British undersecretary named Thomas Whately. In these letters Hutchinson, then lieutenant governor of Massachusetts, made it clear that he believed that firm measures, including "an abridgment of what are called English liberties," were needed in America to maintain its colonial dependence on Great Britain. Otherwise, he continued, "it is all over with us. The friends . . . of anarchy will be afraid of nothing be it ever so extravagant."[80] When Franklin sent the letters to Massachusetts, he included a cover letter in which he argued they were proof that the native colonial officials had traded "away the Liberties of their native Country for Posts" and had therefore betrayed not only the interests of their own colony but also of the crown and "the whole English Empire." These designing men, he wrote, "laid the Foundation of most if not all our present Grievances" and were responsible for instigating the "Enmities between the different Countries of which the Empire consists."[81] Franklin was so convinced he was right that he went so far as to make the outlandish argument that given the extent of the responsibility borne by Hutchinson and his lieutenant governor, Andrew Oliver, they should willingly be the scapegoats and sacrifice their reputations to avert the further disintegration of Anglo-American relations.[82]

That Franklin thought he could engineer reconciliation between Great Britain and the colonies by leaking the private letters between colonial and British officials was absurd in hindsight. On Franklin's part this incident represents a spectacular miscalculation of his own influence and a critical misreading of how the British officials, on whose side Franklin was trying so hard to remain, would perceive the leak. Just as Washington as a young officer was often guilty of dramatically overstating his own abilities in hopes of currying British favor, Franklin made similar mistakes with the Hutchinson letters.

Despite Franklin's stipulation that the letters were to be circulated only among a few men of worth, they were compiled into a pamphlet, printed, and circulated throughout Massachusetts in 1773. The publication sent the colony into an uproar and had the exact opposite effect than what Franklin had hoped. The colonists read the letters as proof of a conspiracy against them instead of seeing them as what Franklin argued — that is, as the isolated opinions of a few powerful men. As a result the Massachusetts radicals began to look for another opportunity to reinvigorate the struggle. That opportunity came in December 16, 1773, after the passage of the Tea Act, when the radicals dumped £10,000 worth of recently arrived tea into Boston's harbor. Almost at the same time, the uproar in Britain over the letters' publication reached fever pitch, and Franklin finally felt he could no longer keep silent. He publicly confessed to being responsible for leaking the letters to the Massachusetts rebels. The confession transformed Franklin into a symbol of colonial treachery. On January 20, 1774, news of the Boston Tea Party reached London, and the meeting of the Privy Council, which was supposed to decide on the Massachusetts petition to remove Hutchinson from office, instead became a full indictment of Franklin. On January 29 the Privy Council summoned Franklin to appear in the Cockpit, a gallery that was packed with many members of the king's court and London high society. Solicitor General Wedderburn berated Franklin for nearly an hour, hurling abuses that had never been heard before in polite English society. Indeed, much of it was too harsh for the newspapers to print. Wedderburn called Franklin "the true incendiary" and the "first mover and prime conductor" behind all the troubles in Massachusetts. He asserted Franklin furthermore had "forfeited all the respect of societies and of men, for he was not a gentleman; he was in fact nothing less than a thief."[83] Franklin stood stock still throughout Wedderburn's entire tirade despite the cheers and jeers from the crowd. His plan having completely backfired, Franklin's humiliation was complete. His hope for being the great reconciler was shattered, as too were his dreams of holding political office or at least of wielding political influence in London. This episode was Franklin's Americanizing moment. He could no longer harbor any delusions of having an English identity.[84]

Although Washington's transformation into an American occurred nearly a decade before Franklin's, and America and Great Britain were not yet on a full-fledged road to war, some striking dissimilarities between the two future founders underscore their respective political growth. Franklin's Americanization happened later than Washington's both in terms of chronology and his age at the time. Having become wealthy and having established an international reputation on the strength of his natural intellectual abilities, Franklin attracted the attention of powerful men in Great Britain first through the Anglo-American academic channels, and they in turn introduced him to the world of British imperial politics. Also his natural abilities gave him a healthy dose of self-confidence, which caused him to clash with those who failed to afford him as an Englishman of letters with due regard. Furthermore, his self-confidence combined with his inexperience in diplomacy led him to seriously miscalculate the degree of increasing hostility between Great Britain and the colonies. Even though Great Britain's intellectual elite feted him and bestowed honorary degrees on him, Franklin was ultimately unable to similarly charm England's political elite into granting him the real preferment that he sought and into treating him with the respect he thought he deserved. From an intellectual standpoint, when Franklin became an American it did not stop him from cultivating a European mind. On the contrary, Franklin was able to use his intellectual gifts and honorary academic pedigree to his advantage during his diplomatic career in France. In contrast to his often-awkward performance in England, Franklin had honed his diplomatic act by the time he arrived in France. Moreover, to his delight the French embraced him in ways that the English never did.

As discussed earlier, during Franklin's residence in London, he made several trips to France, where he received a great deal of attention from the royal family and from the country's intellectual elite. When he returned to France in 1776 on his diplomatic mission for the Second Continental Congress, Franklin found that interest in his scientific achievements had not waned. He also discovered that many at the forefront of the French Enlightenment, including Voltaire, were struggling to reform the ancien régime, and they increasingly came to regard

America as the symbol of everything that France lacked.[85] Franklin's intellectual gifts, his international renown, and his reputation as one of the American Revolution's most eloquent champions helped him mix with these reform-minded French intellectuals. Wearing his trademark fur cap in the carefully orchestrated guise of an American rustic, Franklin used his advantages to become a darling of the French Enlightenment. In other words, Franklin's final acceptance of an American identity coupled with his embrace of emerging European intellectual trends helped make him the successful diplomat that history remembers him as being. His efforts to secure a Franco-American alliance were instrumental to the ultimate success of the Revolution. Undoubtedly, Franklin's tenure in France would have been much more difficult if he had not been able to move so readily in France's intellectual salons. Because Doctor Franklin had made his fortune and his reputation on the basis of his academic talents, it makes perfect sense that his legacy as an American revolutionary leader hinged on his ability to circulate in the highest intellectual circles. His continued embrace of the European mind in concert with his Americanness made Franklin's reputation; however, the absolute opposite is true for Washington.

Washington's Intellectual Pursuits in Context

It is worth noting that Franklin and Washington made similar mistakes in their attempts to prove their Englishness. Franklin's self-assurance, which stemmed from his natural academic ability and positive reception in British intellectual circles, caused him to be overconfident in dealing with political officials, but they did not share the same regard that the intelligentsia had for the American colonial agent with no international political experience. Washington's overestimation of his own abilities arose from his confidence in his physical prowess. He expected that having proved his worth to some of Virginia's most influential men, he would thus enjoy preferment from the British military elite despite his total lack of military experience. Washington's comparative youth made his self-assuredness appear more striking than that of Franklin.

In contrast to Franklin, however, Washington's earlier evolution caused him to reject his contemporaries' interest in cultivating a European-style persona. Instead, he devoted himself to practical subjects that would make his plantations more profitable, thereby enhancing his wealth to such a degree that he would stay at the top of the social ladder that he labored so long to climb. His acceptance of the fact that no amount of battlefield experience or laurels would make him English despite his Virginia birth thus allowed Washington to develop intellectual interests that were more akin to those of his seventeenth-century colonial forebearers than to those of his eighteenth-century contemporaries.[86] Having made his mental break with his Englishness after Lord Loudon harshly dealt him a very personal affront, Washington in that key moment was forced to confront his academic shortcomings. This realization, when coupled with his extreme sensitivity to criticism, drove Washington intellectually inward and toward the subjects that he felt most comfortable with and that, more important, could meet his immediate needs at the time. He was fortunate to have already made his public reputation in Virginia based on his natural propensities for physical bravery and on his leadership experience. Learning to read Latin or becoming an amateur scientist would not sustain that hard-earned reputation in the planter-dominated high society; earning money and being a dedicated public servant would. Consequently Washington focused his reading and intellectual pursuits accordingly, and reading remained an intensely private activity. For example, when in residence at Mount Vernon, he spent on average two hours in the morning and all afternoon alone in his library.[87] Ironically the insecurities that discouraged Washington from ever trying to develop his intellect in the way Franklin had made him a better American revolutionary. Washington's lack of self-confidence in intellectual matters kept him humble enough to realize that he might not be up to the task ahead of him, and he was willing to listen to his advisers' informed opinions in order to make decisions. He learned powerful lessons from his early errors in judgment, a feat that might have been impossible if he had not grasped what his weaknesses were. He may not have had an extensive European education in the military arts, but he had hard-earned American experience in how to form and lead armies of his fellow countrymen. Franklin's Americanness was based on a conscious rejection of Englishness while he still embraced European ideas. Washington's Americanness was based on his conscious rejection of English ideas. In so doing, both men developed identities that they were entirely comfortable with.

Washington filled his library with books to help him confront the challenges that he faced both in his public life and in running his plantations. His library's catalog therefore looks very different from those of fellow Virginians Thomas Jefferson, William Byrd II of Westover, John Mercer of Marlborough, and Councillor Robert Carter of Nomini Hall. Notably, these four contemporaries of Washington's all enjoyed the advantage of university and legal educations. Their great libraries therefore reflect that as readers, they had the training required to facilitate reading across a broader spectrum of genres and languages.[88] Washington's reading also stands in stark contrast to the similarly educationally deprived Franklin, who taught himself to read in several languages and was interested in a variety of subjects. Nevertheless, Washington assembled an extensive library at Mount Vernon. Historians and biographers alike hitherto have not appreciated the library's quality as it reflects the unique intellectual development of the man who, more than any of his fellow founders, epitomizes what it is to be an American.

Chapters 2 through 4 explore the library's contents in the context of the public roles that Washington played over the course of his lifetime. It is interesting that Washington would always be placed in situations that charged him with leading men who were far more intellectually and/or academically qualified than he for his post. Moreover, he was never comfortable with political power. His choice of reading material therefore reflects one of the ways that he met challenges head-on. Deprived of the benefits of a university education, he compensated with a program of self-education to the best extent possible. This chapter examines the development of Washington's early intellect and sense of self and thus the reasons why he engaged in a certain type of reading. Now the stage is set to better understand what he read and how he used the knowledge he gained.

CHAPTER TWO

Provincial Reading

As the first warm rays of the sun that heralded the arrival of spring to Virginia stretched across the landscape, melting away the last of winter's frost, George Washington busily mulled over plans for the ongoing 1759 planting season. He was filled with a mix of anxious anticipation and frustration. Washington loved the land. In his mind, the possibilities of what good land could produce were limitless, and now more than ever he had to be right. The year's crops had to be successful, for he needed the yields to finance his plans for a larger extension to Mount Vernon's main house, which as yet had been only modestly expanded. There was a problem, however, with the cash crop itself, tobacco. Long the staple of Virginia planters since John Rolfe harvested the first meager crop in Jamestown more than a hundred years earlier, overcultivation had since robbed the once-rich soil of its nutrients and reduced subsequent yields to an inferior quality, which drove prices down. Tobacco also demanded hours of intense labor from a large workforce while delivering diminishing returns year after year. This situation simply would not do for Washington, who was brimming with ambitious and expensive plans for the future. That tobacco farming was becoming increasingly problematic constantly nagged at him. He was too much of a provincial Virginian at this point to abandon the traditional cash crop just yet. A man of his social status, however, could not continue raising a tobacco crop that led to diminishing returns. He had to do better and produce crops of the utmost quality, as was expected of one of the leaders of Virginian society. To that end, he dispatched orders to his London agent, Robert Cary of Robert Cary and Company, for among other things "the newest and most approvd Treatise on Agriculture . . . a new System of Agriculture, or a Speedy way to grow Rich."[1]

Cary first sent Washington a copy of Batty Langley's *New Principles of Gardening, or the Laying Out and Planting Parterres* and in 1761 filled Washington's specific request for Thomas Hale's *Compleat Body of Husbandry*.[2] Although Washington found these books useful, when he heard of a new English translation of Henri-Louis Duhamel du Monceau's *A Practical Treatise of Husbandry*, he quickly obtained a copy in 1764.[3] Duhamel's book was of particular interest to Washington, for among other things it outlined a new method for planting that was superior to the old, established common way. Duhamel advocated paying closer attention to soil preparation, rotating crops to preserve the soil, keeping careful records, and being innovative.[4] Washington internalized these lessons and devoted the rest of his career as a planter to transforming Mount Vernon from a one-crop plantation into a multifaceted agricultural enterprise.[5]

These agricultural books provide the best examples of Washington as a "student." His copy of Duhamel's *Husbandry* has more than fifty pages of marginalia wherein he meticulously converted the European measurements into the English system that he could better understand. Given all that we know about his relentless drive to excel at everything he did, it is not difficult to imagine him bent over his book at his desk, pouring over each page with care and making sure that the necessary conversions he made were absolutely right. The notes are mostly found throughout the two hundred pages that make up the book's part 2, which covers the "experiments" with wheat. This extensive and exacting marginalia was unusual for Washington, for due to his defective education he never developed the scholarly habit of marking up his books in the way that Thomas Jefferson and John Adams did. In fact, the evidence suggests that he made extensive notes in only a handful of other works he owned, most notably a harsh critique of his presidential administration by James Monroe. Although slight in comparison to his library's overall size at the end of his life, these isolated books with their examples of marginalia seem to indicate that Washington's most intense reading was done in circumstances when he stood to either gain or lose a tremendous amount. In the case of Duhamel's *Husbandry*, Washington's financial future was on the line. As one of Virginia's preeminent gentlemen, he felt he had a responsibility to maintain a certain lifestyle, which cost money, all while doing his best to enhance his overall fortune and not become entrapped in the endless cycle of debt to British financiers as so many of his fellow planters had. After years of pulling himself up by his bootstraps and more than once by the coattails of others, Washington had reached the top of Virginia society. Now he had to work to stay there — no small undertaking if ever there was one. No wonder he took the study of agriculture seriously.

Chapter 1 of this volume offers an argument as to why he read the materials he did — specifically, why he shied away from some of the classical reading that was so popular among both the colonial elite and the English gentry in favor of more practical subjects that would help him accomplish the short-term goals he outlined for himself. Having therefore established why he read, surveying what he read will hopefully make more sense within this broadly established context. As noted previously, chapters 2 through 4 examine the contents of Washington's library, broken down over three separate phases of his lifetime. This chapter addresses the first forty-three years of his life, before he was given command of the Continental Army and became an American figure. Chapters 3 and 4 explore the period of Washington's life when he was in the national spotlight during the American Revolution and through the end of his presidency. Chapter 5 focuses on his final retirement from public life to his death.

The Library and the Analytical Framework

At his death, Washington's library consisted of more than nine hundred volumes, including books, pamphlets, printed sermons and religious tracts, maps, and periodicals. The first question that must be answered is, did he read all of them? The short answer is no. For instance, the library at Mount Vernon had multiple volumes in various foreign languages, including German, Italian, French, and Latin. As Washington did not speak or read any foreign languages, those foreign-language works can immediately be ruled out. Also many books that Washington obtained later in life were gifts from the authors or from admirers who were hoping to curry favor or win an endorsement of some sort. Now, of course, just because some books were gifts does not mean that Washington failed to read them; however, if he did not take the time to search for and purchase them, the gift books must be closely examined for evidence that he read them and didn't simply thank the giver and place the book on a shelf without ever thumbing through them. Additionally some books that the estate appraisers labeled as the property of the library were women's magazines and literature that in reality belonged to Martha Washington; her daughter, Martha Parke "Patsy" Custis; and other female relatives who periodically resided at Mount Vernon over the years. Furthermore, Washington furnished his stepson, John Parke "Jacky" Custis, with a handsome library to facilitate the young man's education. When Custis died of typhoid in 1781, Washington had some of the books brought back to Mount Vernon, presumably for the education of Custis's son, George Washington Parke "Washy" Custis. George and Martha Washington would rear him and one of his sisters at Mount Vernon.

These are just several examples of the limiting factors discovered during the research for this book that must be taken into account to understand what Washington actually did read. In the end, after paring down the inventory of the library's contents, the remaining list is still extensive and demonstrates that Washington was in fact a deliberate and prolific reader who was discriminating in his selection of reading material and, when circumstances allowed, who read deeply on certain subjects such as agriculture. While he was not in the same intellectual league with Thomas Jefferson, Benjamin Franklin, or John Adams, Washington had a sharp, clear mind and a focus that enabled him to use reading as a tool to refine his image and enhance both his wealth and his social status.

In examining the library's contents, one of the next questions that must be answered is, how did he acquire the various works that filled his shelves? It can be answered with a reasonable degree of certainty by comparing the inscriptions in the individual volumes, the five different book lists that were compiled between 1759 and 1799, Washington's expense accounts, the invoices of goods he ordered from his London agents, and his correspondence. Washington purchased a fair amount of reading material throughout his lifetime, and it can be neatly traced through his meticulously kept expense accounts. He inherited some from his parents and absorbed a few volumes from the extensive Custis library upon his marriage to Martha. The rest were mostly unsolicited gifts.

Determining which of these volumes Washington read is far more difficult. Washington made a habit of writing his name and sometimes the year in which he acquired particular works on the flyleaf or the title page of the books he owned. He also had a bookplate that he used intermittently. In all, 397 volumes have his signature or bookplate or both. One can assume that he at least looked at each of these volumes, indicating maybe just a cursory read if not a careful one, and valued them enough to definitively mark them as belonging to him. That said, Washington did not put either his name or his bookplate in a number of volumes; often these books were gifts. With only a few exceptions that are discussed later in greater depth, there is no indication as to whether Washington read these unmarked books. Also frustrating is a severe dearth of marginalia, which would indicate what books Washington read and how thoroughly he read them. As stated earlier, this lack of annotation is not altogether unexpected. Because of his truncated education, he was never trained to read as a scholar, and on his own, he did not develop the habit of making notes in his books. Only a few volumes prove the exceptions to this general rule — namely, Duhamel's *Husbandry* and James Monroe's *View of the Conduct of the Executive*.[6]

Without extensive marginalia or commonplace books filled with reading notes in his hand, it is difficult to determine with complete certainty all of the books that Washington did read.

By eliminating the books that belonged to other family members who resided at Mount Vernon and those books in foreign languages that he could not read, however, a plausible case as to which books Washington did read can be made by using a carefully chosen set of assumptions based on several established facts. First, members of Washington's family attested to the fact that no one entered the library at Mount Vernon without orders from Washington himself; thus it makes sense to assume that he was not simply collecting yards of unread classics for the sake of appearances.[7] Therefore, with regard to the books he purchased for himself, we can assume that Washington did so with the express reason of wanting or needing to read them. Second, although Washington did not take many notes on his reading and seldom directly quoted anything in his writings, he did make certain literary allusions from works he possessed, such as the Bible and Shakespeare's writings, among others, thereby indicating that he read them carefully and felt comfortable enough with the material to refer to it in his correspondence.[8] Since Washington diligently preserved his writings and understood that his popularity meant that his correspondents would keep his letters as well, it is hard to believe that someone as calculating as Washington would write anything he was unsure of. Third, by establishing the most accurate timeline possible of when he acquired the various works in his library and then putting it in context with what was taking place in his life at the time, reasonable assumptions can be made about how he could have used each particular piece to assist him in whatever occupied him at that point. Again a timeline of Washington's literary acquisitions can be constructed by referencing his expense accounts, his correspondence with his agents and authors, the lists of Washington's book inventory made during his lifetime, and the publication dates of each work. On average, with the exception of the books he inherited from his parents and those that came from the Custis library, Washington seems to have acquired his books within ten years of their publication. Additionally Washington typically received presentation books as soon as they were published in first-edition print runs.[9] All of this information combined with an understanding of Anglo-American print culture shed light not only on what Washington read but also on the significance of each work at various points throughout his life.

Washington's Religious Collection: Growing up Anglican

With this methodological framework established, it is now possible to begin exploring the books Washington collected during the early part of his life in Virginia before he rose to national prominence. As stated in chapter 1, Washington's education abruptly ended with the death of his father. He spent his formative years under the tutelage of his mother. Washington family lore tells us that Mary Ball Washington was a stern, pious woman who, in the tradition of Virginia colonists since the mid-seventeenth century, maintained a small religious library and read to her children daily from the Bible and from several other texts including Sir Matthew Hale's *Contemplations Moral and Divine,* James Hervey's *Meditations and Contemplations,* Offspring Blackhall's *The Sufficiency of a Standing Revelation in General,* and Thomas Comber's *Short Discourses upon the Whole Common-Prayer.*[10] These books were all standard reading for Anglicans in the late seventeenth and early eighteenth centuries and were widely available on both sides of the Atlantic.[11] This early instruction in the Anglican Communion is where the young Washington, as well as the majority of his fellow Virginians, gained his lifelong commitment to orthodoxy.

Although the veracity of Washington's true faith remains a subject of heated debate among historians, that he was a practicing Episcopalian is beyond dispute.[12] Leaving the question of faith aside, it is not difficult to see the impact of the lessons from his parents' religious library on the developing youth. During his adolescence, Washington began to develop the formidable willpower and self-discipline that would become his chief characteristics later in life. Anecdotal sources all pinpoint his mother as the source of Washington's discipline; she certainly imparted it to her son through the Anglican doctrine that she read to him. In direct contrast to Puritan sermons, which were intensely theological and often centered on the subject of salvation, Anglican sermons were shorter, less theological, and more pietistic, emphasizing sound morality as opposed to predestination.[13] For example, Blackall's eight sermons in *The Sufficiency of a Standing Revelation in General* are free of complex structures and concisely make the argument that scripture is the only moral guide that one needs in life. The simplicity of the message in each of his sermons was intended to reach a wide audience and therefore made a good instructional catechism for children.[14] Similarly, Comber's *Short Discourses upon the Whole Common-Prayer* provides a straightforward guide on how to read and use the *Book of Common Prayer*. What is particularly striking about Comber's work is that in addition to teaching readers how to behave in church, he argued that sinfulness must be acknowledged and forgiveness must be asked from God, but in doing so, it was important not to go overboard. Maintaining self-control while living a life of quiet yet reverent devotion was the correct way of living.[15] As Washington was the epitome of self-control, it makes sense to connect that character trait in part with the lessons he learned from reading Comber as a young man.

Growing up a good Anglican was an important quality to Virginia's ruling class, so Mary Washington ensured not only that her children understood the lessons of the Bible but also that they knew how to perform the communicant's role in an Anglican service. After all a Church of England service follows the *Book of Common Prayer*, which is not so much a collection of prayers as it is a playbook, or the "script" that proscribes how worship is done. Although the Anglican liturgy is not as physically performative as its Roman Catholic counterpart, it nonetheless requires participants to know when to stand, sit, and kneel at given intervals; when to pray; and how to do it. Inherent in the prayer book are carefully laid stage directions, collective and individual repetitions, and different speeches made by different individuals.[16] In other words, in order to behave with proper reverence and decorum in these services, one must first be instructed in what to do. Learning how to behave in church without embarrassing oneself was crucial, for Virginia church services featured a veritable who's who in the upper crust of society. Performing well in church would have been doubly important for Washington after the death of his father when his adolescent mind was dreaming of big ambitions that would require the patronage of a powerful benefactor; thus the shy teenager needed to make an appropriate impression if he was ever to transcend his middling position. Being confined to the second tier of Virginia society did not appeal to Washington, for it would likely have meant greater difficulty escaping his domineering mother.

Travel Narratives, Magazines, and Heroics:
Fuel for the Imagination

The prospect of social immobility must have weighed on the youth, whose imagination at the same time was being fueled by stories in the popular magazine *The Spectator* and his reading of Chevalier Ramsay's *The Travels of Cyrus* and Lord Anson's *Voyage round the World*.[17] Founded in 1711 by Joseph Addison and Richard Steele, *The Spectator* was widely read on both sides of the Atlantic and was a great favorite of the Virginia gentry because it communicated current events in an enlightened, erudite manner, bringing philosophy out of libraries and classrooms and into the coffeehouses. The literary style of *The Spectator* inspired Virginia printers to fill their pages with essays and poetry rather than straightforward reprints of old news.[18] Ramsay's *The Travels of Cyrus*, a best-selling fictional work, describes an ideal world populated by figures from ancient Greece. Into the text of the travel narrative Ramsay interwove a discourse on pagan theology, a subject of particular interest to those Virginians who were developing and refining their knowledge of the classics. Therefore the classical setting for this work captured readers' attention, and the fantastical prose held it. Lord Anson's *A Voyage round the World* recounted the details of the British naval expedition of 1739. The British were anticipating that war would soon break out with Spain, and the admiralty decided that the best strategy would be to attack Spain in its colonies in order to deprive it of their wealth and natural resources. Anson was ordered to sail the world and reconnoiter the colonies to determine the feasibility of this plan of action. This book offered readers a contemporary assessment of the world outside the British Empire and a romanticized view of service in the Royal Navy. At the time it seemed possible that Washington would embark on a naval career, so it would have made perfect sense for him to read such a travel narrative.

It was William Fairfax, in consultation with Lawrence Washington, who arranged for George to become a midshipman in the Royal Navy; however, Mary Ball Washington vetoed the plan after her brother informed her that George would be ill-treated and have little hope of advancement in that service because he lacked the necessary connections. Although his mother closed the first window of military opportunity for Washington, he still dreamed of a life in uniform.[19] These dreams were fueled by his first documented book purchase, *A Panegyrick to the Memory of His Grace Frederick, Late Duke of Schonberg*. This slim volume is a eulogy of the persecuted Huguenot Friedrich Hermann, First Duke of Schomberg, who was driven from France and into the service of William III and whose character traits were strikingly similar to Washington's.[20] Schomberg was renowned for his personal bravery on the battlefield. He was praised for his "kind of Capacity for the greatest Trusts" along with his "Worth and Abilities." Moreover, "he was Naturally Active, a great lover of Exercise, Healthful and Temperate to Admiration. He neither Courted nor Fear'd Danger, ever Himself, ever Fortunate, ever preventing the worst, and surmounting the Greatest Difficulties." Schomberg was said to have closely adhered to a set of rules of civility; likely it was similar to the version that Washington copied in his schoolbook. What is also interesting is the short passage dealing with Schomberg's education: "Education makes us truly what we are; and if Nature prepares Men to, it is that that lays the

Foundation of Great Actions."[21] Given the extremely close parallels between the descriptions of the characters and attributes of the two men later in life, it seems plausible that this book was extremely influential in Washington's character development as a young man. The heroic language in which the panegyric was written was deliberately chosen to illicit admiration from readers.[22] As such, it is not difficult to imagine that such a story of a successful life would have captivated the teenage Washington. If Washington was really taken with this memorial to Schomberg, it makes sense that he would seek to follow Schomberg's example and take seriously the admonition that education was the foundation of a man's identity.

Surveying: Employment and Opportunity

Learning how to act in the presence of greatness so that he could curry favor was only one aspect of what Washington needed to master in order to further his lofty ambitions. In Virginia the amount of land one owned also determined one's social status, and being the third son, Washington's inheritance from his father was modest. Thus he needed to earn money so he could begin speculating in real estate. He had his father's old surveying instruments, and from William Fairfax he obtained a copy of William Leybourn's *The Compleat Surveyor, Containing the Whole Art of Surveying of the Land by the Plaine Table, Circumferentor, Theodolite, Peractor, and Other Instruments*. This straightforward handbook for surveyors outlines how to use each tool to determine measurements of a tract of land and how to turn those measurements into maps. It is written in plain language so that anyone could read it, with or without any previous experience in an apprenticeship.[23] It is interesting to think of the influence that this book had on the beginning of Washington's career, for it is from this text that he gleaned enough knowledge of surveying to obtain a license from the College of William and Mary. Once licensed he embarked on his first job, surveying lands for the colony's elite landowners, with Lord Fairfax among them. It is important to note that although Washington's transactions with these wealthy men were only a part of the overall dividend from his early occupation, the most valuable lessons he took from his surveying career were his knowledge of the land and his wilderness survival skills. This expertise made him the right choice when Dinwiddie selected him as the emissary to the French in the Ohio Valley just prior to the start of the Seven Years' War. As was previously mentioned, this service made Washington a household name when his journal cataloging the entire harrowing experience was widely published and read in the colonies and in England.

Military Art and Science

Once war with the French became a reality and Washington found himself saddled with the responsibility of command, he needed guidance. As noted in chapter 1, he obtained a copy of Humphrey Bland's *A Treatise of Military Discipline*. First published in 1727, the book went through nine editions and quickly became known as the British army's bible. It was a foundational text that outlined daily operations at every level of command beginning at platoon level. Almost all British officers serving in the Seven Year's War had copies of this book. Gen. Sir William Howe owned one in 1732, Brig. Thomas Paget in 1741, Lt. Gen. Henry Hawley in 1753, Maj. Gen. James Wolfe in 1756, and Maj. Gen. Alexander Dury and Lt. Col. William Wade in 1758. Col. Samuel Bagshawe in 1751 and Lord John Murray in 1762 each owned two copies. Furthermore the book maintained its popularity through the end of the eighteenth century, as Field Marshal John Ligonier obtained his copy in 1770, Lt. Gen. William Tryon and Capt. George Smith in 1773, Maj. Gen. Sir Charles Hotham Thompson in 1784, Lt. Col. William Calderwood in 1787, and Capt. John Montresor in 1799.[24] Washington also read *Julius Caesar's Commentaries*, one of the most popular military books on the art of war in the eighteenth-century Anglo-American world, and numerous translations were readily available in the colonies. Washington read the book on the advice of William Fairfax, but as many officers recommended, discussed, listed, or cited *Julius Caesar's Commentaries*, it is equally possible that other officers, such as Gen. Edward Braddock, could have recommended the book to him.[25]

There is little evidence to support that Washington did any other military reading during the Seven Years' War. For one thing Washington had to build a regiment from the ground up, so devoting what spare time he had to reading the latest in European grand strategy would not have provided him with any practical knowledge that would have been immediately useful. Also he was away from his regiment from November 1757 to March 1758 with a severe bout of dysentery, which by his physicians' accounts brought him to death's door.[26] By the time he recovered, he went on only one more campaign with General Forbes. Washington viewed it as a chance to showcase his experience as a battle-hardened, frontier combat leader; grand strategy and European tactics were expressly not useful in this situation. Another reason why Washington never returned to military reading in the years before the American Revolution was that he began planning for a future life outside the army.[27] The repeated rejections Washington received to his requests for a regular commission burned him, and as time passed and they kept coming from higher levels of authority, he must have realized that he would never get his wish. He therefore turned his mind to new dreams of prosperity and fulfillment in civilian life. He also began to think of marriage.

Washington was twenty-six years old when he paid his respects to the recently widowed Martha Dandridge Custis. He had met her before at a ball in Williamsburg when he was officially elevated to commander of the Virginia Regiment. Although she was married at the time, she must have made an impression on Washington, for he proceeded straight to her house after doctors pronounced him well following his illness. After that first visit (an overnight stay), she must have given him some encouragement, for he was back within a week. He also made it a point to impress Martha's children, four-year-old Jacky and two-year-old Patsy. Much to the frustrations of historians and biographers, few details are known about exactly what attracted George and Martha Washington to each other. He was well aware that she was the richest widow in Virginia, with an estate valued at £23,632, which would certainly catapult him to the top of Virginia society, but there was apparently more to his interest than that. By all accounts Martha was a gentle person who communicated warmth to those who interacted with her. While her wealth was almost certainly a compelling reason for Washington to consider courting the widow Custis, he must also have found her benevolent personality soothing, especially in light of his cool relationship with his mother. In Martha he would have a supportive partner, and he set out for that definitely worthy goal with his characteristic determination. The extremely brief courtship was fruitful, for the couple became engaged sometime during or shortly after his second visit. His expense accounts record that he ordered a ring from Philadelphia, as well as a suit of new clothes, at about the same time that Martha placed an order for a new dress and shoes.[28] The bachelor soldier was about to become the head of a family and a gentleman planter.

The prospect of marrying Martha posed a problem for Washington: the house at Mount Vernon was too small. He had met and courted Martha and her children in her world, where he could impress them with his grace and impressive physical appearance. But the house at Mount Vernon in 1758 was not yet the architectural manifestation of the man; indeed, it was little altered from its original seventeenth-century appearance. As he was always eager to impress, Washington recognized that he needed to expand — and quickly. Designing and supervising the extension of a house was as arduous a task then as it is now, and complicating matters was the fact that Washington was going away with General Forbes's expedition against Fort Duquesne. While Washington entrusted the supervision to George William Fairfax, his best friend and neighbor, he did most of the planning himself. A fair number of architectural books were available to him, but among others, most likely he relied on Batty Langley's *The City and Country Builder's and Workman's Treasury of Designs* (which is discussed in further detail in chapter 6).[29]

The year 1759 was filled with new beginnings. Washington retired from the Virginia Regiment and married Martha on January 6. Not only was he now a husband and stepfather, but he also was responsible for managing the Custis estates that Martha's first husband had left to her and their children. Washington threw himself into his new roles and the task of running the sprawling plantations. One of the first major duties he had to face following the marriage was the settlement of Daniel Parke Custis's estate, which was still in turmoil because Custis had died without a will. As Washington sifted through the assorted legal hassles to divide the property that belonged to Martha, Jacky, and Patsy, he began to make provisions for his stepson's education by going through the Custis library and taking to Mount Vernon those volumes he thought would suit the boy's future education.[30]

Washington Begins to Build His Library

Through the early years of his marriage, books seemed to take on a new degree of importance for Washington. In 1764 Washington compiled a list of books that were at Mount Vernon. He made this list sometime after receiving Tobias Smollett's eleven-volume *Complete History of England* in the summer of 1763 and before he received the twelve issues of *Country Magazine* that Robert Cary and Company sent to him from London in February 1765. Analyzing this list is a challenge for several reasons. First, the list was apparently made according to the shelf or whatever other container in which the books were stored and not by alphabetical order, by author, or even by genre. Washington arranged his books by size, so the titles do not flow together in a logical sequence. Second, as he made this list, Washington began putting the initials GW or JC after each title to indicate whether they belonged to him or to Jacky; however, Washington stopped doing it approximately a third of the way through the list. Third, Washington abbreviated most of the titles. These abbreviations are in most cases slightly different than the ones he created in the 1759 list and for the subsequent list made of the books at Mount Vernon in 1783, the list of Jacky Custis's books at the time of his death in 1781, and the final list of Washington's books at the time of his death in 1799. Fourth, several volumes are simply listed as "Miscellanies," offering no clue to their actual identities. Despite these problems, however, the true list of which books were Washington's can be deduced with some certainty. Before he stopped placing the initials next to each title, Washington claimed ownership of twenty-nine titles, totaling some thirty-eight volumes. By comparing the 1764 list with the one Washington made of the Custis books in 1759 and that of Jacky Custis's books in 1781, and by eliminating the titles that appear on all three lists as Custis property, about twenty-nine more titles on the 1764 list can be identified as belonging to Washington.

When all of the processes of elimination are complete and the books that belonged to Washington are sifted from the rest, what emerges is a telling picture of Washington's views on reading and what books could offer. Washington's books span several genres: agriculture, history, religion, law, military arts, science, and periodicals with a few literary works. Of the total collection, agriculture, history, and religion dominate his relatively small collection. All things considered, these preferences make sense given the station he occupied. At this point Washington thought that military service was behind him; so in 1764 the only military-related titles he had were the two books that he had owned during the Seven Year's War. He was responsible for managing a complex conglomerate of plantations that he was trying his best to make profitable for not only himself but also for his two stepchildren. He was a member of the Virginia Assembly and had become a vestry-man of Truro Parish in 1762.[31] All of these roles required a certain kind of knowledge, and Washington made a concerted effort to acquire it.

Washington Studies Agriculture, the Great Passion of His Life

Washington more fully immersed himself in the study of agriculture than in any other subject, and books on agriculture were readily available in the colonies. As Washington grew frustrated with tobacco as his staple crop, however, he recognized that in his society, where a planter's reputation hinged on not simply how much tobacco he raised but also the crop's quality, he needed to expand his knowledge in order to properly maintain his social status.[32] Shortly after his marriage Washington wrote to his London agents, Robert Cary and Company, and ordered the latest and most up-to-date agricultural treatise, "Langley's Book of Gardening," and the latest edition of "Gibson, upon Horses."[33] Washington followed up this request on June 12, 1759, with another letter to Robert Cary and Company in which he stated that since his previous order, he "had been told that there is one lately publishd — done by various hands — but chiefly collected from the Papers of Mr. Hale." Washington asked if his information was correct and that if the book "is known to be the best pray send it but not if there is any other in higher Esteem."[34] Washington was so convinced that Hale's latest multivolume work was the best series of books on agriculture available that he felt the need to write again on October 24, 1760, requesting the series by its specific name this time. As it turns out, Washington's information about the series' recent publication was correct. He received the first edition of *A Compleat Body of Husbandry*, published by T. Osborne and J. Shipton in London in 1756, at Mount Vernon on March 31, 1761, to the relief of Washington's anticipation. These agricultural books each offered the latest information on planting experiments, which he hoped would be useful in his attempt to reverse the devastating nutrient-depleting effects that the overcultivation of tobacco had wreaked upon the soil.[35]

This exchange of letters between Washington and his agents in London raises an important question: how did Washington learn about agricultural books that were just becoming available? Most likely he learned of new books by word of mouth. Neither his diaries nor his correspondence contain any details about book recommendations. Agriculture was one of the few areas that Washington would have discussed in public conversation as it was expected of planters. Eighteenth-century Virginia was dominated by an agrarian culture in which tobacco shaped planter society and helped define a planter's place in it. In fact, it was so woven into the fabric of daily life that it was impossible to go anywhere in Tidewater Virginia without hearing conversations about it.[36]

Engrossed in this world, Washington for years sought out the newest and most up-to-date treatises on agriculture, looking for the ways to enhance his tobacco crop's quality. The evidence of Washington's unending search in his reading for solutions to his agricultural questions can be found in his diaries. His diaries from this period are rich with details of his small-scale experiments based on his reading, along with considerable information gleaned from his daily inspections of his farms.[37] These diaries reflect the seriousness with which he approached his new full-time occupation of farming. Unlike many contemporary diarists who included details of their personal lives in daily entries, Washington wove weather reports, farming statistics, and summaries of his social engagements into a somewhat awkwardly structured narrative of his daily routine. Personal or emotional details are simply absent.

What is also interesting is that both before and after the Revolution when Washington resided at Mount Vernon and was fully engaged in managing his plantations, he wrote his diary entries in interleaved copies of the *Virginia Almanack*.[38] Washington's choice of using an almanac as a diary instead of a blank notebook illustrates how important agriculture was to him. While critics have characterized Washington's diaries as uneven or erratic, these diaries instead illustrate the degree to which he loved farming his land.[39] Increasing his plantations' efficiency became a lifelong passion for Washington.

As such, the diaries reveal that he recognized the special relationship that existed between his family and his land. For example, Washington went into detail about the sowing of wheat in his entries on August 3, 1771: "Began to Sow Wheat at the Mill, also steepd in Brine with alum put thereto. This day began to Sow the Brined wheat at Muddy hole. Before this the Wheat was not steepd in Brine at this place. Note. The Brine was made by the directions in the Farmer's guide, as the common method practiced by Farmers; but our Wheat was steepd only 24 hours instead of 35 which he recommends."[40] In contrast, his entry for June

19, 1773, curtly states, "At home all day. About five oclock poor Patcy Custis Died Suddenly."[41] The difference between the levels of detail in these two entries in the same diary does not indicate that Washington had no emotional reaction to his stepdaughter's death. On the contrary, the differences underscore the fact that Washington intended his diaries to be an accurate record of his activities and nothing more. His writing was factual, entered into the blank pages of a practical publication.

Washington instead conveyed the emotions of his loss in a letter to his brother-in-law Burwell Bassett:

> Yesterday . . . the Sweet Innocent Girl Entered into a more happy and peaceful abode than any she has met with in the afflicted Path she hitherto has trod. She rose from dinner about four o'clock in better health and spirits than she appeared to have been in for some time; soon after which she was seized with one of her usual Fits, and expired in it, in less than two minutes without uttering a word, a groan or scarce a sigh — This sudden and unexpected blow, I scarce need add has almost reduced my poor Wife to the lowest ebb of Misery.[42]

These examples demonstrate that Washington viewed farming as the livelihood around which the rest of his life revolved and to which his family's fortunes were tied. The diaries served a purpose in his farming enterprise. In them there was only room for sentiment, not sentimentality.

As noted previously, in 1764 Washington obtained Duhamel's *A Practical Treatise of Husbandry*, another European agricultural book that boasted a radical new approach to soil preparation.[43] Duhamel's book flew in the face of eighteenth-century Virginia's tobacco mentality, arguing that in order to preserve the soil's nutrients, farmers should rotate their crops. This advice struck a particular chord with Washington, for as the price of tobacco continued to drop, he saw that it would be necessary to diversify in order to survive. Shifting away from tobacco was an enormous risk. Reflecting how intensely he debated the potential risks versus rewards of making this transition, Washington covered Duhamel's *Husbandry* with more than fifty pages of extensive marginalia. In part 2 Duhamel addressed experiments with wheat that compared planting wheat in a field the "common way" as opposed to "deep plowing" and worked out the difference between the yields. When utilizing deep plowing, seeds were planted in only two or three rows that were separated from the next group by "alleys" twice their width. The alleys allowed the roots of the plant to expand to collect more nourishment. The benefit of this system was that beds and alleys could be rotated yearly and a field could continuously produce wheat.[44] It is almost possible to imagine Washington bent over his desk with the book in front of him, a quill in his ink-stained fingers, reading this passage and suddenly realizing the keys to the future — rotate crops and diversify. Tobacco alone would not work in the long run, so why not transform Mount Vernon from a plantation into a farm?

Why did Washington make such extensive, exact marginal notes in this one book? Washington did not have a habit of writing in his books, so why write in this volume, especially so prolifically? The answer lies in the circumstances. As a planter, Washington was tied to the seasons, so no matter how fast he devoured the agricultural books he got his hands on, he could still only experiment in accordance with the seasons. In other words, nature allowed him to study his books slowly and deliberately. Again Washington alone was responsible for the production of not only Mount Vernon but also the estates belonging to his two stepchildren and those estates that his wife brought into the marriage. Additionally since he and his peers believed that their respectability was tied to their profit margins, he stood to lose much more than money if his plantations were not productive enough. He was keenly aware that the stakes were high and that the conventional wisdom that his fellow Virginians lived by for so long was no longer sufficient. Concentration and exactness were integral to future productivity.

Besides learning the best way to plant wheat, Washington gleaned other important lessons from Duhamel about soil preparation and record keeping. Above all the most important advice that Washington internalized from his reading was that in order to be a truly successful farmer, he had to be innovative, for "the common farmer is perhaps the least inquisitive of any man."[45] Washington learned this instruction well and became an agricultural innovator ahead of most of his peers. He was among the first in Virginia to turn away from tobacco in favor of wheat and corn. That decision, although agriculturally prudent, did not immediately pay off as Washington had a difficult time finding a good market for his Virginia grain. This setback did not cause Washington to abandon his diversification experiment and return to old ways. He instead expanded his operations to include a fishery and gristmill.

All of this ingenuity was necessary, because try as he might in the first years of his marriage, Washington fell ever more deeply into debt to Robert Cary and Company. Here Washington was the classic Virginia aristocrat — land rich and cash poor. His marriage to Martha brought him substantial wealth and an increase in social status, which obliged him to live and entertain lavishly. The newlyweds went on a spending spree, ordering everything from luxury furnishings, table settings, clothing, shoes, hair accessories, fine wines by the cask, and medicines not available in the colonies.[46] After two years of marriage, he owed Cary and Company the princely sum of £2,000.[47] Before he knew it, he had burned through the money he received through his marriage and then some in the course of expanding Mount Vernon.[48] This profligate spending reveals one of Washington's contradictions. In some ways, he was an innovative thinker, more willing than some of his contemporaries to abandon an English mind-set; yet in other ways, he was totally trapped in the social mores of his day, spending funds he did not have in order to keep up appearances as required for someone of his standing. His mounting debt robbed him of his sleep, yet the orders kept flowing from his desk even as his tobacco prices kept dropping and his profit margin eroded. He vented some of his frustrations in terse letters to Robert Cary and others, but mostly his annoyance manifested itself in his intense work to master the science of agriculture in order to revolutionize his plantations into moneymaking enterprises.

When considering the significance of Washington's agricultural studies during this period of his first retirement from military service, it is important to bear in mind that he was not simply a planter but also a member of the House of Burgesses and a vestryman of Truro Parish. He was first elected to a seat in the House of Burgesses before he even left the Virginia Regiment, but now that his military career was over, he was expected to take more of a direct interest in the running of the colony. As with his militia service, Washington's tenure in the House of Burgesses marks another situation in which he found himself surrounded by men who were more qualified than he was. He had fame and fortune but little else to recommend him for a career in politics. Many of his fellow members were men with at least some college education, and more than a few had been educated abroad in British universities and the Inns of Court.[49] Whatever Washington may have felt about his preparedness for office, duty demanded that he serve to the best of his ability.

Politically Oriented Reading and Service in the House of Burgesses

Once more Washington turned to his books to help him. The list that Washington made of his books in 1764 reveals that in addition to his growing agricultural collection, history, law, and religious books also lined his shelves. On both a societal and personal level, it makes perfect sense that such books would grace Washington's expanding collection. Religious books were the first books brought to Virginia in the earliest days of settlement. Although provincial Virginians were traditionally not as pious as their Puritan counterparts in New England, religious books were present in most private libraries from the seventeenth century onward. It was deemed essential for planters and gentlemen in Virginia also to have a basic working knowledge of the law as they were expected to serve as members of the governor's council, as burgesses, and as justices of the peace. Furthermore their management of extensive land holdings also required that they understand the law specifically with regard to contracts. History, particularly English history, was also a cornerstone of libraries in colonial Virginia. The reason for this is twofold: service in government demanded an understanding of the English constitution, and it was a matter of pride — British pride. Eighteenth-century Virginians were full of patriotic fervor, and Washington was no exception.[50]

With all of this in mind, Washington's library in 1764 seems to be on par with that of his peers in terms of the types of utilitarian books he owned; however, there is a distinction albeit a slight one. Unlike his wife's first husband, Thomas Jefferson, and Landon Carter — all of whom were wealthy enough to acquire and assemble large, broad-based collections — Washington built a library that was quite limited in scope. It had almost no philosophy, little in the way of belles lettres, only a couple of travel narratives, and a few periodicals. In this way Washington's narrowly based collection places him more in line with his seventeenth-century forebearers, who were focused on forging a living in a young colony and thus had no time for leisure reading, than with his Enlightenment contemporaries in the more refined eighteenth century who had reaped the benefit of their forefathers' efforts and embraced a classical education.

The colonists who came to Virginia in the first migratory waves from England almost certainly brought no literature or other books for pleasure with them as freight costs were high and ships had little room for excess baggage. Instead, the evidence suggests that the colonists brought Bibles and books that had a practical application. The high cost of imports also precluded many colonists from purchasing books from England. Furthermore as Virginia did not have a permanent printing press until 1730, there was no alternative to buying imports.[51] Moreover, the early colonists were focused on establishing themselves and making the colony profitable; therefore, they had little time to devote to reading for personal gratification. In this sense, when placed in context with his fellow elite planters, Washington's preference for practical books parallels decisions of an earlier generation.

Washington's religious books are significant not because they yield any insight into his opinions on God and everlasting life — they do not — but because they illustrate one way that Washington approached the issues that confronted the House of Burgesses during his years as a member. The religious works Washington acquired during this period contained valuable information relevant to the political issues swirling around both the church and the state. His choices of reading material make greater sense when placed in context with his initial foray into the House of Burgesses. At the time all Washington had to rely on in the House of Burgesses was his military experience. Nothing else in his background prepared him for playing a role in politics. As a result, he was mostly a backbencher, saying little in the assembly. When he did try to speak publicly, it went badly. During the first session he attended shortly after his marriage in 1759, his colleagues voted on a resolution thanking "the late Colonel of the first Virginia Regiment, for his faithful services to his Majesty, and his Colony, and for his brave and steady Behaviour." Washington rose, choked as panic flushed over his usually pale cheeks, and said nothing but quickly bowed and sat back down.[52] Washington did not have this problem when he was in command of troops, so what was different about the House of Burgesses? He had a talent and a naturally authoritative air for leading soldiers, but he had no such talent for political performances. Those few fleeting moments of humiliation in front of his fellow burgesses must have been agony for a man so accustomed to maintaining his self-control.

As was the case with everything else he did, Washington was driven to succeed in politics. His sense of duty and his social status demanded it.[53] Not wanting to repeat his humiliation, Washington slowly worked his way up through the organizational structure of the House of Burgesses, involving himself in matters he understood, studying for the rest, and all the while preparing to take on a more overt leadership role. It is no surprise that the first issues he expressed interest in were preserving the Virginia Regiment and maintaining the colony's defenses. In his first session Washington lent his support for local bills respecting Frederick

County and sat on several committees charged with responding to the accusations and petitions that came in regarding provincial soldiers and officers. He made himself available so his fellow burgesses could consult him on the legislation that would provide for the continuation of the Virginia Regiment and additional defensive measures for the colony. During the assembly session of 1761, Washington was unmistakably the Virginia Regiment's most ardent proponent. His correspondence with Capt. Robert Stewart reveals the degree of Washington's involvement as the lobbyist in chief for the regiment that he once commanded. At Washington's request Stewart prepared a comprehensive analysis on the state of the regiment after they consulted together on March 12, and by March 27 Washington wrote to Stewart and informed him that he expected the appropriations bill to pass the House. By the beginning of April, the legislature authorized recruiting up to the level that Washington and Stewart wanted, and it made provisions for the Virginia Regiment to be supplied and paid up to December 1, 1761, in the event that a war broke out with the Cherokees.[54]

Washington also worked assiduously for his own constituents during this session, for he would soon face reelection. A special session was convened in November 1761 for the purpose of further provisioning the regiment in case the possibility of a Cherokee war persisted. Here he also had the opportunity to chair a committee that examined the requests made on behalf of disabled veterans and introduced a bill to incorporate a new town, Strasburg, in the Shenandoah Valley. During the nine-day meeting in March to April 1762, he participated in the vote to disband the old regiment and establish a new one. Also during this brief session, Washington again sat on committees having to do with military affairs and chaired one of them.[55] Washington's activities during his first four years as a burgess were of the minor variety, with Washington doing his best to gain legislative experience while minimizing the opportunity of embarrassing himself in front of the full assembly. As the former commander of the Virginia Regiment with years of combat experience, he could rest assured that his colleagues considered him an expert on the military. It gave him a certain degree of comfort as he learned the ropes of how the House of Burgesses operated. During his thirteen years of service in the House of Burgesses, Washington slowly became more influential. It must be kept in mind that his ascendency was indeed gradual, for no matter how much experience Washington gained, he never was comfortable with political power. This is not to suggest that he was apathetic; rather, he felt no amount of legislative experience could make up for the fact that he was not university trained or a member of the bar. Since the majority of his colleagues did meet at least one of these qualifications, the thin-skinned Washington was constantly in fear of embarrassment. Still serve he must, so he did the best he could. Knowing that increasing his participation in House proceedings would require him to branch out into other issues beyond those of his constituents and the militia, Washington did as he had always done and turned to reading for the answers.

As nearly all Virginians, Washington was raised with a healthy respect for his British heritage and history. Anyone who read *The Oceana of James Harrington and His Other Works* would have been well aware that history was useful; indeed, knowledge of history was a prerequisite for a politician. The book, written during the interregnum, is an exposition on an ideal constitution. Harrington argued for an agrarian state where power is vested in landholders for limited amounts of time. While the book is utopian, Harrington made a definite argument that political leaders need to be educated both in history and on current events so that they may lead with understanding.[56] If Washington was not exposed to much history in the little formal schooling he did have, his English-educated half-brothers, Augustine and Lawrence; his mentor, William Fairfax; or any number of Virginians in his social circle would certainly have introduced him to it. They would have encouraged Washington to read history and not simply listen to the conversations of those around him at the dinner table, for books were the high road to knowledge. John Adams asked in his diary in 1761, "How can I judge . . . how can any man judge, unless his mind has been opened and enlarged by reading."[57] This aspiring Massachusetts lawyer's rhetorical question would have resonated just as much in Virginia. English history permeated colonial Virginia life especially during this period after the Seven Years' War when royalism reached fever pitch up and down the Eastern Seaboard.

In order to better prepare himself for the House of Burgesses, Washington attempted to broaden his historical knowledge through his purchase of Smollett's *Complete History of England*.[58] This multivolume work was difficult to acquire in Virginia and even in Williamsburg, which did not boast the number of booksellers and print shops that could be found in Philadelphia and Boston at the time. Washington ordered the full series along with the *Annual Register* from Robert Cary and Company in 1762 and received them in 1763, shortly before he began compiling his list of books at Mount Vernon in 1764.[59]

This newest work of English history reflected the most current research at that time. David Hume also began a series that chronicled English history since the Norman conquest, but he died before completing *The History of England*. Although Hume's volumes were published in many editions, his work was heavily criticized in England. Hume's generous treatment of the English monarchy would also become fodder for America's future revolutionaries. Reflecting on the trend in historical reading during the 1760s, John Adams explained to Thomas Jefferson his dislike of Hume's "elegant Lies," which "had nearly laughed into contempt Rapin Sydney and even Lock[e]."[60] Such criticism aside, Hume's work rendered other editions of English history obsolete, so some enterprising publishers in London commissioned Tobias Smollett to pick up where Hume left off. Smollett's volumes have a far less monarchical overtone, so much so that critics and historians often have a hard time deciding what Smollett's political leanings actually were.[61] As soon as his volumes were published in London, they were immensely popular and soon read on both sides of the Atlantic.[62]

Smollett probably intended to obfuscate whether he was a Whig or a Tory, but there was no disguising his scathing critique of Britain's entry into the Seven Years' War, as well as its prosecution by English officials. It is a frustrating fact that Washington left no record of his reaction to Smollett's treatment of the war in North America, for Smollett painted a brief and unflattering picture of him as the inexperienced young man who started the whole thing. Smollett mentioned Washington by name only for his haphazard construction of Fort Necessity, his subsequent surrender of it, and his involvement in the Jumonville massacre:

> Colonel Washington was detached from Virginia with four hundred men, and occupied a post on the banks of the river Ohio, where he threw up some works, and erected a kind of occasional fort, in hope of being able to defend himself in that situation, until he should be joined by a reinforcement of New York, which however did not arrive. While he remained in this situation, De Viller [sic], a French commander, at the head of nine hundred men, being on his march to dislodge Washington, detached one Jumonville, an inferior officer, with a small party, and a formal summons to Washington, requiring him to quit the fort, which he pretended was built on ground belonging to the French, or their allies. So little regard was paid to this intimation, that the English fell on this party, and, as the French affirm, without the least provocation, either slew or took the whole detachment. De Viller [sic], incensed at these unprovoked hostilities, marched up to the attack, which Washington for some time sustained under manifold disadvantages. At length, however, he surrendered the fort upon capitulation.[63]

Smollett also took General Braddock to task for his unbending arrogance and poor judgment, which directly led to the catastrophic loss that would prove to be Great Britain's greatest defeat in the eighteenth century. It is worth noting that in his description of Braddock's defeat, Smollett did not mention Washington once, although he was the one officer left standing who had enough sense to organize the retreat and prevent a total rout:

He [Braddock] marched on with so much expedition, that he seldom took any time to reconnoiter the woods or thickets that he was to pass through; as if the nearer he approached the enemy, the farther he was removed from danger. On the eighth of July he encamped within ten miles of Fort Duquesne; and though colonel Dunbar was then near forty miles behind him, and his officers, particularly Sir Peter Halket, earnestly entreated him to proceed with caution, and to employ the friendly Indians that were with him, by way of advanced guard, in case of ambuscades; yet he resumed his march the next day, without so much as endeavoring to get any intelligence of the situation or disposition of the enemy, or even sending out any scouts to visit the woods and thickets then on both sides of him, as well as in his front. With this carelessness he was advancing, when, about noon, he was saluted with a general fire upon his front, and all along his left flank . . . the panic and confusion . . . became general. . . . As to Braddock himself, he discovered at once the greatest intrepidity, and the highest imprudence; for, instead of ordering a retreat till he could scour the thickets and bushes from whence the fire came, with grape shot from the ten pieces of cannon he had with him, or ordering flanking parties of his Indians to advance against the enemy, he obstinately continued upon the spot where he was. . . . At last the general, whose obstinacy seemed to increase with the danger, after having five horses shot from under him, received himself a musket shot through the right arm and lungs, of which he died four days after, having been carried off the field by lieutenant colonel [Thomas] Gage, and another of his officers [Washington].[64]

Knowing what we do of Washington's personality, it is easy to imagine him seething privately in his chair as he was confronted with yet another reminder of how little the British valued his service to the king and empire. These earlier volumes of Smollett's contribution to the series gave Washington and his contemporaries a healthy lesson in British patriotism of the parliamentary variety. Such examples would have been eminently useful to the inexperienced burgess as he tried his best to learn the ropes of colonial government, which was modeled on the English system.

In order for Washington to develop his understanding of both colonial and British government more fully, he also had to acquire a working knowledge of the law. This enterprise was typical for an eighteenth-century gentleman, for in that day English history was infused with a healthy veneration for the common law. Sir Edward Coke, the famous English common lawyer, made a name for himself, as well as an indelible mark on British legal tradition, with his argument that English law was purely English and therefore the best in the world. His sentiment echoed that of Fortescue, who asserted that English laws were the best in the world because they were the most ancient and never altered by the Romans or the Normans.[65] Now this explanation is not to suggest that Washington studied Coke as aspiring law students did in preparing for examinations before the bar; on the contrary, it is simply intended to highlight the extreme degree to which history and the law were intertwined in the minds of eighteenth-century Britons.

In Washington's specific case, gaining an understanding of how the legal system operated on a day-to-day basis was crucial, for he was not only a large landowner and a burgess but also a justice of the peace. To this end, prior to making his 1764 list, Washington had obtained copies of Thomas Pearce's *The Justice of the Peace's Pocket Companion, or the Office and Duty of a Justice Epitomised* and Henry Crouch's *A Compleat View of the British Customs.*[66] Sometime later during this period Washington acquired William Fairfax's copies of George Webb's *Virginia Justice* and Thomas Goodinge's *Law against Bankrupts* and procured George Meriton's *The Landlord's Law* and the two-volume *Attorney's Pocket Book.*[67] These practical legal guidebooks were all written for nonlawyers who needed a working knowledge of the law to facilitate their regular operations as landowners, landlords, and justices of the peace. These books address how to write deeds and wills, to probate estates, and to conduct real estate transactions. Washington required this level of legal knowledge and nothing more.

While the history and law books provided Washington with a rich appreciation for the British tradition he was a part of and how the mechanisms of government operated, they still would not have provided him with all of the tools he needed to fulfill his duties as a public servant. This gap turns the analysis to the most tantalizing genre in Washington's collection — the religious works. It is true that the core of Washington's religious collection was inherited from his parents as discussed earlier. However, in the period following his marriage, Washington made several purchases of religious books that require a broader explanation in context.

It is possible to assert that Washington acquired these specific works for a non-spiritual purpose. During this period in which he was both a burgess and an active vestryman in two parishes, Virginia's government faced profound issues with the church that had direct ramifications on the state.

After George Whitefield's momentous tour through the colonies that began in 1739, the ruling elite in Virginia unhappily found their world profoundly altered by the Great Awakening. Whitefield's emotional preaching style, which saw him reach out to all regardless of socio-economic status, ushered in a wave of itinerant preachers; they trooped through the colony and lured parishioners away from the established church. One such itinerant was Samuel Davies, an evangelical Presbyterian who came to Hanover, Virginia, in 1748 and led the fight to preach freely. Davies envisioned an alternative parish system of Presbyterian churches that would have legal recognition in the colony. He tried to comply with the regulations of the Virginia establishment by obtaining licenses to preach at the various meetinghouses in Hanover County. He reasoned that if people were free to choose their own doctors, they should be equally able to choose a physician for their souls. By trying to work within the established laws of the colony, Davies posed a new and arguably more dangerous challenge to both the Virginia elite and the

Anglican clergy because he attempted to use the law to undermine the established church. Davies cited the freedom guaranteed by the 1689 Act of Toleration in England, arguing that it provided the grounds for evangelical rights in Virginia. He forced the ruling elite to confront a legal protest rather than a simple act of lawlessness by a traveling preacher.

Davies's activism in Virginia coincided with another crack in the establishment's foundation: some of the vestrymen (who were also members of the ruling elite) were beginning to clash with their priests. For years the clergy had received their salaries in tobacco, but in 1758, the House of Burgesses passed the Two Penny Act, which stipulated that cash payments were to replace tobacco at the rate of two cents per pound, or well below the then current market price of tobacco. Some clergymen protested to the Privy Council in London, which then invalidated the Two Penny Act. Afterward several parsons filed suit to recoup back pay. The colonial officials retained Patrick Henry, a young lawyer, who railed against the Privy Council's interference in colonial affairs. In building his case against the clergy, Henry argued that in invalidating a colonial statute King George III had degenerated into a tyrant. As far as Henry was concerned, the meddling of the king and his Privy Council in this case signaled their willingness to use the church as a political weapon to deprive the colonists of their liberties.[68]

In the wake of Davies's challenge and the fallout from the Two Penny Act, the Anglican clergy in Virginia grew vindictive toward the growing number of dissenters that poured into the colony in the 1760s. Although the leaders of the established church grudgingly reconciled themselves to the permanence of Presbyterians, the encroachment of the Baptists was a different matter. Unlike the Presbyterians, the Baptists felt no need to comply with Virginia's licensing laws. Instead, the Baptists flourished because the public perceived that they were being oppressed by an unfeeling establishment. The Baptist itinerants' reputation rose dramatically, even to the extent of having mystical powers. Over time they drew more congregants away from the Anglican parish churches. The colonial authorities, egged on by the disgruntled Anglican clerics, physically abused and arrested the Baptist preachers at every opportunity in the 1760s and the 1770s.[69]

This development was disconcerting to the colony's elite on several levels. First, Virginia law stipulated that attendance at the established church was mandatory, so the persistence of these competing denominations for more than two decades constituted a challenge to colonial authority. With the church tied to the state, the colonial elite had another means of governing the people, for the vestries ensured among other things that the obligatory tithes were collected and compulsory attendance was enforced. Therefore as lower-class congregants began to drift from the established church toward the more egalitarian style of worship that the itinerant competitors offered, the elite's degree of control seemed to erode. Second, although the archbishop of Canterbury never really had a firm grasp on the colonial churches, the elite recognized the possibility that if church attendance continued to wane while nonconformity continued to rise, the church officials in England might become interested in asserting more direct control and thus revoke a degree of colonial autonomy that had been enjoyed for more than 150 years. After all the king and his councillors had already demonstrated their willingness to reach all the way down into colonial pews with their response to the Two Penny Act.[70]

This threat of interference appeared more and more likely by the late 1760s when rumors began to circulate throughout Virginia that the Church of England was considering the appointment of a bishop to take control over colonial churches. This bishop controversy would be incorporated in the list of colonial grievances against the increasingly tyrannical British rule. While this conclusion seems obvious given that the bishop's possible appointment was couched with the string of parliamentary measures aimed at tightening British authority over America, the idea of a bishop was not universally despised and held as another example of tyranny. Some High Church Anglicans welcomed the idea of more centralized control. In 1771 a group of Anglican ministers even passed a resolution requesting a bishop from Canterbury.

When the issue was first brought before the House of Burgesses, it highlighted deep divisions among its members. Some were convinced that appointing a bishop to oversee the colonial dioceses would simply be the beginning of the move to end the colonies' autonomous rule in not only spiritual but all matters. Still despite the persuasiveness of that argument, others were just as devoted to the Church of England as the clergy who had made the request, and those burgesses saw that the appointment of a bishop could actually help revitalize the suffering establishment and relieve some of the vestries' duties.[71]

Given the divisiveness of the religious issues facing the House of Burgesses while Washington was a member, his purchase of certain religious books during this period makes more sense. That he added to his religious collection by ordering Gilbert Burnet's *Exposition of the Thirty-nine Articles of the Church of England* from Robert Cary and Company in 1766 had less to do with matters of faith than with matters of politics. While it is infused with theology, Burnet's *Exposition* provides a breakdown of how the Anglican Church's hierarchy operated, specifically how ecclesiastical power was delegated from the crown to the bishops who exercised authority over the parishes. The book is about church law, an understanding of which would prove crucial in the days ahead.[72] The timing of Washington's purchase coincides with the growing numbers of dissenters in Virginia and the lead-up to the bishop controversy. Washington was clearly trying to enhance his understanding of the scope of the Church of England's authority in both spiritual and temporal matters — more specifically, how a bishop might exercise that power on behalf of the archbishop of Canterbury, the Privy Council, and the king. Such foundational knowledge would be vital to determining the exact implications for Virginia's government if a bishop was in fact appointed.

Washington also made use of the Custis library to assist him in this particular situation. Washington kept Daniel Parke Custis's copy of *The Trial of the Seven Bishops* from the collection and did not turn it over to Jacky. The book chronicles the trial of Bishops Sancroft, Lake, White,

Turner, Ken, Lloyd, and Trelawny of the Church of England. James II committed them to the Tower of London in June 1688 because they opposed his Declaration of Indulgence, which allowed a certain degree of religious toleration, primarily so Catholics could worship openly. James's government pressured the jury for a conviction, but they were acquitted anyway.[73] This volume encapsulates many of the issues that the Virginians faced after the Great Awakening and in the lead-up to the American Revolution. The arrest and trial of the seven bishops for exceeding the limits of their authority when they opposed a royal decree for religious toleration demonstrated not only the degree to which politics and the church were intertwined but also the willingness of kings to use the legal system to manipulate the church (and vice versa) to ensure their royal will was done. This case also showed the willingness of bishops to politicize their pulpits in order to speak against the laws. In this case, it was the issue of religious toleration. There could not have been a better English resource for Washington to consult.

Besides English resources, Washington also needed to understand how his fellow Virginians felt about the issues plaguing the religious and political establishments of his colony. To this end in 1764 he also purchased in Williamsburg copies of Peyton Randolph's "Letter to the Bishop of London" and Richard Bland's "Letter to the Clergy"; they lay out the case against the clergymen who brought suit for back pay in the wake of the Privy Council's handling of the Two Penny Act. Washington also bought additional pamphlets on the bishop controversy written by John Camm, who actively opposed the Two Penny Act in 1758 (and was instrumental in persuading the Privy Council to strike down the statute), and Landon Carter's angry response, titled "The Rector Detected."[74] It is worth noting that in their respective pamphlets, Carter and Bland both claimed that royal instructions could only be issued to the colony's governor, who served as the only royally appointed official. As the colonists elected the legislators, they did not fall under the direct jurisdiction of the king and his Privy Council. Moreover, Carter and Bland pressed the case that it was unconstitutional for the crown to require the assembly to follow instructions that would in fact be harmful to the colony. These arguments would certainly have resonated with Washington, who also had previously chafed under the control of stubborn British officials who dictated high-handed strategy without deferring to those colonial leaders who had sufficient experience to act independently and with authority.[75]

In addition to the internal threats from itinerant preachers and disgruntled parish priests and the annoyance of external interference from the Privy Council over the Two Penny Act, Washington and his fellow burgesses faced other substantial issues in the late 1760s and early 1770s. In April 1764 shortly before Washington delivered his chairman's report from the commission charged with certifying for payment the accounts of the militia forces that had fought under Pontiac's warriors, Parliament adopted the Currency Act of 1764. It was a comprehensive policy aimed at imposing order on the colonies and, among other things, prohibited the issuance of paper bills as legal tender currency. It was followed in short succession by the Stamp Act in March 1765. Between the announcements of these new fiscal policies, the burgesses, in anticipating the Stamp Act, claimed that they had sole jurisdiction in matters of "internal polity" and taxation. Here Washington actively took part in the development of the revolutionary ideology that Americans had the right to political self-determination.

Washington Becomes a Revolutionary

Washington's personal political views at this stage were evolving steadily in the direction of becoming a revolutionary although he did not yet share in the militancy of his friend and neighbor George Mason. Washington was outraged over the Stamp Act but remained convinced that it would be repealed in the wake of continued colonial protests. He was right. By September 1765, however, he was seeing more of a direct correlation between his personal indebtedness and increasingly strained relationship with Robert Cary and Company and the increasing level of hostility between England and the colonies. In an extraordinary

letter to Cary, Washington argued that given that Cary was responsible for keeping tobacco prices low and ensuring he would remain in
debt, Washington was evaluating alternative means of increasing his
personal independence. He was also considering different ways for
the colonies to obtain greater self-determination.[76] Interestingly at
this point Washington finally did shift away from growing tobacco and
began aggressively investigating other cash crops and moneymaking
ventures on a significantly larger scale than before on his plantations.
He also began exploring other markets, so his studies of agriculture took
on a renewed importance. He was determined to rid himself of debt.
Meanwhile, Washington became more vocal in his opposition to the
Stamp Act, the Currency Act, and the Sugar Act of 1764. He called the
Stamp Act an "unconstitutional method of Taxation [,] and a direful
attack upon their Liberties" that was "imposed by the Parliament of
Great Britain." He would later call it an "Act of Oppression."[77] Washington also predicted that the Stamp Act itself would cause colonial
judicial proceedings to grind to a halt, because even if the colonists
were willing to pay the tax, they lacked the hard currency to do so
thanks to the Currency Act. The closing of the courts would therefore
prevent debts from being collected on behalf of British creditors; thus
the British merchants would feel the pain of the Stamp Act even more
than the colonists would.[78]

Additionally Washington became one of the most outspoken
advocates for adopting a nonimportation agreement in the wake of
Parliament's passage of the Townsend Acts of 1767. On the whole, likely
based on his own futile pursuit of a royal commission years earlier, he
thought that making repeated petitions to the Parliament and even to
the king were useless. Instead, he favored increasing colonial opposition
through economic coercion. Washington and George Mason worked
together to delineate the details of how a nonimportation association
could work for Virginia. Washington's proposal and advocacy of the
association reflected his growing standing within the House of Burgesses. He was now a regular dinner guest of the governor, Speaker

of the House, and other members of the council. Furthermore, he was also appointed to more high-profile, powerful committees such as Propositions and Grievances, Privileges and Elections, and the newly constituted standing Committee for Religion.[79]

Washington's appointment to the Committee for Religion likely had little to do with his faith and more to do with his ability to solve problems. The committee was created to address the still-increasing numbers of dissenters that were contributing to the declining influence of the established church, the charges of corruption and immorality against the Anglican clergy, the debt scandal involving Speaker John Robinson, and the perceived corruption in the sensationalized murder case against John Chiswell. The committee responded by increasing its regulation of the established church and by enhancing its oversight of the parish vestries. In order to keep the church under colonial control, the committee also composed a plan to block renewed calls for an Anglican episcopate. It further sought finally to diffuse the long-simmering tensions over dissenters by extending religious toleration to the Baptists. In his work on this committee, Washington undoubtedly relied on his religious reading and his belief in the public virtues of organized religion.[80]

Out of this evidence of Washington's increasingly public political activity in opposition to Great Britain, his 1765 letters to Cary and to Francis Dandridge and his co-authorship of the nonimportation measures reveal a coming together of Washington's studies with his personal experience to form his political philosophy. His reading of British history and law led him to the conclusion that Parliament had no authority outside of Great Britain. His agricultural reading and frustrating experience with his increasing indebtedness to Robert Cary and Company within the constraints of the stilted tobacco markets convinced him that it was both possible and necessary to turn away from tobacco in favor of a new system of industries and markets that would help him become more self-sufficient. If he could do it, then the rest of the colonists could too. His increasing militancy earned the respect of his peers, so much so that by 1774 he was one of Virginia's delegates to the Continental Congress, and by 1775 he received command of the newly formed Continental Army forming in Cambridge, Massachusetts.

Practical reading in conjunction with personal experience led Washington to logical conclusions concerning the real problems facing his world. From boyhood he applied himself and studied subjects that would help advance him in Virginia's social ranks. Once his father died, Washington pursued his studies as never before. He combined reading with a sustained effort to learn from his experiences, both positive and negative. With this method he successfully built the Virginia Regiment, and he would use it again in the future to build the Continental Army and to serve as the nation's first president. During this Virginia phase of his life, Washington's rise was surprising given where he began. Born the third son of a middling planter in 1732, by 1774 he had achieved wealth, property, military fame, and political influence, and he moved in the uppermost circles of Virginia society. He may not have been a bibliophile in the same vein as Jefferson, Franklin, and Adams, purchasing and treasuring as many books as they could acquire, but Washington's actions indicate that he understood that he owed much of his success to the useful knowledge he learned through deliberate reading. This self-study, combined with his natural maturation over time, provided the necessary confidence that enabled him to become the leader of a resistance movement. Indeed, this conjoining of practical knowledge with life experience would prove to be the key to Washington's success throughout the rest of his public life.

CHAPTER THREE

Revolutionary Reading

As spring gave way to another sultry summer in Philadelphia in 1775, the city buzzed with activity, and rumors swirled around the Second Continental Congress. All talked about what the American response would be to the latest developments in the ever-increasing hostility between Great Britain and the colonies. Shortly before Congress convened on May 10, the rapidly rising tensions centered on the British occupation of Boston had finally sparked a war. In the early morning hours of April 19, the British had sent troops from their base in Boston to seize the stores of arms and ammunition in nearby Concord and two leaders of the Sons of Liberty — Samuel Adams and John Hancock. Gen. Thomas Gage, the British commander, did not yet know that his operation had already been compromised before the first troops embarked on their short trip across the Charles River. The Sons of Liberty had an effective intelligence network and knew many details of the British orders in advance. They used express riders — most notably, Paul Revere — to spread the word throughout the area between Boston and Concord that the British were on the move. In response to the warnings, local militias mustered in the predawn hours and waited. The British first had to pass through Lexington, where they came face to face with the armed minutemen. At some point during the short, tense exchange, the "shot heard 'round the world" was fired, and the war that seemed to be looming over the colonies for years had finally begun. After a second deadly encounter, the British army retreated to Boston, and the swelling patriot militia units began hastily occupying the heights overlooking the city.[1]

When this explosive news reached the delegates who were about to travel to Philadelphia, reactions were mixed. For his part, George Washington was apprehensive of what lay ahead. He foresaw that the killing of British soldiers would bring the full force of imperial retribution down on the colonies. Yet despite the sense of foreboding, he felt the familiar sensation of duty calling. He wrote to George William Fairfax, "Unhappy it is though to reflect, that a Brother's Sword has been sheathed in a Brother's breast, and that, the once happy and peaceful plains of America are either to be drenched with Blood, or Inhabited by Slaves. Sad alternative! But can a virtuous Man hesitate in his choice?"[2] However uneasy Washington was about the colonies' future, his fellow Virginians had been preparing for war. In the previous months, county militias had begun to organize, calling themselves "independent companies." Washington seemed the obvious choice to lead them, and by March, five of the companies had formally requested that he take command. Also in March the Virginia Convention had voted to put the colony on a military footing. From that point forward, Washington had rapidly become one of the foremost leaders of the colonial resistance movement. He recognized and accepted, if not relished, this fact. Upon arriving in Philadelphia as a member of Virginia's delegation to the Continental Congress, Washington made a habit of attending the sessions in his uniform as a physical demonstration of his willingness to serve if called upon.[3]

Washington stood out from the crowd of delegates assembled in the Continental Congress. He was a full head taller than anyone else in the room and the only one there in uniform. He was also the only native-born American with any real military experience, which made him the obvious choice to command an American army. Moreover, that Washington was a Virginian implied that he would marshal the support of the southern colonies to what had previously been a Massachusetts effort. The only other possible candidates with significant active military experience besides Washington were Charles Lee and Horatio Gates. Both were professionally trained officers who had served in European armies; however, they were British by birth. The image of a British expatriate at the head of America's brave volunteers would have sent the wrong message. Washington was the natural choice.

After Congress unanimously approved John Adams's motion naming Washington as the commander of the yet-to-be-formed army, the overwrought new general gave a short speech in which he made a key point intended to be ingrained in the collective American memory: "[B]ut lest some unlucky event should happen unfavourable to my reputation, I beg it may be remembered by every Gent[lema]n in the room, that I this day declare with the utmost sincerity, I do not think myself equal to the Command I [am] honored with."[4] The case for the sincerity of his self-doubt is bolstered by his letters to both Martha and John, his favorite younger brother, in which he described his appointment as "a trust too great for my capacity."[5] Interestingly he was even more descriptive to his brother-in-law Burwell Bassett: "I am now Imbarked on a tempestuous Ocean from whence, perhaps, no friendly harbor is to be found. . . . It is an honour I wished to avoid. . . . I can answer for three things, a firm belief in the justice of our Cause — close attention to the prosecution of it — and the strictest Integrity — If these cannot supply the places of Ability & Experience, the cause will suffer & more than probably my character along with it, as reputation derives its principal support from success."[6]

Even if Washington was trying to delude himself into believing that he really did not have any ambitions for this high command, despite his doing nothing to discourage the buzz about his uniformed appearance and his military fame in Congress, these strikingly honest letters reveal his deep apprehension regarding his ability to meet the challenge. This ambivalence further reflects his attempts to balance his pride with the sense of honor that he had learned from his reading, particularly the courtesy manuals and histories that documented the conduct of the great men and women of the past.

Although his diary entries for the date of his appointment are unhelpful in that they provide no insight into Washington's state of mind, one can only imagine how heavily he felt the weight of the task that bore down on him. The days of his unbridled martial enthusiasm and over-brimming self-confidence were long since behind him. He was supremely responsible for the conduct of a war against the most powerful military force on earth, and there was little margin for error. He had not previously led an entire army, and now before he could lead this one, he had to build it first. How was he ever going to do it? Washington had to compensate for his lack of experience quickly, for the war had already begun, and his army was beginning to take shape in Cambridge. As had become his habit when faced with a new challenge, Washington turned inward to private study. In preparing to leave Philadelphia and go off to war, he began to purchase books on the military arts.[7]

Chapter 2 explored Washington's reading during the first phase of his life when he was a Virginia provincial. Building on that chapter's themes regarding his selection of reading material based on whether it offered immediately applicable knowledge, this chapter examines Washington's reading during the period of his life when he transcended his colonial status to become an internationally recognized leader from 1774 through 1783. Washington's library collection as a whole grew tremendously over the course of those nine years. The additions Washington made to his collection presents interesting possibilities for analysis, as well as several potential pitfalls.

Washington Takes Command

The pressure on Washington was staggering. As the military leader of a revolution, the stakes were infinitely high. He needed to read but had little time to do so. Therefore, it can safely be assumed that if he sought to purchase a particular work, he intended to read it. Conversely, given the demands on Washington's time during this period, the analysis of the numerous works he received as gifts requires greater scrutiny. As demonstrated throughout the chapter, some of the gifts were sent by well-intentioned friends who thought the works would be helpful. A vast majority of these gifts, however, were sent by authors who were either hoping to curry favor with Washington or seeking an endorsement that would potentially help boost their sales. It would be too simplistic to assume that because Washington had little leisure time at this point, he would have disregarded the printed gifts sent to him. Likewise, it would be too sweeping to assume that just because Washington kept these gifts, he must have read them. The truth, I think, lies somewhere in between. Based on what is known about Washington's preference for reading material that offered practical knowledge, a reasonable case for determining which presentation copies he did read can be made by aligning his previous reading preferences both with the situations he faced during the Revolution and with the gifts themselves in the order that they were received. While a certain amount of ambiguity is inherent in this method of analysis, unfortunately there is no more clear way of narrowing Washington's reading down because his writings yield few direct connections.

What becomes apparent from this analysis is that Washington's focus remained largely centered on the same genres that he had read before becoming a national figure. During this period, works on the military arts, politics, and religion dominated his collection. As this chapter illustrates, the works on politics and religion are intertwined due to the politicization of the pulpits during both the revolutionary and early national periods.

This analysis also reveals a picture of a very fragile Washington. As stated earlier, the evidence indicates that he was deeply pessimistic about his ability to carry out his commission successfully. Indeed, the year 1776 nearly proved him right as he and his fledgling army suffered a series of humiliating losses at the hands of the British until a small surprise attack on the sleepy Hessian garrison at Trenton gave the Americans a surge of momentum. Although Washington ultimately emerged victorious from the Revolution, he lost more battles than he won, and his pride took the heaviest beating over the course of the long war as he weathered storms of criticism and conspiracies to replace him. The problems associated with the sometimes fractious civil-military relations and the general staff's infighting during the Revolution put immense burdens on the commanding general, who was still learning how to lead on such an immense scale. In short, for Washington, the Revolutionary War era was filled with as much strife as triumph. This truth must be carefully remembered when considering how susceptible he was to criticism and the degree to which he was driven to succeed. To sustain him in his high-profile position while presenting a public image of the quintessential leader with masterful self-control, Washington needed both knowledge and a healthy reassurance that what he was doing was right. His reading provided them both during this phase of his life.

Military Reading: Preparing for Generalship

Even before the Continental Army was an idea, Washington understood that the die seemed to be cast for war, and duty would demand his service.[8] As Virginians began to ready themselves for war, Washington also turned his attention back to military matters. In November 1774 he ordered a copy of Thomas Webb's *A Military Treatise on the Appointments of the Army*, originally published in Philadelphia in 1759.[9] Webb, a lieutenant in the British army, wrote this book to offer his observations on the current state of the army's level of training and organization and on what changes he thought should be made in the event that war did break out in North America. Webb premised that "it is the Duty of every Military Man, to endeavor to make himself Master of his Profession, and freely to impart any Knowledge he may have acquired, which can be of the least Advantage to the Service."[10] Lieutenant Webb wrote from the standpoint of an officer who commanded ordinary soldiers in battle, and as he implemented the policies he was commenting on, he was in an excellent position to offer an opinion on their effectiveness. Such a commentary would have been potentially useful to Washington if he had to constitute an army. Also in 1774 Washington ordered six copies of *The Manual Exercise, as Ordered by His Majesty, in the Year 1764*. Shortly thereafter in May 1775, Washington ordered eight copies of Thomas Hanson's *The Prussian Evolutions in Actual Engagements*.[11] These works would have been most useful in teaching new sergeants and company officers how to train their soldiers, for the books break down into simple steps how to perform the manual of arms. Additionally, immediately prior to the outbreak of the Revolution, Washington acquired a copy of Sir William Young's *Manoeuvres, or Practical Observations on the Art of War*. This book is of particular interest because it offers another example of Washington's making marginal notes. These notes reveal Washington's self-education in the art of command. He paid attention to the size of the different formations referenced throughout the book, and his notes show that he tried to determine how to scale those numbers proportionally given the number of soldiers he had so that he could maneuver units on the battlefield in accordance with the manual's instructions. To fully appreciate the significance of this book and Washington's notes, it must be remembered that his experience was in building a regiment from the ground up, and he had never led a larger unit.

With these military treatises and drill manuals that he acquired during the first two years of the Revolution, we see Washington applying the same diligent study method he had used previously with Duhamel's *Practical Treatise of Husbandry* when he sought to make his plantations profitable. In other words, he read these military books for the sake of immediate practical problem solving. There is nothing philosophical or reflective about them. They are tactical field manuals, not massive theoretical tomes on the art of command as it evolved over the centuries.

Washington also acquired twenty-four other works on military science. They gave Washington an overview of the latest European battlefield tactics and plans for military administration. It is interesting to note that the target audience for most of the books was company and field grade officers, not generals. For example, Edward Harvey wrote *A New Manual, and Platoon Exercise: With an Explanation* for infantry lieutenants. He instructed them how to move their soldiers into a formation, how to issue battlefield commands, and how to march a platoon in formation. In the plainest terms, the book taught new officers to "seize the Firelock with the right Hand, and turn the Lock outward, keeping the Firelock in the same position as before."[12] When considering the importance of this volume and the other military books Washington read during this period, it is indeed critical to remember the scale and complexity of the task facing him. Washington was quite literally learning how to build an army as he went along. While his command experience with the Virginia Regiment provided a useful foundation in the basics of military administration, it was not a sufficient solitary resource to rely on when constituting a much larger, more complex army. As such *A New Manual, and Platoon Exercise* and *A System of Camp-Discipline, Military Honours, Garrison-Duty, and Other Regulations for the Land Forces*, which describe how the army operated on a daily basis, were useful but only to a point. Washington was rapidly trying to educate himself about how to raise, administer, and maneuver armies in European-style battles, and these manuals gave him a place to start. Moreover, these manuals would also provide an approach to training junior officers. That knowledge, however, was the limit of what Washington could gain from such books; these works would not teach him how to be a commanding general.

The only other assets that Washington had when assuming command were his experiences in the Seven Years' War, his reputation, and his ability to see the overall strategic picture very well. He had to use those assets to forge a coherent fighting force made up of men from across the colonies who represented a broad spectrum of different cultures and traditions. He had no experience in maneuvering troops on an open battlefield, and neither did the majority of his subordinate officers. Moreover, many people expected him to fail. Of course his British adversaries assumed they would defeat him handily, but there were Americans who also did not want to see him succeed—the staunch loyalists and even some members of his own staff who coveted his position and were jealous of his fame. Naysayers were not the only source of stress for Washington. Those who supported his nomination and those devoted to the patriot cause wanted him to rise to the occasion and secure victory no matter the odds. No less significant was the stress he also placed on himself. As with every endeavor, his reputation was linked to the war's outcome, and it would have been a nagging worry. With all of these factors in mind, it is no wonder that he devoted what little time he had for reading to straightforward manuals such as *A New Manual, and Platoon Exercise*; *A New System of Military Discipline Founded on Principle*; and *Essay on the Art of War: Principles of All Operations in the Field*.[13] In particular, *Essay on the Art of War*, a collection of essays by an unknown author, defines what honor and valor should mean to officers, explains the duties and responsibilities of senior army leaders, delineates how an army staff operated, and expounds on how to administer military justice and how to conduct battlefield maneuvers. The author wrote that his wish was that "every young Officer will here find Lights sufficient to conduct him on the most difficult Occasions."[14] With regard to discipline, the author argued, "Military Discipline consists properly in maintaining good Order and Policy, without which the most beautiful Body of Troops would become a Band of Robbers and Assassins. Military Discipline comprehends, 1st, The regularity of Manners of those who follow the Profession of War. 2ndly, The perfect Obedience of the Inferior to the Superior, relatively to each Rank. 3rdly, The Vigilance of the Chiefs, in executing the Ordonnances of the Prince, against Military Crimes and Delicts. 4thly, The Chastisement with which those who are faulty are punished."[15]

This single volume is a succinct reference that addressed all aspects of army life. The author's stated intent of reaching an audience of new officers made this book another logical choice for Washington if he was looking for a basic text that he could possibly use in training his army. He also purchased the order of merit list of all general and field officers in the British army for the years 1772, 1777, and 1778, presumably to determine which adversaries he would face. With these purchases he was attempting to gain a complete understanding of his situation and determine how to best move forward.

Washington's Military Reading Put to Use

The evidence of how Washington utilized this reading is best illustrated by looking at the earliest days of his command when the newly consti-tuted Continental Army was encamped around Boston. Washington arrived shortly after the Battle of Bunker Hill and discovered that the information he had regarding the number of able soldiers was incor-rect. Although he was told that there were twenty thousand volunteers, only fourteen thousand men were actually fit for duty. Almost every regiment was incomplete. Most of the soldiers were old men or young boys, and even more shocking to the new Virginian general was the surprising number of free blacks in their ranks. The men were filthy in their threadbare clothing, and they did not know the first thing about how to present their rusty arms for inspection. They slept in an odd conglomeration of rude huts and half tents scattered about the muddy, open fields. Horses and other animals wandered throughout the cantonment, eating the strewn spare garbage. Latrines were open, everywhere, and highly unsanitary. The smell of human waste forever hung heavy in the humid summer air.[16]

Worse than the appearance of the encampment was the behavior of the men. The officers had limited authority indeed because the very soldiers they commanded had elected them. Men came and went as they pleased. They looted and destroyed property, felt free to leave their posts, and fell asleep on duty. Before long Washington was being inundated with complaints from the locals that Connecticut soldiers skinny-dipped in the river in full view of the respectable ladies. Wash-ington remarked that the New Englanders especially were "an exceeding dirty and nasty people."[17] Washington set to work to instill discipline and order into his camp. His first general orders specify the duties of his officers, based on what he read in his British manuals. For example, his general orders for July 4, 1775, stated that

> exact returns to be made by the proper Officers of all the Provi-sions, Ordnance, Ordnance stores, Powder, Lead, working Tools

of all kinds, Tents, Camp Kettles, and all Other Stores under their respective care, belonging to the Armies at Roxbury and Cambridge. The commanding Officer of each Regiment to make a return of the number of blankets wanted to compleat every Man with one at least.... It is required and expected that exact discipline be observed, and due Subordination prevail thro' the whole Army, as a Failure in these most essential points must necessarily produce extreme Hazard, Disorder and Confusion; and in the end in shameful disappointment and disgrace.

The General most earnestly requires, and expects, a due observance of those articles of war, established for the Government of the army, which forbid profane cursing, swearing and drunkenness; And in like manner requires and expects, of all Officers, and Soldiers, not engaged on actual duty, a punctual attendance on divine service, to implore the blessings of heaven upon the means used for our safety and defence.

All Officers are required and expected to pay diligent Attention, to keep their Men neat and clean — to visit them often at their quarters, and inculcate upon them the necessity of cleanliness, as essential to their health and service. They are particularly to see, that they have Straw to lay on, if to be had, and to make it known if they are destitute of this article. They are also to take care that Necessarys be provided in the Camps and frequently filled up to prevent their being offensive and unhealthy. Proper Notice will be taken of such Officers and Men, as distinguish themselves by their attention to these necessary duties.[18]

Washington clearly had his work cut out for him, and there were precious few able and experienced minds to assist him. The two voices of experience Washington had to rely on were Maj. Gen. Charles Lee and Maj. Gen. Horatio Gates, the two British-born and educated officers who saw active service on the continent and North America during the Seven Years' War. Lee was experienced, but he was vain, spiteful, filthy, and vulgar. Gates, who would be known to the army as "Granny Gates" because of his age and his propensity to move too slowly, was a pudgy but capable administrator with a greater talent for instigating political intrigue than for battlefield command. Of course Washington's military family included other generals and staff officers. There were two other major generals from Massachusetts—Artemas Ward and Israel Putnam. Ward had no military talent but wasted no time in communicating his disapproval of Congress's appointment of a Virginian to command an army made up largely of New England men. It would not take long for the dislike to become mutual. Putnam was a local hero in Massachusetts thanks to his frontier exploits, but behind the myths he had limited military abilities and was hindered by his illiteracy. Congress also commissioned Maj. Gen. Philip Schuyler, a wealthy landowner from New York with little else besides his wealth to recommend him. There was also Maj. Gen. John Sullivan, a lawyer from Durham, New Hampshire, who had less of a talent for command than getting himself into trouble. He knew nothing of the military arts. Brig. Gen. Nathanael Greene would in time prove to be one of Washington's most capable lieutenants, but he came into the war with little more than a good mind, solid education, and physical bravery in his favor. Washington made a surprising move and plucked the rotund but talented Boston bookseller-turned-self-educated-artillerist Henry Knox from the ranks. In the early days of the war Washington also had two primary aides-de-camp—Joseph Reed and Thomas Mifflin—who were the first of a large number of aides who would have to keep pace with the sheer volume of paper that circulated through the headquarters on a daily basis.[19]

This group composed the general staff that was to assist Washington in raising an army that could face the British in open battle. Not only were the majority of his officers completely inexperienced but also the two with experience would prove to be critical, taciturn, and eventually conniving. Washington therefore had to do the bulk of the work himself, and as he believed that there was a "kind of stupidity" among many officers throughout the ranks, he did not delegate the task of establishing the code of conduct to a subordinate.[20] This dearth of able staff officers and subordinate commanders therefore makes Washington's military reading more significant. It is also interesting to note that Washington's desire to manage the army's daily operations personally stems from the fact that in his new role, establishing discipline was a subject he felt the most comfortable about, for here he could couple the knowledge that he had gained from his reading on the issue with his experience in the Virginia Regiment. His popularity increased among the local people of Cambridge as he cracked down on those soldiers who roamed the countryside, looking for horses and chickens to steal and dismantling fences for firewood as they went.[21] He admonished his subordinate officers to be strict with their men and to

> [r]equire nothing unreasonable of your officers and men, but see that whatever is required be punctually complied with. Reward and punish every man according to his merit, without partiality or prejudice; hear his complaints; if well founded, redress them; if otherwise discourage them, in order to prevent frivolous ones. Discourage vice in every shape, and impress upon the mind of every man, from the first to the lowest, the importance of the cause, and what it is that they are contending for. . . . Be plain and precise in your orders, and keep copies of them to refer to, that no mistakes may happen. Be easy and condescending in your deportment to your officers, but not too familiar, lest you subject yourself to a want of that respect, which is necessary to support a proper command.[22]

Washington's advice to his officers reflects exactly how Washington put his reading to use. All of his books — including Bland's *Treatise of Military Discipline, A New Manual, and Platoon Exercise, A New System of Military Discipline Founded on Principle,* and *Essay on the Art of War* — provided in similar terms the foundation of Washington's guidance to his officers.

As he organized the army, Washington's mind simultaneously raced ahead to what he would do with it. The British were entrenched in Boston, and the long-suffering citizenry, along with Congress, expected Washington to eject them. Washington was an aggressive commander by nature, and this instinct caused him to devise an amphibious attack to force the British out of the city. The harsh reality was that he could not do it. His army was yet untrained and ill equipped. The siege of Boston, which had been under way even before Washington arrived to take command, had yielded no progress. Washington was plagued by inaccurate reports of both the British strength and his own, but the intelligence that he could verify about the British position was not encouraging. The American forces were too small and did not command all the key terrain necessary to dislodge the British from the city. Another problem was that he did not have sufficient artillery to cover the river crossing until Henry Knox pulled off the seemingly impossible task of retrieving the guns from distant Fort Ticonderoga.

With this sudden, improbable infusion of artillery, Washington put the knowledge he gained from reading his copy of John Muller's *A Treatise of Artillery* and, much to the British surprise, fortified the Dorchester Heights over the course of one feverish night of hard labor. Similar to the infantry manuals that Washington read, Muller's book is a basic text intended for entry-level artillery officers. The entire introduction, for example, is devoted to a technical description of the British army's different types of land cannons and includes simple charts with the different maximum ranges that each type of cannon could hit. Muller also explains how to read the charts and how to put the information to use. Parts 7 and 8 specify in great detail how to use artillery on the battlefield to the greatest effect. The treatise further describes how to properly construct gun emplacements and artillery batteries both for sieges and for the construction of defensive fortifications.[23] This book would have been a highly useful reference for Washington as he did not have much experience with artillery.

The plan of attack for Boston offers an example of how Washington attempted to put his tactical reading to use. Although he was a strategic thinker who maintained a more clear-eyed vision of the Revolution than any of his fellow revolutionaries (both military and civilian) had, his vision was sometimes clouded by a curious hybrid of boredom, frustration, inexperience, and the adverse effects of his lacking a formal military education. Washington wanted a fast, decisive end to the war because he knew that a protracted struggle was fraught with uncertainties for the Americans. His experience in Cambridge thus far had taught him that his army was in a precarious situation. The number of capable soldiers fluctuated, and the Continental Congress had yet to determine how the soldiers would be paid or resupplied. A quick engagement resulting in a decisive victory was therefore in the Americans' best interests. Annoyed by the problems associated with an ineffective siege that produced a stalemate, Washington proposed hurling his army across the Charles River into the main British position in Boston. At the same time he planned to bombard the city from the heavy guns mounted on Dorchester Heights. Yes, Boston might be burned to the ground in the process, but if successful, the British would be forced to surrender or risk being consumed in the flames.[24] Washington's assessment was correct: in order to achieve a quick victory he had to destroy or force the surrender of the British garrison in Boston. His aggressive instincts combined with his ignorance of the proficiency and overall size of a force required to conduct such an amphibious attack successfully, however, made the plan unfeasible from the beginning. His military reading taught him the fundamentals of army administration and tactical field maneuvers, but it was not enough to keep him grounded in reality when facing both an anxious citizenry that demanded action and an endless litany of complaints and issues that arose each day from his untrained, ill-disciplined army. Consequently, he downplayed or ignored the fact that many soldiers in his army either were from Boston or had family in Boston. When he proposed his plan to his staff, Lee scoffed at him. When the visiting congressional delegation heard his plan, Benjamin Franklin put him off, discounting the plan entirely.[25]

Even though Washington's force did not mount an attack on Boston, the increasingly desperate British, holed up with dwindling supplies and increasingly hostile hosts, evacuated. Americans rejoiced as the last British ship slipped away into the horizon, but Washington knew the war was not over yet. Both adversaries would face off again while seeking that elusive defining victory, and the next episode would again show that Washington's rudimentary self-education on military matters was not sufficient to make him a successful commanding general. Time would prove that he would only prevail when he used his reading knowledge to develop a different strategy from that of the European commanders. He had built an army that operated on a completely different set of principles from that of the British, so he had to come to terms with the fact that he also had to use his army differently if he was going to win the war. This process resulted from a combination of his reading of European manuals and his developing experience. As the summer and fall of 1776 would prove, this intellectual leap was difficult for Washington. What follows is a case study of the campaign of 1776, for it provides the best insight into this formative stage of the development of Washington's military thinking.

New York: A Lesson in Defeat

When the British evacuated Boston, no one in the American camps knew where they were going or if they were coming back at all. Some deluded themselves into believing that the British had simply given up and returned to England. Washington, however, assumed correctly that they would go to New York City and thought it would provide an opportunity for an American victory. This hope, however, would prove fleeting. From the British perspective, New York offered several key advantages. To be sure, New York had a large, deep natural seaport perfectly suited to serve as the headquarters for the Royal Navy. Additionally any attack on New York City would require an amphibious assault, a task made difficult by the tidal rivers swirling around Manhattan. Finally New York City sat at the point where the Hudson River connects to the harbor, and the Atlantic beyond was an ideal position from which the British could isolate New England from the rest of the colonies and thus pursue a divide-and-conquer strategy to regain the colonies one by one. Upon concluding his analysis, Washington hurried his army south from Cambridge to take up new positions on Manhattan and Long Island.

Although Washington was right about the British selecting New York as their destination, neither he nor any of his staff were prepared for what the British were about to hurl at them. Furious that its troops had lost Boston to the "rebels," the ministry deployed the largest expeditionary force the world had ever seen. To make matters worse, Washington realized that New York was virtually indefensible given the forces he had at his disposal. He was on an island surrounded by two navigable rivers and a harbor, but he had no naval support. He had no idea how large the combined British force would be or when it would land.[26] Nevertheless he had to do something.

From the outset, Washington's defense of New York was plagued with problems. Major General Lee was in command prior to Washington's arrival, and he struggled to erect effective defenses of this complex and critical terrain. When Washington arrived, he began to consult widely with others, and as he did so, Lee's plan began to change. The most likely reason why Washington struggled was because the military reading he had done to this point was insufficient for the task of defending this particular area. Muller's basic artillery treatise did not offer Washington any possible solution as to how to use his limited number of cannon in such a complex defense. Nor did Washington's other book by Muller, *A Treatise Containing the Practical Part of Fortification in Four Parts*, which offered technical guidance on constructing adequate defenses but not on selecting their placement on a battlefield.[27] Washington also could not use the knowledge he gained from his infantry manuals because he lacked the soldiers and resources to carry out the tasks that the authors proscribed. For instance, in *Manoeuvres, or Practical Observations on the Art of War*, Young instructed that when occupying a new area, an officer should "ride forward with his Cavalry, observing the proper precautions; he will send out Patroles, to find out the Enemy's nearest Posts; examine all Roads, and even foot paths, leading from the Enemy, to the Army he belongs to; he will endeavor to learn from the Peasants, everything the Enemy has been doing, and form conjectures, upon what their intentions may be; and think nothing but his profession, till relieved."[28] Washington, however, was unable to gather much intelligence before the attack began. He therefore was unable to deploy his troops to the best possible advantage. This lack of situational awareness led to chaos throughout the American lines. The result was a series of major defeats that ultimately led to the loss of Long Island when General Howe's army flanked around to the rear of Washington's position and took the Americans by surprise.[29]

In the immediate aftermath of the defeats on Long Island, the Americans had fallen back to strong defensive positions on Brooklyn Heights. They occupied the high ground and had clear fields of fire; trenches, redoubts, and star forts at intervals along the line; and double palisades and small fortresses at critical positions. Additionally they had plenty of supplies, ammunition, and guns. Some British officers wanted to storm the American lines in an attempt to complete the victory begun on Long Island. General Howe would hear nothing of it. He did not want another costly victory similar to Bunker Hill, where the British eventually drove the Americans out of their fortified positions after sustaining a ghastly number of casualties. Instead, Howe opted for a conventional siege of Brooklyn Heights and ordered his engineers to proceed methodically, being careful to find the weaknesses in the American lines. As that happened, Adm. Lord Richard Howe prepared to send his fleet into the East River. The Americans were quickly about to be surrounded. The weather shifted, and driving rains began to fall. Washington observed how close the British engineers were through the storm and decided to convene a council of war to discuss the possibility of evacuating the entire army across the river back to Manhattan.

After Washington outlined his many reasons for such a plan, he asked for the opinions of his senior commanders present: Major General

Putnam, Maj. Gen. Joseph Spencer, Brigadier General Mifflin, Brig. Gen. Alexander McDougall, Brig. Gen. Samuel Parsons, Brig. Gen. J. M. Scott, and Brig. Gen. James Wadsworth. Immediately, they raised their doubts and questions. Some thought evacuating the army before the British detected what was going on was impossible. The river was nearly a mile wide with strong currents, the Americans had too few boats, the British army could attack at any moment during the evacuation and slaughter the entire army in the open, or the British navy could catch the army in the water and likewise destroy it. Putnam argued that the fortifications were strong, and he was confident that the Americans would be better at fighting from behind defensive works. After hearing all opinions, Washington weighed in again, this time with a decision: the army would evacuate to Manhattan. The boats were already being gathered, and the operation would begin immediately in the strictest secrecy. They deliberately kept the soldiers in the dark, telling them only to pack and prepare for a shift in positions. At ten o'clock at night in a driving rain, the Americans began making their escape.[30]

Col. Benjamin Tallmadge would later recall, "It was one of the most anxious, busiest nights that I ever recollect, and being the third in which hardly any of us had closed our eyes to sleep, we were all greatly fatigued."[31] Besides exhaustion, the Americans had other factors working against them. Rain reduced the ground to a sea of mud, making mobility difficult and sinking the gun carriages down to the hubs. They dragged the small cannon out but left the larger ones behind. The bad weather was both a blessing and a curse for the Americans. The sudden northeaster masked their movements from the British, but it slowed them down. The mariners from John Glover's Fourteenth Massachusetts and the fishermen in Israel Hutchinson's Twenty-seventh Massachusetts did their best to keep the boats moving against the wind and the currents in the darkness, but the operation was still slow going. At first light, many of the best American troops still held positions as rear guard security and were in real danger of being discovered and captured by British and Hessian patrols. Then, as if by divine intervention, a dense fog began to rise and settled over both the British position and the American point of embarkation. Even as the sun rose, the fog persisted and shrouded the Americans in an unusual yellow light as they slipped farther away from the Brooklyn shoreline. A separate evacuation rescued American troops on Governor's Island. British cannon fire sank only one boat, but nearly all the soldiers on board survived.[32]

The exhausted Americans would not get a decent respite after their hairbreadth escape from the British. Washington reported the loss of Long Island to Congress on September 6 and called another council of war to determine what to do next. Washington realized that given the strengths and weaknesses of his army, risking the men against the British again in the open field made no sense. He also reported that he did not have the capability to defend even strong positions at all costs because his troops were not willing to die for either honor or duty. In his report to Congress on September 8, 1776, Washington wrote, "That we should on all occasions avoid a general action, or put anything at risqué, unless compelled by a necessity into which we ought never be drawn. . . . [W]hen the fate of America may be at stake on the issue . . . I cannot think it safe or wise to adopt a different system."[33] He resolved to keep his army alive by means of retreat, defending what it could, yielding what it must, and watching for an opportunity to strike the enemy whenever there was any probability of success.

It is interesting to note that Washington's decision to evacuate Long Island in the middle of the night rather than waiting until daylight ran counter to the conventions of eighteenth-century warfare. A commander who ordered his troops to abandon the field under cover of darkness in order to escape rather than risk having to surrender did not behave honorably. It was one thing to undertake a night operation for the purpose of going on the offensive; it was quite another to simply run away. With the full weight of the war on his shoulders, however, Washington wanted not only to win but also to do so decisively. With that option not really being possible, he had to resort to running the British ragged, to stinging them where and when he could, to securing enough small victories to keep the American people vested in the cause and the army, and to risking as little as possible in the meantime. Building on the lessons he learned from his humiliation in New York, Washington would make an even better use of surprise as an unconventional weapon.

After the Americans had evaded the British in Harlem, escaped from the losses of Forts Washington and Lee and a separate engagement at White Plains, and made it all the way to safety on the Pennsylvania side of the Delaware River, doubt spread through both Washington's army and the American people. The presence of the British force in Trenton, just a day's march from Philadelphia, sent the residents of Trenton into a panic. More bad news came from New England when reports circulated that the British had in fact taken Rhode Island without much resistance. Members of the Continental Congress muttered about Washington's fitness to command. Loyalists became more outspoken, and pessimism began to infect patriot strongholds throughout the colonies. People seemed increasingly inclined to believe that the cause was lost. These pressures weighed heavily on Washington, who had yet another massive problem: the majority of the soldiers' enlistments would be up at the end of December 1776, and if they did not reenlist, the Continental Army would cease to exist.

The enlistment problem reached a crisis level quickly. As the autumn days slipped rapidly toward December, Washington's army shrank by the day. Some help came from British pamphleteer Thomas Paine, who previously had caused a sensation with a forty-six-page pamphlet titled *Common Sense*.[34] Although Paine, with his poor habits, sloppy appearance, and hatred for both authority and orthodoxy, was not the sort of man Washington would have ordinarily befriended, Washington recognized Paine's talent for stirring the emotions of the people through the written word, a skill that he sorely needed to keep the cause alive at this critical juncture. Paine had been traveling with Washington's army and had written a new essay, *The American Crisis*. It began, "These are the times that try men's souls. The summer soldier and the sunshine patriot will, in this crisis, shrink from the service of his country; but he that stands it now, deserves the love and thanks of both man and woman."[35] Paine arranged to have it printed in Philadelphia and sold for just two cents, only enough to meet the printer's costs and nothing more. Upon reading Paine's work, Washington ordered that it be read to his troops as an inducement to reenlist. It circulated widely, both in the camps and among the people, and it had a limited but positive impact. Some of the soldiers returned, but the larger problem of their enlistment contracts still loomed.

As Christmas Eve approached, Washington began mulling over a plan to strike a blow at the Hessian garrison at Trenton in order to galvanize his soldiers to stay in the army.[36] His decision to launch a surprise attack in winter — on Christmas night no less — was inherently risky as it hinged on both secrecy and precision timing. Moreover, Washington's planning ran counter to the lessons taught in his military reading. Because of the dangers associated with travel over snow-covered terrain and the logistical difficulties of keeping an army supplied, healthy, and fed in winter, all eighteenth-century military books advised against undertaking offensive campaigns during those months. All British commanders heeded that advice; thus, the Hessians calculated that the rumored American attack would be unsuccessful. Washington's choice to defy such conventions reflected the extreme circumstances he was in and the need to produce victories to keep soldiers in his ranks and to sustain the war.

The plan was that the operation would commence at midnight on Christmas night with the army attempting to cross the Delaware at three different points. A thousand Pennsylvania militia and five hundred veteran troops under the command of John Cadwalader and Joseph Reed were to cross the river at Bristol and advance toward Burlington. A second force of seven hundred Pennsylvania militia were to attack directly across the river at Trenton, hold the bridge over Assunpink Creek at the foot of Queen Street, and cut off a possible escape route. The third and largest force of twenty-four hundred Continental troops under the command of Washington, Greene, Sullivan, and Stirling would cross the river nine miles up from Trenton at McKonkey's Ferry. Halfway to Trenton, this force would divide into two columns—one led by Sullivan taking River Road and the other led by Greene on Pennington Road. Washington would ride with Greene. Four cannon were to be at the advance of each column. The two columns had to arrive at Trenton no later than five o'clock and the attack to commence at six, or an hour before daylight. Officers were to wear white paper in their hats to distinguish them. Absolute secrecy was required, and no man could quit his ranks on pain of death. The password for the night was "Victory or Death." The latest intelligence estimates indicated between twenty-five hundred and three thousand enemy troops were in Trenton.[37]

From the outset the weather took a severe toll on Washington's complex plan. The driving snow combined with ice that choked the river caused such delays that only Greene's column went forward. Once across the river, the increasingly severe conditions significantly slowed the troops' progress. They did, however, finally reach Trenton. The attack began just after eight o'clock. Greene's men charged across an open field toward a Hessian patrol that fell back to the town once the men could make out the size of the force bearing down on them through the driving snow. Hessian soldiers came pouring out of their barracks, falling into formation at their officers' commands, only to be scattered with devastating rounds from Henry Knox's cannon. As the stunned Hessians fled to the side streets, they ran headlong into Sullivan's men, and savage house-to-house fighting raged for a brief time. Hessian commander Col. Johann Rall, roused from his bed, mounted his horse and ordered his panic-stricken men into a nearby orchard to regroup. Hessians fell all around him, and soon Rall fell, mortally wounded. The Hessians in the orchard surrendered. The attack was over in less than forty-five minutes. Twenty-one Hessians were killed, ninety wounded, and nine hundred taken prisoner. Another five hundred Hessians escaped over Assunpink Bridge, which the Americans should have been guarding. Only four Americans were wounded, and two died from exposure. Washington quickly ordered his exhausted troops to march the nine miles back to McKonkey's Ferry and cross back to Pennsylvania, for he knew that once word of the defeat spread, it would not be safe for his tired army to remain in New Jersey.[38]

Washington highly praised his soldiers' performance in his general orders on December 27 and assured them that they would receive a proportionate amount of the value of what was captured at Trenton in cash.[39] The victory at Trenton breathed new life into the American cause. It was celebrated throughout the colonies as the improbable story of crossing the river in the snow to overwhelm the Hessians and achieving such a surprising result was repeated in nearly every newspaper, church, tavern, and home in America. Bolstered by the success of Trenton but still mindful that his army's enlistments were within days of expiring, Washington decided to keep up the momentum and go after the British again. On December 29 Washington, Greene, Sullivan, and Knox crossed the Delaware at McKonkey's Ferry again in an operation just as dangerous as the previous one had been. In Trenton, Washington made a personal appeal to his troops to reenlist. He offered a bounty of ten dollars to anyone who would stay for six more months, thanks to the money Robert Morris sent from Philadelphia. The willing were asked to step forward. The drums rolled, but no one moved. Then riding before the men, Washington changed his approach and spoke to them in the most affectionate terms: "My brave fellows, you have done all I asked you to do, and more than can reasonably can be expected, but your country is at stake, your wives, your houses, and all that you hold dear. You have worn yourself out with fatigues and hardships, but we know not how to spare you. If you will consent to stay just one month longer, you will render that service to the cause of liberty, and to your country, which you can probably never do under any other circumstance."[40] The drums rolled again, and nearly every one of the soldiers in the formation stepped forward. This speech to the troops offers another example of how Washington put rhetoric to practical use. The oratorical flourishes of this speech echoes the writing in Paine's pamphlets, which had previously proven to be an effective bolster to the American cause.

By January 1, 1777, Gen. Charles Cornwallis arrived in Princeton with eight thousand men. On January 2 Cornwallis took fifty-five hundred troops and set off after Washington at Trenton. By dusk the Americans retreated back through Trenton and, thanks to Knox's cannon, were able to hold the British advance at the Assunpink Bridge. As the sun set, Cornwallis convened his officers to decide whether it made sense to try one last attack on the bridge to destroy Washington. Even though some at the meeting, including Sir William Erskine, predicted that if they did not press the attack immediately, they would not find Washington in the morning, Cornwallis decided not to risk a night attack. Instead he would "bag him in the morning."[41] True to the predictions, Washington's army was nowhere to be found when the sun rose. Having left enough men behind to create the illusion that the army was encamped for the night, Washington pulled out of Trenton on a large, daring northward movement around to Cornwallis's rear in Princeton. Washington planned to divide his force once again, with Sullivan's column going to the right and Greene's going to the left. The fighting broke out at daybreak on January 3 as Greene's column ran into some British forces a couple of miles outside of Princeton. At the end of the battle, the Americans had lost twenty-three men; the British, considerably more. It was another stunning, improbable success for the Americans. Washington was sorely pressed to push on to Brunswick and capture the British supplies there, but the army was too exhausted. Any such operation was way too risky, so Knox talked Washington out of it. Instead, the bedraggled yet victorious Americans slipped back into the hills near Morristown to spend the rest of the winter there, tucked safely out of reach of the British.[42]

The victories at Trenton and Princeton were of small tactical consequence to the Americans in the short term. The British were dealt two surprise blows that took a toll on the officers, yet in the broader context of the overall size of their force during the entire war, the losses were relatively minor. In the long term, however, the victories at Trenton and Princeton forced Howe to fixate on holding New Jersey and on taking Philadelphia in the face of Washington's army, which had not simply disappeared as he had hoped. Washington's army survived and was holding out in New Jersey; therefore, Howe had to re-array his forces to counter Washington's presence. Furthermore, in order to take Philadelphia, Howe was obliged to sail around to the city's port.

Washington's Reading and the Development of His Strategy

The significance of these battles for the Americans is hard to overstate. After the dismal performance of Washington and his army in New York that very nearly ended the Revolution in the late summer of 1776, Washington turned everything around by the end of the year and kept the cause alive by delivering two stunning victories that had a tremendous psychological impact on both the army and the people. He adapted his strategic thinking to embrace a defensive strategy designed at wearing away the British will to fight while keeping the survival of his own army paramount. He was learning the art of high command.[43] Washington's reading was a critical component in the evolution of his generalship, which had failed him in 1776. His lack of a military education had caused him to make costly mistakes, resulting in defeat after defeat. Washington's eventual shift toward a defensive strategy was largely due instead to his experience. This strategic transition, however, would have been more difficult if he had had an extensive military education, for combined with his aggressive nature and desire for victory, such a background arguably would have inhibited his ability to see clearly the weaknesses in his army that could not be ignored.

In this way, Washington in 1776 was going through the same type of intellectual shift that he had experienced nearly twenty years earlier when he lost his fight for a British commission. At the point when he realized he could not transcend his colonial birth and become British, he readily abandoned the idea of cultivating a European-style intellect in favor of pursuing the Virginian ideal of gentry living — that is, turning profits as a planter while dedicating the rest of his time to public service. In 1776 he had to become a leader whose abilities would be recognized not just by his countrymen but by the British as well. As such he initially did not take the lessons learned from his practical reading on military tactics and adapt them to his unique situation. Forced to recognize that he must do so after suffering the staggering defeats in New York, Washington began to evolve into the leader that history remembers.

These early years of the Revolution were the most trying in Washington's life. He shouldered an immense burden and had few people he could confide in. Over time the whispered criticism of his performances in 1776 and 1777 grew louder. For all the disparagement, however, Washington carried the hopes of many of his countrymen, and grateful admirers inundated Washington with printed sermons, political tracts, and newspaper articles that celebrated the cause, the army, and the commander in chief himself. That said, although the business of the headquarters was unceasing, Washington added more military books to his reading collection throughout the war. In attempting to assess which texts Washington actually made the time to read, it is important to remember the extreme circumstances he faced on a daily basis. Washington was often despondent during the long campaign months that were filled with defeat and disheartening news, and no one was there to cheer him. His outlook improved when his wife joined him in his winter quarters, but for long periods in between he was most certainly alone with his dark thoughts. For all of his strength, Washington was someone who needed security and reassurance. He mentally escaped to Mount Vernon whenever possible, sending pages of instructions to his overseer not only to enjoy a bit of a distraction in making plans for the home he loved but also to regain some sense of control. With the war going badly and its ultimate success anything but a foregone conclusion, it is possible that he made time to read some of the sermons and periodicals he received in order to regain some positive perspective on his task. This assumption makes sense especially for printed works that were either written or sent by someone he knew.

Besides the matter of ego, Washington had a practical need as commander in chief to keep his finger on the pulse of the Revolution as it intensified. Although he maintained his belief in subordinating his role as a general to civilian authority, in the eyes of many Americans Washington embodied the Revolution, and he knew it. The materials he read and the news he received constantly reinforced the knowledge that the people were more focused on him than they were on John Hancock as the president of Congress; so he necessarily had to stay abreast of precisely how his countrymen thought about the Revolution. As such both his position and his reputation demanded that he maintain at least a cursory knowledge of the latest expositions on current affairs as they became available from the presses across the states.

The Rhetoric of the American Revolution

Any analysis of Revolutionary War–era writings must be conducted with a thorough understanding of how language was both used and understood to describe the evolving American mentalité. The writers during this period went to extreme lengths to lay the discursive foundation of national legitimacy with their careful use of both the spoken and the written word.[44] Washington, who was likewise striving to establish both his legitimacy as a leader and that of the Continental Army, would have certainly recognized the writers' efforts to establish national credence. Furthermore, he was not the only one to appreciate that language was one of the Revolution's most effective weapons. John Adams correctly asserted that the American Revolution had taken place in the consciousness of the American people: "What do We Mean by the Revolution? The War? That was no part of the Revolution. It was only an Effect and Consequence of it. The Revolution was in the Minds of the People, and this was effected, from 1760–1775, in the course of fifteen Years before a drop of blood was drawn at Lexington."[45]

Even though Adams was in large part championing his own role in the Revolution when making this assertion, he was nonetheless correct in the sense that a revolution can only be carried out by people who have been convinced that doing so is both possible and right.[46] This intellectual process is what qualifies the war that it sparks as being a true revolution and not simply a rebellion. Adams's argument is further proven by applying it to Washington, for as is argued earlier in this chapter and in chapter 2, he became a revolutionary ahead of many of his fellow countrymen. When he accepted the appointment as commander in chief of the Continental Army, he did so as an American and not as a Briton seeking the restoration of the old colonial status quo.

The self-consciousness that Adams, Washington, and the rest of the revolutionary elite felt about the idea that language was the contested site for political action was not reserved to them alone; it was also crucially a part of popular propaganda as well.[47] When the colonies began resisting British policies and finally demanded independence, they did so not just as individuals but also as members of particular local counties or congregations. This of course does not suggest that all colonists were united at all times; rather, the effort to stage a successful revolution encompassed far more than simply the elite who were at the vanguard of the movement.[48] Colonists across class lines understood that the language used either to support or to decry the Revolution was politically charged in a distinct, eighteenth-century manner. For instance, given that a considerable cross section of colonial American society widely read and understood the law, not only was the practice of law far more difficult then as opposed to more recent times but it also had a profound impact on the way that revolutionary discourse was written.[49] The combined effect of this revolutionary rhetoric, which uniquely interwove legal, political, and religious discourse, allowed the people living through these times to be a part of a sophisticated rhetorical culture wherein everyone — lawyers, legislators, military officers, planters, and merchants — had a particular understanding of distinctive political nuance.[50]

Washington's Collection of Revolutionary War Sermons

When examining the religious writings of this era that Washington collected, it is critical to bear in mind that the printed sermons had as much or more to do with politics than with theology. Nearly every pulpit in

America was politicized during this period either for or against the patriot cause. Therefore, when considering the reasons why Washington may have read these works, he may have sought more than religious inspiration. These sermons could have provided Washington with a sense of reassurance that the public still held him and the cause that he embodied in high regard. That encouragement would have been sorely needed during the long retreat across New Jersey, the winter at Valley Forge, and the even harsher winter at Morristown. Washington's wanting to know whether the public was still on his side, moreover, was not out of simple vanity. He also needed to determine that the American people still supported the war because, for the most part, it was not obvious. States routinely failed to meet the recruiting quotas that Congress set forth, and the army chronically lacked everything it required: pay, uniforms, weapons, ammunition, food, medicine, and horses. Washington sought evidence that the people were still behind the war so that he in turn could reassure his troops, who were torn between their duty to support their families and the obligation they felt to serve — service that often entailed suffering with little tangible reward. Washington strived to keep his troops in the army, but he and his recruiting officers had to rely largely on rhetoric to do so. The very writing style of the many sermons, pamphlets, and newspaper articles Washington collected included many ideas and turns of phrase that would have been useful to him and his recruiting staff. Moreover, the literary style of these works, along with their ideological undertones, would have been familiar to most of the men in their target audiences.[51]

Also striking when considering Washington's sermon collection as a whole is how closely it chronicles the transformation of the American Revolution from a struggle to restore English liberties into a war to achieve complete independence from Great Britain. The earliest example in Washington's collection is William Smith's *A Sermon on the Present Situation of American Affairs, Preached at Christ-Church, June 23, 1775.* Preached just nine days after Washington's appointment as commander in chief and the formal establishment of the Continental

Army, Smith's sermon argues vehemently for the justice of the American cause but clearly states that independence was not the goal; rather, the Americans were engaged in a struggle to restore the old status quo of British rule.[52] At that time Smith spoke to men who thought they were the rightful inheritors of the Glorious Revolution of 1688. In other words, the struggle that had just begun on the far-flung battlefields around Boston was to restore the glory of the English constitution.

Another example in Washington's collection that justifies rebellion to restore English liberties is Thomas Coombe's *A Sermon Preached before the Congregations of Christ-Church and St. Peter's, Philadelphia.* Coombe drew on a passage from 2 Chronicles to make the argument that as with the ancient Israelites who cast their eyes to God to deliver them in the face of an approaching superior enemy, the colonists also stood against a mightier power that unjustly demanded submission from their brethren who had been loyal members of the same family. The sermon is constructed with language about loyalty, family, constitutionality, and Providence. Weaving together passages from scripture with contemporary political events, this sermon plainly imbues the American cause with a sense of righteousness but yet stops short of calling for independence.[53] In the same vein as the previous example from William Smith, Coombe's sermon reflects the current situation in 1775. Therein lies a key to understanding both the language and the purpose of these political sermons: the clergy simply reflected upon the political situation of the moment. The pulpit served as a platform for announcing the goals of the American Revolution, but others elsewhere often developed those goals. For the most part, the clergy saw themselves not only as the link between God and the people but also as necessary intermediaries between the revolutionary leaders and the citizens who were being asked to choose sides. Thus they instilled a sense of sacredness into a war being waged over political principles.[54]

As the war transformed into a struggle for independence from Great Britain, the message of the sermons likewise changed to reflect this ideological shift. Two examples from Washington's collection are William

Gordon's *The Separation of the Jewish Tribes, after the Death of Solomon, Accounted for, and Applied to the Present Day, in A Sermon Preached before the General Court, on Friday, July 4, 1777; Being the Anniversary of the Declaration of Independency* and Chaplain John Hurt's *The Love of Our Country: A Sermon Preached before the Virginia Troops in New Jersey*.[55] These sermons were written by army chaplains and therefore reveal the degree to which revolutionary rhetoric began to resonate within the ranks. Additionally Washington's decision to keep copies of these chaplains' sermons indicates his thinking about what the role and significance of the clergy and organized religion were in the Revolution. When Congress authorized the appointment of chaplains to minister to the regiments of the Continental Army, Washington mandated attendance at Sunday services for all soldiers. Furthermore, he insisted that they afford the chaplains the proper degree of courtesy on pain of God's wrath, for "the blessing and protection of Heaven are at all times necessary but especially so in times of public distress and danger — the General hopes and trusts, that every officer and man, will endeavor so to live, and act, as becomes a Christian soldier defending the dearest rights and liberties of his country."[56] Here Washington's choice of language in this general order was a reflection of the message emanating from the pulpits across the Continental Army encampments each Sunday morning. Moreover, even before Congress officially sanctioned the chaplains, Washington recognized and welcomed the evangelical clergy's contribution in promoting the American cause. He specifically commended Abiel Leonard of Connecticut, a minister who would become one of his favorite chaplains, for his particular talent for explaining to the soldiers the inherent sacredness of their political rights.[57] Therefore, whether Washington was theologically aligned with his chaplains or not, he clearly viewed organized religion as a key to the successful outcome of the war. He saw it would go a long way toward inspiring both a regard for discipline and a sense of duty in the soldiers.

It is interesting to note that Washington's collection includes revolutionary sermons written by authors from both sides of the Atlantic.

For example, he received two copies of a political sermon delivered by Richard Price in England, printed first in London in 1776 and reprinted in Philadelphia shortly thereafter, that is titled *Observations on the Nature of Civil Liberty, the Principles of Government, and the Justice and Policy of the War with America*. Price was a dissenting minister in England who was known to many of the American revolutionary leaders as a friend of the colonies. This sermon in particular recognizes the legitimacy of all the colonial grievances against the king and Parliament for trampling on the colonists' collective English liberties. It further delineates the staggering amount of money that Great Britain spent during the Seven Years' War while negating the argument first advanced by Lord Grenville that as the war had been fought on behalf of the colonies, they should therefore "welcome" the various taxation acts as just payment for services rendered. Price argued instead that the ministers were "strangely misinformed" and that it should have come as no surprise that the Americans resisted.[58] Price's arguments must have been reassuring to the Americans, who persisted in waging what at the time appeared to be a losing war. For Washington in particular, it would have been heartening to know that an Englishman's recognition of the justice of the American cause was circulating in print throughout England, Ireland, and the colonies.

Washington seemed to have a set of favored authors. For example, his collection includes several works by Uzal Ogden.[59] Among them are *A Sermon Delivered at Roxbury, in Morris County, March 19, 1781* and two different sermons similarly titled *A Sermon on Practical Religion* (the first delivered at Newark, New Jersey, on August 15, 1779, and the second in 1782).[60] These sermons use similar tones to extol Christian virtues and the benefits of maintaining a devotion to Christian worship.[61] The straightforward texts urge adherence to disciplined orthodoxy as a means for living a good life and achieving a good death. The message made perfect sense for Washington, who, as the previous example from his general orders demonstrates, worked so hard to instill these values in his troops. Even *Sermon Delivered at Roxbury*, a funeral sermon for a colonel's wife, reinforces the ideals of liberty, virtue, and piety, using terms that were linked to patriot rhetoric. The sermon promises eternal life in Heaven to those men who lived according to these qualities.[62] As such this same sermon could have just as easily been delivered to eulogize any soldier killed in battle; therefore, it offered an opportunity for a practical application for Washington, who, as mentioned earlier, was constantly in search of rhetoric to bolster his recruiting efforts.

Another cleric who is heavily represented in Washington's religious collection is Granville Sharp, an English Anglican priest whose writings are even more overtly political than Ogden's sermons are. Sharp was an outspoken critic of the British policies toward the colonies and of the prosecution of the war specifically. Washington had in his collection seventeen of Sharp's works, mostly on the subject of the American war. Of interest is his *An Appendix to the Representation (Printed in the Year 1769) of the Injustice and Dangerous Tendency of Tolerating Slavery, or, of Admitting the Least Claim of Private Property in the Persons of Men in England Addresses the Immorality of the Institution of Slavery Both in America as Well as Britain's Toleration of It.*[63] It is one of twenty volumes on the subject of slavery in Washington's collection, and all address, in one way or another, the moral inconsistencies of the system, either hinting at or directly calling for the need for its abolition. The significance of Sharp's and other works on slavery is explored more fully in chapter 6, which discusses Washington's decision to free his slaves in his will.

Washington also had in his collection five works by the Methodist leader John Wesley. Wesley's sermons were printed at the conclusion of the Revolution and, unlike the majority of the others discussed in this chapter, are centered on religious themes. What makes them noteworthy is that, first, their number indicates Washington's great interest in Wesley's writing. Second, the two men never corresponded with each other; so unlike many of the other authors whose work from 1775 to 1799 appeared in Washington's collection, the five sermons were not gifts from Wesley himself. Third, the sermons became available during the period around the end of the Revolution when Washington's home state of Virginia debated enacting Thomas Jefferson's Statute of Religious Freedom into law. Although Washington was in the process of retiring and withdrawing from public life and was therefore not a member of the Virginia Assembly that passed the law in 1786, he still actively followed developing political affairs. Moreover, after his tenure with the Continental Army, which exposed him to various forms of Christian worship, he possibly followed the movement in Virginia to disestablish the Church of England once and for all and sought to learn more about the increasing popularity of one of the Anglicans' chief rivals, the Methodists. Having been a burgess in Virginia when the bishop question dominated the agenda and pitted the church against the state and the will of the people, he understood both the significance of disestablishing the church and the impact that religious questions had on society.

Washington's Collection of Revolutionary War Political Tracts and Periodicals

Washington's need to follow all of the latest developments in current affairs throughout the Revolutionary War era meant that he had to read more than just sermons. He also amassed a considerable number of political pamphlets and copies of the records of the Continental Congress, as well as those of the House of Burgesses and later the Virginia Assembly. Of the legislative records that Washington collected, he probably read only those passed by the Continental Congress as they had immediate application to his army's activities. Richard Henry Lee sent the records of Virginia to Washington, but he likely had little time to read them and follow the legislative affairs of one state, albeit his home state, as he was too occupied with the war effort.[64]

Washington's collection of political tracts outlines the scope of the ideological debate on the American crisis with Britain. He seemed interested in developing an understanding of both sides of the conflict with Great Britain. For example, William Milnor, Washington's Philadelphia agent, sent him a copy of Thomas Bradbury Chandler's (attributed to Myles Cooper) *A Friendly Address to All Reasonable Americans, on the Subject of Our Political Confusions*. Milnor also provided Charles Lee's refutation, *Strictures on a Pamphlet, Entitled, "A Friendly Address to All Reasonable Americans, on the Subject of Our Political Confusions."*[65] In *Friendly Address* Chandler flatly condemned the revolutionaries' rash actions and argued that it was "high time therefore to awaken the thoughtless to a sense of danger, and to think of providing for our common safety." Chandler further asserted that "our own misconduct has brought it forward; and our immediate reformation must stop its progress. He must be blind, that is not convinced of this; and he must be infatuated, that will pursue the road, which evidently terminates in darkness and destruction."[66] Lee countered Chandler's argument point by point in similarly plain language. Lee maintained that "the design of his Pamphlet is manifestly to dissolve the spirit of union, and check the noble ardor prevailing through the continent; but his zeal so far outruns his abilities, that there is the greatest reason to think that his Reverence has labored to little effect."[67] Lee drew a parallel between the commonly held views that Charles I was a tyrant and the popular opinion of George III's conduct in order to decry Chandler's call for passive obedience to the monarch as "a mark of lunacy."[68] Washington also had another pamphlet written by Chandler, *What Think Ye of the Congress Now, or, an Enquiry, How Far the Americans Are Bound to Abide by, and Execute, the Decisions of the Late Congress?*[69] Chandler's pro-British arguments in this pamphlet were counterbalanced in Washington's collection with the writings by some of Washington's fellow delegates to the Continental Congress. One example is John Dickinson's *A Declaration by the Representatives of the United Colonies of North America Now Met in General Congress at Philadelphia, Setting Forth the Causes and Necessity of Their Taking up Arms*. Washington found Dickinson's argument so persuasive that he forwarded a copy to his closest friend, George William Fairfax, who had returned to England because of his loyalist leanings.[70] Along with Dickinson's pamphlet, Washington also sent a copy of the Continental Congress's address to the inhabitants of

Great Britain that made a direct appeal to the British people to accept the justness of the American cause. Washington included a letter to Fairfax with the pamphlets in which he noted his appointment as commander in chief of the Continental Army and reported the casualties sustained at Bunker Hill, because he was certain that Fairfax would "have a very erroneous account transmitted, of the loss sustained on the side of the Provincials." Washington expressed his confidence that on the American side there were no more "than 139 killed[,] 36 missing and 278 Wounded; nor had we, if I can credit the most solemn assurances of the Officers that were in the action, above 1500 men engaged that day." He went on to state that "the loss on the side of the Ministerial Troops, as I am informed from good authority, consisted of 1,043 killed and wounded, whereof 92 were Officers."[71] Although the language of this letter is terse, on second reading it appears that Washington was attempting to make his friend understand his rationale for accepting the command. Despite Fairfax's decision to return to England, the two men remained close, thus it makes sense that Washington would do so.

Washington also kept copies of his fellow Virginian Arthur Lee's pamphlets, which Lee had originally composed and published in England in 1775 for British audiences: *An Appeal to the Justice and Interests of the People of Great Britain in the Present Disputes with America; A Second Appeal to the Justice and Interests of the People, on the Measures Respecting America;* and *A Speech, Intended to Have Been Delivered in the House of Commons, in Support of the Petition from the General Congress at Philadelphia.*[72] Lee's writing bears all the hallmarks of an American fully trained in English common law, and it therefore brims with that particular brand of rhetoric used during this period to justify the colonists' claims against Great Britain. In addition to Lee's legalistic arguments on the justness of the American position, Washington had copies of Thomas Paine's *Common Sense* and *The American Crisis*. Paine's masterful use of plain language distills the rhetoric into a heated condemnation of George III and the need to carry on the war. Both pamphlets had a profound effect on the people at large.[73] These different works presented

Washington with the full range of opinions on the Revolution in both learned and popular language. Together they provided him with a well-rounded understanding of how the people understood the conflict as it changed over time.

Besides religious tracts, printed sermons, and political pamphlets, Washington subscribed to multiple periodicals as another means of keeping track of current events. During the Revolution he maintained subscriptions to multiple periodicals, including *Monthly and Critical Reviews, Annual Register for 1781, Annual Register for 1782, Pennsylvania Packet,* and *Political Magazine.*[74] Of these publications, publisher John Dunlap expressly established a subscription of the *Pennsylvania Packet* for Washington's particular use during the war. It is interesting that the other four periodicals were all English publications. The disproportionate number of English journals is perhaps indicative of Washington's need to maintain an awareness of how the popular press on both sides of the Atlantic presented the war's events.

The Significance of Washington's Revolutionary-Era Reading

Washington's growing personal library during the revolutionary period when taken as a whole is revealing. By concentrating his energies and what free time he had to reading military field manuals, political pamphlets, overtly political religious works, and periodicals, Washington was able to maintain an understanding of the total progress of the Revolution both within and beyond the army. He combined this self-directed reading with his natural penchant for leadership to become the very personification of the Revolution itself. As commander in chief of the Continental Army, he had to realize that success hinged on his abandoning the attempt to be a European-style general and instead develop a plan that would preserve his army. He did so by building his force from the ground up while relying on both a handful of the latest tactical guides to lay the necessary foundations and his previous experience as commander of the Virginia Regiment. He further shaped his strategy by maintaining an awareness of public opinion as expressed through various forms of print media from periodicals to pamphlets to sermons. His reading always had an immediate application to the circumstances he faced, and he learned to adjust his thinking as he combined his reading knowledge with his continually developing understanding of his circumstances. Just as his conscious rejection of classical reading in favor of a practical study of subjects such as agriculture brought him wealth and status before the war, his reading during the revolutionary era helped him succeed as a general.

CHAPTER FOUR

Presidential Reading

All of Manhattan was abuzz with anticipation the morning of April 30, 1789, for it was the dawn of a new era for Americans who had lived through decades of revolutionary upheaval and uncertainty to see a new nation born against incredible odds. At precisely nine o'clock, church bells rang out across New York City for the better part of a half hour, summoning congregations to assemble and pray for President-elect Washington. The faithful dutifully answered the call, then made their way down Broadway to Federal Hall, and awaited the much-anticipated inauguration of the republic's favorite son. An estimated ten thousand people crowded the street beneath the balcony where the ceremony was set to take place and hoped to catch a glimpse of the great man although, of course, they had no hope of hearing a single word of his speech. Among the crowd was a self-professed Washington enthusiast who described the event as being nothing short of a religious experience. In a letter that was published in newspapers throughout the nation, the enraptured citizen wrote:

> The scene was awful, beyond description. It would seem extraordinary, that the administration of an oath, a ceremony so very common and familiar should, in so great a degree, excite the public curiosity. But the circumstances of his election — the impression of his past services — the concourse of spectators — the devout fervency with which he repeated the oath — and the reverential manner in which he bowed down and kissed the sacred volume — all these conspired

to render it one of the most august and interesting spectacles ever exhibited on this globe. It seemed from the number of witnesses, to be a solemn appeal to Heaven and earth at once. . . . I confess, that I was under an awful and religious persuasion that the gracious Ruler of the universe was looking down at that moment with particular complacency on an act, which to a part of his creatures was so very important. Under this impression, when the Chancellor pronounced in a very feeling manner, "Long Live George Washington," my sensibility was wound to such a pitch, that I could do no more than wave my hat with the rest, without the power of joining the repeated acclamations which rent the air.[1]

This exuberant observer was not the only one overawed by the scene on that warm, spring afternoon. The newly minted president Washington was described by those closer to him on the balcony as being so moved by the immensity of both the crowd and the task he was about to undertake that he did two things that were distinctly out of character. After taking the oath of office, he suddenly seized the hefty pulpit Bible from the hands of the unsuspecting secretary of the senate Samuel Otis and kissed it, likely taking everyone by surprise.[2] Following the ceremony the nerve-wracked president Washington returned to the Senate chamber to deliver his inaugural address. His performance was at best described as hesitating and at worst as embarrassed and clumsy. He frankly admitted to the assembly that nothing had ever made him as anxious as the news of his election; he had grown despondent as he considered his own "inferior endowments from nature." He drew strength from God, however, who, as the "Great Author of every public and private good," had bestowed his blessings on the people of the United States and the new government.[3]

In the end those who witnessed Washington's first official performances as president were not overly inspired.[4] The question that everyone in the assembly (not to mention Washington himself) must have been asking is, why was he so awkward? He was after all America's great hero, and he had previously mastered the art of public appearance as he had demonstrated time and again. He had put down the Newburgh Conspiracy, bade farewell to his officers, submitted his resignation to the Continental Congress, and presided over the Constitutional Convention. What then had made the inauguration so difficult for him?

By setting all the criticism aside and looking at the event itself, it is not difficult to see why Washington was so hesitant. It was not easy to be first. Not only was he the most famous man in America but also he was well aware that the success of the presidency and the federal government as a whole depended on him.[5] He had nothing to guide him. The United States was attempting a republican experiment that was utterly different from the closest examples from history: ancient Rome, Cromwell's protectorate, and the Dutch Republic.[6] One can just imagine the thoughts that had run through Washington's mind immediately after he was notified of his election to the presidency: How was he supposed to conduct himself? How was he supposed to make his inauguration and his subsequent public appearances sufficiently ceremonial without too closely invoking images of monarchy?

It is important to remember that Washington's nervousness ran deep. He had never been comfortable with political power, and becoming the nation's first chief executive brought him an overwhelming command of it. The Constitution was deliberately vague as to executive (and judicial) responsibilities because the founders had paid greater attention to the composition and powers of the national legislature and had little precedent for defining presidential powers. That vagueness would be a source of difficulty for Washington to negotiate at different times throughout his presidency. Moreover, he doubted his ability to do the job.[7] His solution was characteristic, given the way that he approached his command of the Continental Army during the Revolution: he surrounded himself with the most talented minds to assist him. As a general he had called his staff his military family; as president, he would call his staff members his cabinet. His decision to engage a cabinet was fortuitous for several reasons. First, it would be overwhelming for any president to execute his duties without advisers. Second, by surrounding himself with qualified individuals whose opinions carried significant weight in his decision making, Washington was carefully trying to avoid any criticism that he sought to hoard power in order to rule alone. He believed in this great republican experiment, had no desire to be a king or dictator, and was fearful of doing anything that could besmirch his hard-earned reputation.

Washington's awareness of history and his developing place in it relates again to his reading. He had been raised with an appreciation of his British heritage and, as noted previously, had purchased Tobias Smollett's *Complete History of England*. In it he would have read the celebratory descriptions of Elizabeth I's political skills as queen during one of the most tumultuous periods in the history of the realm.[8] Indeed, much of Smollett's characterization of Elizabeth's leadership can be similarly applied to Washington:

> She was endowed with a great share of natural penetration: she had observed the characters of mankind. Knowing how to distinguish merit, she made choice of able counselors. She administered justice impartially, without respect of persons: she regulated her expense with such economy as could not but be agreeable to her subjects . . . and having been accustomed to dissimilation she not only assumed the utmost complacency in her deportment, but affected such an ardor of love and regard for her subjects, as could not fail to produce the warmest return of confidence and affection. Her frugality was not so much the effect of her natural disposition, as the result of good sense and deliberate reflection.[9]

While the lessons of English history thus informed Washington, still it was monarchical history. He would therefore need contemporary sources to draw upon in order to determine if his performance as a republican head of state hit the mark with the American people, who still lived under the long shadow cast by the crown.

Just as he had done during the American Revolution, Washington incorporated reading into his execution of public duties. As president he was of course inordinately busy, but he did make time to read when possible, especially periodicals. Newspapers, pamphlets, and political sermons were the primary means by which he could gauge how the American people responded to his performance as he did his best to forge a republican future out of a monarchical past. That Washington would be setting precedents for all of his successors was a daunting prospect, but the presidency would prove to be vastly different from the challenges that he had faced when given command of the Continental Army in 1775. This time Washington had the enormous benefit of his reputation to rely on. The task he faced as the first president, however, was to establish the parameters of the office in order to legitimate the Constitution as a form of government that would prove resistant to republican excesses on one extreme and the potential for despotic rule on the other. Accomplishing this task would require a delicate balance of investing the office with dignity by incorporating familiar signs and symbols of authority into the presidential routine while giving them a uniquely American twist. He had to exude authority without appearing too much like a king. This territory was uncharted, and in order to be successful, Washington had to maintain an awareness of public opinion, which he would glean from an array of sources outside of his presidential office.

What follows is an examination of what Washington read during the years between the end of the Revolution and the end of his two terms in office. It offers an opportunity to delve into the construction of the American presidency as an institution and to determine how early republicans saw themselves and the new nation they were building. Washington's collection during this period expanded tremendously in size, for he received a deluge of gifts from authors eager to secure his endorsement and from others who sought to curry his favor in general. Washington's daily schedule did not permit him time to read many books during this period, but he did read as often and as much as he could. Unlike his first foray into politics as a member of the House of

Burgesses, Washington could not take his time to study law, political philosophy, and religion and gradually become more involved in issues as he grew more comfortable in his role. This time he had to focus exclusively on the contemporary issues as they developed.

Washington's Homecoming

When Washington took his leave from public life in Congress in 1783, he was eager to return to Mount Vernon. After he arrived home, Washington faced the reality that his estate was in disarray. The financial toll exacted on Washington's fortune as a result of the war and his refusal to accept a salary was substantial. He remarked to his nephew Fielding Lewis Jr., "I made no money from my estate during the nine years I was absent from it and brought none home with me."[10] Washington soon figured out that he would not be able to remedy the situation quickly. More than a year after returning home, Washington despaired in a letter to Henry Knox that his business affairs could "no longer be neglected without involving my ruin."[11] By 1785 Washington nudged aside Lund Washington, his estate manager for more than twenty-one years, and began personally managing the five farms that constituted the seven-thousand-acre Mount Vernon estate: Muddy Hole, Dogue Run, Union, River, and Mansion House. At this point Washington's land holdings had expanded so greatly that he was unable to personally oversee all of them, so he implemented a weekly reporting system from each of his respective overseers that demanded "an account of the stock and every occurrence that happens . . . minutely detailed . . . every Saturday."[12] He had a bottomless appetite for details regarding his estate, and he longed to devote all of his energies to remodeling it to such a degree that it would surpass its prewar glory. He began corresponding with the English agricultural reformer Arthur Young, who sent Washington multiple volumes of the series *Annals of Agriculture*, to which Young was a major contributor. Young was a proponent of advancing the science of agriculture as opposed to relying exclusively on time-honored techniques. Washington eventually owned thirty-two of these volumes and diligently studied them, copying out entire passages that were of a particular interest, as he had done before with other agricultural texts.[13] Washington and Young conducted transatlantic conversation about plows, farmyard design, soil, seeds, and crop rotation. Washington's main problem was the exhausted soil of his farms, which had not been properly managed during his long absence. He began an ambitious program of revitalization by conducting his own experiments with fertilizers made from manure and soil dredged from the bottom of the Potomac River. To restore the soil with nutrients, Washington also devised a complex system of crop rotation that called for planting the following crops in succession: corn with potatoes and carrots, buckwheat, wheat, peas, barley, oats, and red clover.[14]

Although the business of rebuilding his fortune was endless, Washington never did have the chance to truly immerse himself in the task. For one thing he was besieged by visitors, including friends, family members, and associates, as well as many strangers who simply wanted to be able to say that they had seen Washington. Eighteenth-century hospitality rules dictated that no matter how beleaguered he was with the constant stream of people, he could turn none of them away. The visitors taxed both Washington's patience and his finances as the constant flow of guests devoured his food, drank his wine, and stabled their horses in his barns. The catalog of guests reads like a hotel registry. Indeed, he and Martha finally dined alone for the first time on June 30, 1785, a full year and a half after he retired from public life.[15]

Washington's Preoccupation with His Postwar Reputation

The hordes of guests kept Washington well informed of the latest political and diplomatic developments, and increasingly it seemed he was not yet out of the public eye forever. He therefore felt the need to act and set a certain tone in accordance with what he thought the public still expected of him. For example, he resigned his position as vestryman of Truro Parish during this period, a position that he had held for twenty-two years. Washington never explained his decision to give up the post, although his motives were likely both political and image related, for vestrymen were still required to swear an oath of obedience to the "doctrine and discipline of the Church of England," of which George III was the head.[16] Although this technicality may not have been obvious to the average parishioner, it would certainly not have escaped the notice of the political elite, and Washington could not be seen to doing anything to undermine his status. Safeguarding his reputation in this manner was especially necessary should he ever be recalled to public life. Another example was Washington's agony over the question of whether to accept the state of Virginia's gift of fifty shares of Potomac Company stock and a hundred shares of James River Company stock in recognition of his wartime service to the state. Washington's first reaction was that "no circumstance has happened to me since I left the walks of public life, which has so much embarrassed me."[17] On the one hand, while he did not want to offend his fellow Virginians by rejecting the gift, he also felt that he could not accept it as he had refused a salary during the war. On the other hand, his refusal might be interpreted as "an ostentatious display of disinterestedness or public virtue."[18] He did not want people to think that "sinister motives had the smallest influence in the suggestion."[19] He dashed off frantic letters to an astonishing number of confidants about what to do, going so far as to make the point that he did not need the money. As he told Henry Knox, "I have nobody to provide for and I have enough to support me through life in the plain and easy style in which I intend to spend the remainder of my days."[20] After much consultation and deliberation, Washington came up with a solution. He decided to hold the gift shares in trust for public education. Specifically he wanted to create "two charity schools, one on each river for the education and support of the children of the poor and indigent," especially children who had lost their fathers in the war.[21]

Washington's Interest in Literature and Legacy Building

Further evidence of Washington's preoccupation with his reputation and his recognition of the weight of his celebrity can be found in what he was reading during the period between the end of the war and the convening of the Constitutional Convention. In the spring of 1783 he placed an order for several books advertised in a gazette including Voltaire's *Letters of M. de Voltaire, to Several of His Friends,* John Locke's *An Essay Concerning Human Understanding,* and Edward Gibbon's *The Decline and Fall of the Roman Empire.* He also ordered biographies of Charles XII of Sweden, Louis XV of France, and Peter the Great of Russia.[22] He further added several travel narratives to his collection, among them two by John Moore — *A View of Society and Manners in Italy: With Anecdotes Relating to Some Eminent Characters* and *A View of Society and Manners in France, Switzerland, and Germany: With Anecdotes Relating to Some Eminent Characters.*[23] At first this somewhat eclectic reading list seems to indicate that Washington intended to broaden his horizons in retirement. This list demonstrates that Washington wanted to gain a better understanding of European affairs so that he could cultivate an appropriate frame of reference for responding to inquiries he received from foreign luminaries, leaders, and observers (many of whom were visitors to Mount Vernon during this period) to comment on the American situation.

The biographies on this list also illustrate Washington's growing interest in how key literary figures could assist in the cultivation of his image. Washington's initial interest in biography began when he was a teenager, and he purchased *A Panegyrick to the Memory of His Grace Frederick, Late Duke of Schonberg.* Now as a mature man who had achieved fame in his own right, Washington renewed his interest in the genre. In selecting biographies of renowned leaders at this juncture, it is possible that Washington wanted to read them not for the purpose of learning life lessons from these subjects but to see how the production of biographies contributed to the subjects' lasting fame. Further evidence of Washington's interest in the benefits of biographical and historical writing is seen in his entertaining, sometimes at great length, some of the most prominent writers of the day. In these engagements he exhibited none of his previous inhibitions that stemmed from being

in the company of intellectuals. In May 1785 he entertained Noah Webster, who visited Mount Vernon to solicit Washington's support for a
copyright law in Virginia and probably also to provide him with a copy
of his *Sketches of American Policy*.[24] The next month Washington welcomed famed British historian Catharine Macaulay Graham and her
husband to Mount Vernon for a ten-day visit. Unlike the scores of other
guests who were little more than expensive intruders, he was clearly
taken with Macaulay. He wrote to Henry Knox that "a visit from a lady
so celebrated in the literary world could not but be very flattering to
me."[25] Macaulay, an expert in both English and Roman history, was also
a radical Whig and a known friend of the American Revolution. She
and Washington engaged in extensive political conversations much to
Washington's delight. "It gave me pleasure to find that her sentim[en]ts
respecting the inadequacy of the powers of the Congress . . . coincided
with my own," he told Richard Henry Lee.[26] It is also worth noting here
that Washington very well might have taken an interest in Macaulay
as a potential biographer, for one of his diary entries from the visit
indicated that he placed his "military records into the hands of Mrs.
Macaulay Graham for her perusal and amusem[en]t."[27]

Additional evidence to support the argument that Washington did
in fact appreciate the ability of biographers to enhance their subjects'
reputations is found in Washington's letters to Lafayette in 1788. In recommending the American poet Joel Barlow to Lafayette, Washington
described the poet as being "one of those bards who hold the keys to the
gate which patriots, sages, and heroes are admitted to immortality. Such
are your ancient bards who are both the priest and doorkeepers to the
temple of fame. And these, my dear Marquis, are no vulgar functions."
He went on to say, "In some instances . . . heroes have made poets, and
poets heroes."[28] These examples illustrate not only Washington's continued drive to maintain his reputation but also, more fundamentally, the
idea that the seemingly eclectic reading that he pursued immediately
after the Revolution had eminently practical purposes.

Further examples of Washington's attempts to connect his legacy with leading writers of the time can be found in his exacting instructions for transporting his wartime papers to Mount Vernon. He ordered the lieutenant in charge of the mission not to attempt the two river crossings in inclement weather. The orders also stipulated that "the wagons should never be without a sentinel over them; always locked and the keys in your possession."[29] Just after the shipment arrived at Mount Vernon, two writers showed up at Mount Vernon, looking to solicit his cooperation on their would-be projects. The first offer was more problematic than the second. John Bowie sought Washington's cooperation for a biography; however, Washington was evidently uncomfortable with Bowie's ideas, for he declared that he would not open his papers until Congress did the same with its archives.[30] The second project, William Gordon's proposal to write a history of the Revolution, seemed to have far less self-aggrandizing potential but still could foster Washington's legacy. Washington offered to open his papers to Gordon as long as Congress authorized him to do so. Gordon had been a staunch supporter of the independence movement, so Congress did not hesitate in granting Washington's request. Gordon was a scholar with an eye for detail, and he wasted no time in immersing himself in Washington's papers for two straight weeks, pausing only for meals. When the four-volume work came out in 1788, Washington bought two copies for himself and recommended it to all of his friends, distributing the forty-two sets that Gordon sent to him.[31]

The Gordon project made it painfully clear that Washington's papers were in disarray. Washington began the arduous process of organizing the "thirty and three volumes of copied letters ... besides three volumes of private, seven volumes of general orders, and bundles upon bundles of letters" that were sent to him. The task, however, was simply too overwhelming for him to do alone while trying to run his plantations.[32] He decided to hire a secretary, eventually settling on a former aide-de-camp Lt. Col. David Humphreys. Having distinguished himself at Yorktown, Humphreys earned the privilege of presenting the captured British battle flags to Congress. He was also a talented writer who had drafted many of Washington's remarks for the numerous victory celebrations that took place in and around New York City. Once Washington hired him to serve as his private secretary, it did not take long for Humphreys to convince Washington to collaborate on a biography in 1785. After Washington spurned the first offer of a biography, what caused the sudden change in attitude? It was a matter of personal affinity. Washington both understood and appreciated loyalty, and Humphreys had served him well in the past. After he gave Humphreys his assent, Washington lavished attention on him, affording him unfettered access to his papers: "And I can with great truth add that my house would not only be at your service during the period of preparing this work, but I should be exceedingly happy if you would make it your home. You might have an apartment to yourself in which you could command your own time. You would be considered and treated as one of the family."[33] Unfortunately Humphreys's biography is thoroughly unimpressive on its own merits; it is far too brief and celebratory to be of great value to scholars. However, far more important than Humphreys's work are Washington's editorial notes, which actually run longer than the text itself and are mostly centered on setting the record straight in the passages dealing with the Seven Years' War. Washington also amended some of Humphreys's characterizations of his childhood and early life. Specifically he corrected Humphreys's statements regarding who originally proposed that Washington should join the Royal Navy as a teenager and other details from childhood, including his age at the time of his father's death.[34]

Calls for Government Reform Recall Washington to Public Life

As Washington collaborated with these projects, he also became aware that his enormous celebrity would not allow him to remain out of public life for long. The loosely united confederation of states was in crisis. Congress's powers under the Articles of Confederation seemed insufficient to many observers when it came to handling national issues. Congress did not have the power to compel delegates to attend its sessions, let alone levy taxes or regulate the economy in order to begin repaying the staggering war debts. A commercial crisis gripped the northern states thanks to the trade sanctions that Great Britain put in place in the last days of the Revolution, and the southern states felt that the confederation government relegated them to the status of a sectional minority with nothing and no one to protect the region's interests. Furthermore, the citizenry was increasingly becoming disenchanted with the manner in which both the confederation and the state governments were functioning. In Virginia James Madison complained to Washington about the "dark and menacing . . . evils" that these newly elected legislators were introducing "under the name of relief to the people." He continued to rail that "men without reading, experience, or principle" were generating laws that were "a nuisance of the most pestilent kind."[35]

The situation became much more critical in Massachusetts with the outbreak of Shays' Rebellion in 1786. Shays and his rebels took up arms to prevent the courts from sitting and from foreclosing on western farms, many of which were owned by veterans of the late war. After those in power in Boston made a series of blundering decisions, the Massachusetts government deployed an army to put down the rebellion. The desperate rebels were easily routed. Upon hearing the news of this explosive situation in Massachusetts, Washington was horrified. "Good God!" he exclaimed. "There are combustibles in every State, which a spark may set fire to." Additionally he expressed thanks that the rebellion had "terminate[d] entirely in favor of Government by the suppression of insurgents."[36] Although Shays' Rebellion is often credited with being the catalyst for calling what would become the Constitutional Convention, in truth it was instigated after the various state governments failed to adequately handle the endless stream of issues that began with the peace in 1783. Washington, who reacted to the events in Massachusetts with a mix of fear and disgust, and others were not simply disconcerted by the armed citizens' staging an uprising; rather, they were shocked at the inept handling of the crisis by the government of Massachusetts. Moreover, they all knew that if similar rebellions broke out elsewhere, the national government was power-less to assist. They had to prevent democratic excesses from ruining the new American national experiment.[37]

However, while many were dissatisfied with the downward spiral that the new nation seemed to be in, Washington's opinion that it needed a strong central government was somewhat exceptional as it was based on his long history of mostly unpleasant dealings with the Continental Congress during the war. From Washington's standpoint as commander in chief, Congress had been incapable of coercing the states into making their recruiting quotas and supplying sufficient funds consistently to keep the army in the field.[38] Not everyone, though, shared Washington's conviction that a strong central government was in the best interest of the states. Any move to create a national government with the power to tax and raise armies seemed all too similar to the parliamentary tyranny that had precipitated the Revolution. Therefore, when the first conven-tion at Annapolis met in September 1786 for the purpose of revising the Articles of Confederation, only five states sent representatives. An exasperated Madison turned to Alexander Hamilton, who called for another convention to be held in Philadelphia in the spring of 1787, this time to scrap the articles completely in favor of devising a new framework for the national government.

Madison deduced that part of the problem with the Annapolis Convention was that Washington was not there. In order for the new convention even to garner the participation of the states, Washington had to be a part of it. Madison therefore visited Washington for three days in October 1786, hoping to coax him out of retirement and back onto the national stage. In November 1786 Madison informed Wash-ington that Virginia unanimously decided to place his name at the head of the state's list of delegates. For his part Washington was somewhat annoyed that he had been backed into a corner. As much as he wanted the convention to succeed, he did promise the American people upon his resignation from the army in 1783 that he was leaving public life for good. How could he go back on that pledge? Additionally he had declined to attend a meeting of the Society of the Cincinnati that was scheduled to meet at the same time in Philadelphia. How could he show up to attend a governing convention after refusing an invitation to meet with his former comrades in arms? Finally what if this convention proved to be another unmitigated disaster? Washington was not about to stake his reputation on a potential failure.[39]

Madison's response to Washington was masterful. He conceded that Washington of course had the final say; however, he suggested that it would be extremely helpful if Washington allowed his name to remain on the list of delegates for the sake of gravitas, thereby encouraging other prominent men to sign on also. Additionally keeping his name on the list would allow the possibility "that at least a door could be kept open . . . in case the gathering clouds should become so dark and menacing as to supersede every consideration, but that of our national experience and safety."[40] Washington agonized over the decision for four months; he finally decided to serve in March 1787. It is interesting to note that once he decided to serve, he made it clear that the convention should "adopt no temporizing expedient, but probe the defects of the Constitution to the bottom, and provide radical cures, whether they are agreed to or not."[41] If he was willing to stake his reputation on this convention, it needed to produce a real result.

The Constitutional Convention brought together prominent men from across the states to devise a new system of governance for the infant republic. They wasted no time in selecting Washington as the president of the convention. His selection made perfect sense because of his celebrity, but it was also perfect for him personally. As president of the convention, he presided over the debates but demurred from wading into them, except on two occasions. He knew that the greatest contribution he could make to this process was not in offering his thoughts but his presence. His reputation had reached its zenith in his lifetime, and at this particular juncture, before he became the nation's first president, he no longer needed to prove himself. As the most astute legal minds in the nation debated the way ahead, the best way for Washington to contribute was to sit magnanimously above the proceedings and not appear the least bit partisan toward any of the plans being introduced. Nevertheless, Washington was still a diligent delegate. Before the proceedings commenced, he took the plans that Madison, Knox, and John Jay offered to him and condensed them into a sort of ready reference. He also read the latest political tracts that offered different proposals for the upcoming convention including Charles Pinckney's *Observations on the Plan of Government Submitted to the Federal Convention, in Philadelphia, on the 28th of May, 1787.*[42]

The Virginia delegation arrived in Philadelphia on time; the other delegations did not. While the Virginia delegation waited, its members — Washington, Madison, Edmund Randolph, and George Mason — met for two or three hours per day in order to work out a cohesive position. These sessions yielded the Virginia Plan, which Madison drafted. Washington supported Madison in these internal delegation sessions and countered protests from Mason and Randolph, who did not favor a strong central government.[43] When the written Constitution was finally adopted on the convention's last day, September 17, 1787, Washington was hurt when two of the convention's three holdouts — Randolph and Mason — were his fellow Virginians and personal friends. In particular, Washington and Mason's friendship did not survive after Mason predicted flatly that this new government "would end either in monarchy or a tyrannical aristocracy" and that the Constitution "had been formed without the knowledge . . . of the people."[44]

It is interesting to note that during the convention, Washington seemed to sense that he was not going to be able to simply retreat to Mount Vernon forever when the meeting adjourned. The presidency was plainly in his future, and he began to act like a head of state. For example, he attended different religious services on various Sundays, including those of his own Anglican denomination and a Roman Catholic Mass on one of his first Sundays in Philadelphia. He dined with Jewish merchants and accepted invitations to join fraternal dinners hosted by the Irish Society of the Friendly Sons of Saint Patrick. Moreover, he accepted General Mifflin's invitation to review the city's militia forces. He also visited museums and frequented the theater whenever possible.[45] While Washington embarked on some of these visitations out of his own interests, he was no doubt cajoled into some of the other outings. Already he knew that maintaining his reputation partly hinged on his ability to appear nonpartisan and visible to the people. He was, in fact, beginning to exhibit a new form of performative leadership that is best described as an Americanized hybrid of a royal progress. Over the coming years, Washington would work assiduously to turn his very particular brand of statecraft into an art form that would sculpt the presidency. Once in office he would pay special attention to reports in the different forms of available contemporary print media of how the people received his performances.

Washington and Ratification

During the various ratification conventions that followed, Washington began to collect the published writings that outlined both sides of the ratification debate. He obtained a copy of John Adams's *A Defense of the Constitutions of Government of the United States of America* and Noah Webster's *An Examination into the Leading Principles of the Federal Constitution Proposed by the Late Convention Held at Philadelphia, with Answers to the Principal Objections that Have Been Raised against the System.* Furthermore, Washington, who had always been an avid subscriber to newspapers and periodicals, began receiving copies of Noah Webster's *American Magazine: Containing a Miscellaneous Collection of Original and Other Valuable Essays in Prose and Verse, and Calculated Both for Instruction and Amusement* and Mathew Carey's *The American Museum, or Repository of Ancient and Modern Fugitive Pieces* and his *The Columbian Magazine.*[46] These periodicals reprinted political essays from across the nation that centered on the Constitution. That Washington paid such close attention to how the ratification debates progressed is not surprising. First and foremost he believed that the Constitution was the way forward for the United States if it were to survive as a nation. He was sure that the strengths of the Constitution far outweighed its weaknesses. In his defense of the Constitution, Washington remarked that "the general Government is not invested with more Powers than are indispensably necessary to perform the functions of a good Government," and as such, "no objections ought to be made against the quantity of Power delegated to it." As the powers of the government were balanced between its respective branches, tyranny was impossible "so long as there shall remain any virtue in the body of the People."[47] Washington further believed that by granting the federal government the power over taxation and commerce, the new nation would be able to effectively defend itself, extend trade networks through formal concessions, protect rights to property, and encourage economic growth and prosperity.[48] In Madison's view, "no member of the Convention appeared to sign the instrument with more cordiality than he [Washington] did, nor to be more anxious for its ratification. I have indeed the most thorough conviction from the best evidence that he never wavered in the part he took in giving it his sanction and support."[49]

One voice of dissent that Washington found potentially damaging was that of George Mason. Mason's staunchly anti-federalist stance was hurtful to Washington, for the two men had been friends and neighbors for years, and Mason was a member of the Virginia delegation that was involved in all the meetings that produced the Virginia Plan. When the convention drew to a close, Mason not only refused to sign the Constitution but also published an essay condemning it as a frame of government with a paltry system of checks and balances. In Mason's view the House of Representatives was too weak, the Senate was too powerful, and the Senate's and the president's responsibilities seemed oddly comingled. He also wanted three additional measures: a bill of rights to safeguard the people's liberties, the president restrained by a council of state, and the South protected against unfair commercial laws that would disproportionately benefit the North. Mason concluded his

essay by repeating his prediction that ratification would almost immediately lead to a monarchy and an aristocracy.[50] Upon reading the essay,
Washington angrily forwarded it to Madison, writing that it appeared to
be an attempt "to alarm the people." He further suggested that "sinister
and self-important motives governed Antifederalist leaders." Madison
concurred and further suggested that Mason had "a vain opinion . . .
that he has influence enough to dictate a Constitution to Virginia and
through her to the rest of the union."[51] Washington further laid blame
at the feet of the Anti-federalists as he wrote, "The ignorant have been
told, that should the proposed Government obtain, their lands would
be taken from them and their property disposed of."[52] Washington's
palpable anger emanates from these letters and underscores the degree
of anxiety that he felt over the possibility of failure in the ratification
conventions.

Through his experience in public life, Washington had long recognized the value of print media, and he saw that the best way to sell
the new government to the people was through the newspapers. The
Anti-federalists had already begun waging a newspaper war and had the
reading public's attention; thus the Federalists took up their pens in the
gazettes. In New York, Hamilton wrote a set of newspaper articles that
defended the Constitution. Madison and Jay joined him in this effort;
collectively their essays became known as *The Federalist* (*The Federalist
Papers*). The three collaborators sent Washington copies of their work,
with Madison urging that Virginians needed these arguments as much
as New Yorkers did. Washington, however, needed no prodding on
this point. He forwarded the papers to Fairfax County representative
David Stuart and recommended that "if there is a Printer in Richmond
who is really well disposed to support the New Constitution he would
do well to give them a place in his Paper."[53] Stuart passed the essays
to Augustine Davis, who published them in the *Virginia Independent
Chronicle* in December 1787. The essays were subsequently reprinted
in papers throughout the state.[54]

Washington continued to play an active role in the ratification effort even though he knew that if ratification were achieved, then his election as the first president would follow. Thus he had to maintain the proper degree of disinterestedness in order to safeguard his reputation so that he would be able to serve effectively once more. Washington was compelled by his sense of both duty and self-preservation; however, he simply hated to leave Mount Vernon. In 1788 he was still in the process of making his plantations profitable, and more important, he did not want to leave his family again. He and Martha were rearing two of their grandchildren. His health was questionable, and age was catching up with him. But how could he refuse the presidency if elected?

President Washington Takes Office

Washington did not have to wait long to see the inevitability of his election. On July 4, 1788, the minimum number of nine states ratified the Constitution, and the people of Wilmington, Delaware, began toasting Washington in hopes that once again he might set aside his plow to lead his people. In New York's grand federal procession on July 23, a flag bore an image of Washington and a line expressing the wish that he would be elected the first president of the United States. The pleas became more insistent by the fall of 1788, with some coming from Washington's friends, including Lafayette; Hamilton; Henry Lee, Jr.; and Benjamin Lincoln. By early 1789 Washington asked David Humphreys to draft an inaugural address.[55]

The strange history of Washington's inaugural address hints at a degree of nervousness, for he realized that by accepting the presidency, the manner in which he preserved his reputation had to change. This statement is not to suggest that Washington was driven by sheer vanity; rather, he knew from the start that in becoming the first president, he would have to use his image to legitimize the new government. In other words, if his performance as the elected leader of a republican government did not strike the right chord with the people, the future of the nation could become imperiled. Serving as the president would involve a delicate balancing act between establishing himself as the head of state with certain performative measures that would be familiar to the people who had lived under a monarchical past and setting a new precedent for how chief executives should behave. In this endeavor he had nothing to guide him. The primary factor that worked in his favor was the mythology that already surrounded him; however, one false step could nullify that advantage. In the interest of setting the right tone from the beginning, Washington sought the advice of writers he trusted for assistance with his inaugural address.

David Humphreys produced the first draft of the inaugural address, and Washington immediately recognized problems with it. The first was that it was seventy-three pages long. Humphreys included an analysis of the weaknesses of the Articles of Confederation, a defense of the Constitution, specific recommendations for various pieces of legislation, and a defense of Washington's 1783 retirement pledge. He also mentioned that his presidency would not be the start of a monarchy because he had no biological children. Washington read it, made a copy, and sent it off to Madison for his review and suggested revisions.[56] Madison was appalled at the draft. He wrote to Washington that he concurred "without hesitation in your remarks on the speech of 73 pages, and in the expediency of not including it among the papers selected for the press." Madison went on to call the draft a "strange production."[57] Many years later Madison reflected that Humphreys's work was "certainly an extraordinary production for a message to Congress, and it is happy that Washington took counsel of his own understanding and of his friends before he made use of this document."[58] Washington summoned Madison to Mount Vernon, and as soon as he arrived, they set to work on a new address, completely scrapping Humphreys's draft. Madison wrote and Washington edited the final version that Washington actually delivered. The address was only four pages long. Washington emphasized that he accepted the presidency only out of duty. He asked God for continued blessings on the nation, admonished the members of Congress to avoid local prejudice, requested that he not receive a salary but only the reimbursement of his expenses, and called for amendments to the Constitution to protect the people's rights.[59]

In terms of the inauguration, it is worth noting the degree to which Washington and his inaugural committee paid attention to their British monarchical heritage when designing the ceremony. In many ways, it strikes a deep contrast to a coronation and a state opening of Parliament. English monarchs are crowned behind closed doors in Westminster Abbey, but Washington took the oath of office in an outdoor ceremony, in full public view. In a state opening of Parliament, the monarch reads an address while seated on a throne, and the joint assembly of the Houses of Lords and the Commons remains standing. Washington, however, stood to deliver his inaugural address after insisting that the assembled members of the House and Senate take their seats. The ceremony was appropriately solemn and, most important, American, even though it bore a certain resemblance to the British traditions that the former colonists were used to. The extensive celebrations that day were exuberant as the people seemed to conflate their love for Washington with that for the new federal government.[60] Washington's first act as president was, therefore, a successful performance.

During his two terms in office, Washington was inordinately busy and at times in ill health, so he did not have the opportunity to do much reading even though he was inundated with gifts of books from well-wishers and office seekers. As Washington was constantly preoccupied with public perception, however, he made time to read as many newspapers as were available, as well as many printed political sermons. These two forms of print media were critical resources for Washington, for they offered the most current reflections of public opinion at the time. He remarked to Catharine Macaulay Graham, "In our progress toward political happiness, my station is new; and, if I may use the expression, I walk on untrodden ground. There is scarcely any action, whose motives may not be subject to a double interpretation. There is scarcely any part of my conduct which may not hereafter be drawn into precedent."[61] In light of this awareness, Washington needed to stay abreast of how his performances were received, and print media was the primary means available. Interestingly as Washington penned the letter to Graham, the first serious test of his ability to perform as president well was about to begin. As the federal government slowly came together, debates arose as to how to best shape the American future. Washington appointed Alexander Hamilton to head the Treasury Department, and Hamilton wasted no time in devising a plan to shore up the utterly unstable American economy. He ultimately favored industrialization on the British model, but first he had to deal with the matters arising from the states' conflicting systems of finance and their staggering war debts. On January 9, 1790, responding to a congressional request, Hamilton submitted a report on the public credit to Congress. In it he called for a comprehensive system of finance that would nationalize all war debts still unpaid by the states and would create a national bank.[62]

Washington Shores Up Support for the Federal Government

Hamilton's plan received instant criticism from those who feared it was only the first part of a larger plan to limit states' rights. Tench Coxe, Hamilton's future deputy, wrote from Pennsylvania that local public creditors were "against assumption" because they feared it would "produce the old demon, consolidation," and that many people were opposed to it because they owed "so little as a state, and possess federal securities to a greater Amount."[63] Such opinions were not limited to Pennsylvanians. During the confederation period, states such as New York and New Jersey adopted as state debt the federal certificates that were issued as payment to the ex-Continental soldiers for their service. Connecticut reportedly assumed $640,000 specie value, and Maryland paid an estimated $266,000 to holders of those certificates. Redeeming the certificates was even more important to the southern states. Virginia assumed nearly all debts and had only $171,000 left unpaid. Similarly North Carolina's remaining federal certificate debt was only $8,695, and South Carolina assumed all manners of certificates, leaving a mere $65 to become national debt under Hamilton's 1790 plan. The South therefore had less interest than the other regions in any national system of finance that would guarantee payment to federal creditors.[64] Debate raged in Congress. Madison delivered a lengthy address to the House of Representatives that summarized the southern position on the subject, and it was promptly printed in the *New York Daily Advertiser*, *New York Daily Gazette*, and *Gazette of the United States*.[65]

As the debate continued and the press printed more speeches both for and against the passage of Hamilton's plan, the ramifications became apparent. The debate split the nation along a North–South sectional line. As 1790 unfolded, national politics rapidly became bitterly partisan. Washington hated partisanship and in his inaugural address had admonished congressmen and senators to avoid it. The debate also divided Washington's cabinet. Washington had been gravely ill with pneumonia during much of this period, and after weeks of recovery, when he returned to work he was appalled at the divisiveness among his councillors.[66]

In December 1790 almost a year after Hamilton submitted the first phase of his financial plan, he sent Congress a request to establish both a national bank and an excise tax on distilled liquors to raise funds to pay off the debt. The bank was the cornerstone of the entire program and greatly alarmed those who were previously opposed to the funding and assumption program because it was an even larger step toward federalizing the entire financial system under the powerful Department of the Treasury. Hamilton squarely faced Madison over the bank proposal. Madison fought the bank on terms of constitutionality in Congress, and the bill produced a sectional response. Predictably the northern states were overwhelmingly in favor of the bank, and southerners were steadfastly against it.[67]

Throughout the debate Washington was able to remain above the fray. He solicited advice equally from Hamilton, Jefferson, and Attorney General Edmund Randolph and waited as long as possible to sign the bill, taking time for serious consideration. In the end, however,

Washington did sign it. Criticism immediately rang out that by putting a select group of men in charge of federal money, Hamilton was actively seeking to manipulate the Constitution in order to transform the United States into a monarchy.[68] The extreme degree of bitterness around the bank seemed to deepen the sectional divide between the North and South and to increase the growing partisanship between Hamilton, Madison, and Jefferson. Together these developments thoroughly alarmed Washington. As such he decided the time was right to make good on a promise that he had previously made to visit every state in the union, and he embarked on a tour of the southern states in the spring of 1791.

At this critical juncture Washington could have done nothing better to shore up southern support for the federal government. He knew very well that the people would find reassurance in his presence and that their faith in the federal government would be restored, because to the people, Washington embodied the government.[69] It was not Washington's first tour; he had made a similar journey across the northern states in 1789 to "acquire knowledge of the country and of its attitude towards the new government."[70] During that tour Washington took copious notes in his diaries, paying particular attention to the honors that the people paid to him. His entries chronicling his stop in Boston are filled with descriptions of the lavish display laid out to welcome him, complete from the archway at the statehouse that hailed him as "the Man that unites all hearts" and as "Columbia's favorite Son" to the procession that began with an "ode composed in honor of the President."[71] With this previous tour experience to guide him, Washington evidently believed that a similar effort in the South would produce the palliative effect that was so necessary after the sectional debate over the nation's financial future.

It is extraordinary to note how much Washington's tours of the northern states in 1789 and the southern states in 1791 resembled a British royal progress; however, as with the inaugural ceremony, he observed certain customs to project a wholly American image. For example, on the tours the reciprocal nature of Washington's receptions represented a new American patriotism. When Washington approached a town, a mounted delegation would typically ride out to escort him. Before they came into view, however, Washington would get out of his carriage and mount his horse so that he could meet the men on the same level. Moreover, the carriage itself bore the presidential insignia in place of Washington's family coat of arms. The empty presidential carriage clearly reinforced the constitutional fact that the venerable man and the office were, in fact, separate. Furthermore Washington's riding on horseback made him more visible to the crowd that gathered to merely catch a glimpse of his face. This reception would turn into a full-scale civic procession complete with military salutes along the way. In the evenings Washington would be obliged to attend dinner parties with the local elite, at which thirteen toasts would be offered in what became a standard format.[72]

In addition to the manner in which Washington traveled, the timeline of the southern tour is also symbolically important within a republican construct. Before departing Washington sent his itinerary to Jefferson, Hamilton, and Knox for their review. While he planned to spend at most a few hours in each location, he did arrange two long stops. He stayed in Charleston for five days; in Savannah, he stayed for two. He intended to return to Philadelphia via a completely different route so as not to pass through any location twice.[73] The points where Washington planned to stop were a matter of convenience because they were all located along the post road, but his travel on the main thoroughfare also offered maximum exposure to the people. The point of the entire tour was to make Washington's efforts at promoting the federal government known to the widest possible audience.

In addition as the new government was still in its infancy and all of Washington's actions (and nonactions) were interpreted as sending some sort of message, it was better for him to avoid prolonging his stay in any one place. By passing through the South in a progressive manner, Washington was able to preserve a carefully calculated degree of aloofness from the people. They could find reassurance in his presence, perhaps hear him speak, and maybe share his table; however, no one could get too close. This method of carefully controlling physical access to an elite figure is again highly reminiscent of royal etiquette of the past, and it made sense that Washington presumably chose to perform this way because he felt he could anticipate the reaction of his audience.

Although Washington spent only a night at most stops and said little in public, he did communicate with the people through letters that were intended for publication. William Jackson, a former Continental Army officer and Washington's secretary, drafted them all.[74] Washington's choice to have Jackson draft the letters on his behalf was simply another way to maintain that official aloofness from the people. Although the reading audience may not have known that Washington was not the original author, Washington was carefully setting a precedent for his successors that a president should not do anything that could establish an overly familiar relationship with any of the people. Presidents must remain above even the perception of partisanship at any level and not allow local affinities or allegiances to develop. All of the public letters Washington sent throughout his southern tour share certain common elements. The letters all managed to communicate effectively with the people through the evolving language of republicanism. Each letter thanked the people for their expressions of warmth and welcome, and imbued in each was also a call for national patriotism. For example, Washington wrote to the people of New Bern, North Carolina, that he was "much indebted" to them for their "polite attentions." What gratified him the most, however, was their "patriotic declarations on the situation of our common country." The state of the union seemed especially hopeful when compared with "past scenes" from the Revolution. In comparison how much better he found "our present happy condition, and equally so is the anticipation of what we still may attain, and long continue to enjoy."[75]

A closer reading of Washington's other official letters from the tour reveal that they did more than promote patriotism. These letters express

Washington's support of a strong central government and hinted at the need to develop a strong international standing, thus echoing two tenets of Hamilton's financial program. Washington wrote to the people of Wilmington, North Carolina, that there was "a well founded expectation" based on the federal government's record of "every aid which a wise and virtuous legislation" would lead to enhanced "individual industry" and "the growing dignity and importance of our country."[76] Similarly his letter to the citizens of Fayetteville, North Carolina, declared that "the very favorable change already manifested in our political system, justifies the prediction that the future operations of the general government will be alike conducive to individual prosperity and national honor."[77] Letters to the officials of Charleston, South Carolina, and Savannah, Georgia, bear sentiments that suggest Washington believed national stability was contingent on the public's affirmation of the new federal government. The letter to the officials of Charleston stated, "It is the peculiar boast of our country that her happiness alone [is] dependent on the collective wisdom and virtue of her citizens, and rests not on the exertions of any individual." Furthermore "our natural and political advantages . . . cannot fail to improve them; and with the progress of our national importance, to combine the freedom and felicity of individuals."[78] To the Savannah officials, Washington hinted his support for the funding and assumption program. Referring to the federal government's relief of Georgia's state debt, he wrote, "It was with singular satisfaction I perceived that the efficacy of the general government could interpose effectual relief, and restore tranquility to so deserving a member of the Union."[79]

These official letters conveyed Washington's nationalist agenda in plain language. As these letters were intended to reach a broad audience through the newspapers, consistency in both word choice and message was critical. Washington was asking all the people to keep faith with the federal government as the way to a prosperous future. Words and phrases such as "national honor," "dignity," and "national importance" would have struck a particular chord with early republicans, so

Washington ensured that his message was both received and understood.[80] These letters further demonstrate how Washington developed an appreciation of the power of the press based on his habit of widely reading newspapers and periodicals. As with the ratification debates, Washington understood how to use the power of the press to act on his political agenda. Here, as in other examples in the previous chapters, Washington turned practical reading into practical application.

Washington's reputation and his public behavior, which always maintained the perfect balance between dignified distance and accessibility to the people, allowed the American presidential tours to succeed. His performance and communications, in conjunction with the deferential nature of society at the time, allowed Washington to connect certain political practices from the bygone colonial era with the evolving principles of American republicanism. In effect, all of this effort was comforting to the people; they could exalt him as the nation's father while remaining confident in the knowledge that he was not seeking a throne.[81] Such pageantry would have been an abject failure if Washington and the people had not shared a knowledge and appreciation of British history. For Washington's part, that knowledge came from his reading of Smollett's *Complete History of England*.[82]

The Press Attacks Washington for the First Time

While Washington's southern tour can be considered a success in that some of the rancor over the funding and assumption plan died down and that, in general, faith in the federal government was enhanced, not all acclaimed Washington's public performances as setting the right tone for the new nation. He faced an increasing number of critics, mostly coming from the growing Anti-federalist ranks and proving just as capable as Washington in using the power of the press to their advantage. Early into Washington's first term, an opposition press began to criticize the new government's protocol, and before long, the most outspoken critics began to focus negative attention on the Washingtons themselves, accusing them of trying to foist a monarchy on the country.

The first barbs were over Washington's weekly levees and Martha's Friday evening receptions for ladies. The *Daily Advertiser* bluntly warned that "in a few years we shall have all the paraphernalia yet wanting to give the superb finish to the grandeur of our AMERICAN COURT! The purity of republican principle seems to be daily losing ground. . . . We are on the eve of another revolution."[83] The press also attacked Martha Washington for hosting "court like levees" in her "queenly drawing rooms."[84] Washington, who had always blanched at criticism, was outraged that both he and his wife were being pilloried in the press. He complained to David Stuart, "Would it not have been better to have thrown the veil of charity over them, ascribing their stiffness to the effects of age . . . than to pride and dignity of office, which, God knows, has no charms for me?"[85] To Thomas Jefferson, who would later orchestrate some of the attacks on Washington in the hostile press, Washington reportedly said that "nobody disliked more the ceremonies of his office and he had not the least taste or gratification in the execution of its function; that he was happy at home alone."[86]

Washington later decried "the extreme wretchedness of his existence while in office."[87] He could not understand why the public misinterpreted his actions as reported in the newspapers. At this point he felt that his actions and reputation together should have made it clear to all that he was no monarchist.

The Newspaper War and the Rise of Partisanship

At first these personal attacks on Washington seemed to be limited to those voices of opposition near the seat of the government itself. As time went on and partisanship both within and outside the federal government grew, however, the chorus became both louder and larger. The rise of factionalism in the new United States can be traced to the increasing conflict between Jefferson and Hamilton over the nation's future. Over time Washington's cabinet split, with Hamilton and Secretary of War Henry Knox on one side and Secretary of State Jefferson and Attorney General Randolph on the other. Jefferson,

Randolph, and Madison, Washington's once-trusted friend, came to believe that the expanding federal power under Hamilton's programs was indicative of a sinister plot to discard the Constitution in favor of an American monarchy modeled on the British system. Jefferson characterized Hamilton and his supporters as Anglophiles. Hamilton shot back with charges that Jefferson was involved in a Jacobin conspiracy emanating from Paris.

Hamilton's new faction, the Federalists, came to represent support for the Constitution and national unity through a robust federal government headed by a strong executive. They favored banks and industry but still recognized the importance of agriculture. They were predominantly political elitists who doubted the wisdom of the common people. Furthermore, the party incorporated a growing number of opponents to slavery. By contrast members of Jefferson's party called themselves Republicans, suggesting that they believed in saving the nation from devolving into a monarchy. Republicans favored a limited federal government and vesting more power in the legislative branch than any other. They also championed states' rights while decrying the corrupting powers of banks, federal debt, and industry. Moreover they believed in the wisdom of the common people. Over time Jefferson and his Republicans observed Hamilton's growing influence on Washington with apprehension.

The two parties declared war on each other in the newspapers. The Federalists could count on John Fenno's *Gazette of the United States* to promote the Hamiltonian system and make the case for strengthening the power of the federal government. To counter this argument, Jefferson and Madison arranged to hire Philip Freneau, a poet and College of New Jersey classmate of Madison's, as a State Department translator. Freneau's real purpose in moving to the nation's capital was to launch the *National Gazette*, which became the Republicans' trumpet.[88] In the next few months the two parties waged an ugly newspaper war, firing some salvos directly at Washington himself. The Jeffersonians ramped up their attacks on the Washington administration after a speculative fever arose when the Treasury Department began selling shares in the new national bank. When the news broke that William Duer, Hamilton's former deputy and now governor of the Society for Establishing Useful Manufactures, had been involved in a scheme to corner the market on government bonds, the speculative bubble burst, and share prices plummeted. Hamilton did in fact restore order in the system, but thanks to his former association with Duer, the damage to his reputation was done.[89] In the *National Gazette*, Freneau seized this opportunity to lambast the Hamiltonian system, which he blamed for "scenes of speculation calculated to aggrandize the few and the wealthy, while oppressing the great body of the people."[90] Hamilton went on the offensive in the July 25, 1792, edition of Fenno's *Gazette of the United States* by posing a simple question about Freneau's State Department salary: "Whether this salary is paid him for translations or for publications, the design of which is to vilify those to whom the voice of the people has committed the administration of our public affairs — to oppose the measures of government, and by false insinuations, to disturb public peace?"[91] By August Hamilton charged that the *National Gazette* was established to be Jefferson's mouthpiece and that Madison had been the agent responsible for bringing Freneau to the State Department.

Washington felt wounded by the escalating degree of hostility toward his administration. His best lieutenants were at each other's throats to such an extent that it disrupted the cabinet's ability to function. Moreover the voices of dissent came from his fellow Virginians, indicating that Washington's star had fallen in his home state. After all it was Jefferson and Madison who had hatched the plan to install Freneau in the State Department and enabled him to launch his Republican-supported newspaper. Madison, for his part, penned more than eighteen essays that ran in the *National Gazette* excoriating Washington's administration.[92]

Washington, who had grown weary of the presidency and longed for retirement again, admonished both Hamilton and Jefferson to end the bickering. Both men defended themselves to Washington in extensive letters filled with heated language, each accusing the other of treachery.[93] The only point that they and their respective supporters could agree on was that Washington needed to serve a second term to keep this growing political divide from splitting the nation. Only after a long time of brooding and with a little cajoling from his friend Eliza Powell did he agree to accept a second term if elected.[94]

It did not take long before Washington's hopes for a peaceful second term were dashed. The newspaper war raged on, and Washington became the primary target of Freneau's attacks. Making matters worse was the fact that other newspapers, including the *General Advertiser* and later Benjamin Franklin Bache's *Philadelphia Aurora*, began to follow Freneau's lead. Bache went even further than Freneau in maligning Washington, characterizing his performance in the Revolution as incompetent and even doubting whether Washington really supported independence.[95] Shortly thereafter the opposition press had more than alleged presidential ostentation to focus on.

The French Revolution and the American Press

When the French Revolution began, many Americans thought the United States should throw its support behind the revolutionaries. As the French Revolution began to spiral out of control and war between France and England broke out, Washington wasted no time in declaring that the United States would remain neutral. His announcement sparked criticism from those who believed that the United States owed the French a debt of gratitude for their alliance during the American Revolution. The critics, of course, did not see the situation from Washington's point of view: the United States was simply not prepared to enter into the war on either side, and the safety and security of the still fragile nation depended on a policy of strict neutrality. The chorus of pro-French critics only grew louder with the arrival of the new French ambassador Edmond-Charles "Citizen" Genêt in 1793. He flagrantly disregarded diplomatic protocol in order to wage a popular campaign for French support among the American people, all the while outfitting private American vessels to challenge the British navy on the high seas. In order to placate his cabinet members, who were predictably split over the issue, Washington decided that he would receive Genêt, but it would be the coolest of receptions.

Washington's firm adherence to the neutrality proclamation in the face of Genêt's arrival infuriated the editors of the opposition press. The *National Gazette* lambasted Washington's supposed Anglo mania and his utter ingratitude toward France, urging that the United States should not sit back and "view with cold indifference the struggles of those very friends to support their own liberties against a host of despots."[96] A few days later the paper accused Washington of being isolated from the people. An open letter to Washington stated, "Let not the little buzz of the aristocratic few and their contemptible minions of speculators, Tories, and British emissaries, be mistaken for the exalted and general voice of the American people."[97]

Genêt's flamboyant arrival in Philadelphia stirred up pro-French mobs that led riots and even marched on the presidential mansion. Day after day some threatened to drag Washington out of his house and force another revolution. Genêt added fuel to the fire by violating Washington's express order that American vessels could not be commissioned as privateers to fight the British navy and by threatening to go over Washington's head and ask the American people to overturn the neutrality proclamation. This latest of Genêt's indiscretions turned out to be a sort of windfall for Washington and the Federalists. John Jay and Rufus King leaked Genêt's threats to the Federalist-affiliated press, and the people balked at the very idea of flouting presidential authority. The cabinet unanimously voted in favor of demanding Genêt's recall. The removal of Genêt did not, however, end the protests against Washington's administration over the subject of the French Revolution. New political groups calling themselves Democratic-Republican Societies sprang up. While organizers intended to bring back the spirit of the Sons of Liberty, Washington viewed them as illegitimate critics of the government who sought to destroy the peoples' faith in public servants. He acknowledged their right to protest, but Washington nonetheless regarded them as dangerous because they represented permanent hostility to the government.[98]

The Whiskey Rebellion and Domestic Discord

The political situation did not improve much for Washington by the middle of his second term. Jefferson resigned as secretary of state on December 31, 1793. Then a series of violent encounters between hostile Native Americans and Anthony Wayne's soldiers provided another series of diplomatic crises for Washington. The largest crisis, however, came in 1794 when backcountry settlers rose up to oppose the excise tax on whiskey passed in 1791 as part of Hamilton's program for paying down the national debt. Interestingly as the storm over the whiskey tax was brewing in Pennsylvania, Washington was, in fact, analyzing the best way to ensure that farming was a productive industry for both the federal government and landowners. Having received an initial gift from Sir John Sinclair of several reports on the agricultural surveys conducted in various counties in Scotland, Washington wrote to Sinclair asking for more. Sinclair sent Washington copies of nearly every survey conducted by the Board of Agriculture, and some were specially bound at Washington's request.[99] By reading the survey from across the United Kingdom, Washington was able to gain a better understanding of how a national government approached the development of agriculture as an industry. Although landholding patterns in Britain were different from those in the United States, Sinclair's surveys nonetheless provided Washington with a broader understanding of agricultural management beyond the knowledge he had gained from running his plantations. However, Washington's attempt to determine how to make agriculture a profitable industry for the nation was not going to provide him with a solution to the immediate problem of rebels rising in western Pennsylvania.

Violence broke out in mid-July 1794 in Pennsylvania when a revenue inspector named Col. John Neville and U.S. Marshal David Lenox tried to serve processes against farmers who had not registered their stills as was required by law. Protesters burned Neville's house to the ground and fired at Lenox. On August 1, 1794, six thousand whiskey rebels assembled outside of Pittsburgh in Braddock's field and threatened to seize the nearby federal garrison and force the resignation of anyone attempting to enforce the whiskey tax. A few of the hotheaded radicals among them even called for a French-style revolution. Washington had no tolerance for such lawlessness. After a tense meeting of his cabinet, he met with Associate Justice of the Supreme Court James Wilson, who reassured Washington that it was within his power to call out the militia. Washington did so on August 7, 1794.

After negotiators failed to reach a peaceful resolution with the rebels and the violence continued to escalate, Washington issued a final warning to the whiskey rebels, who after utterly dismissing the peaceful overtures extended to them now constituted a "treasonable opposition."[100] He interpreted their actions as a challenge to the Constitution, posing the question of "whether a small proportion of the United States shall dictate to the whole Union."[101] Determined to end this standoff quickly, Washington decided to lead the troops himself. He had a new uniform made and, in the temporary absence of Henry Knox, rode out of Philadelphia with Hamilton, who served as acting secretary of war. For Washington's part, despite the overwhelming size of the force he deployed to put down the rebellion, he placed his emphasis on ensuring the operation was a show of force that properly showcased the state militias under their respective commanders. He had no desire to see the situation deteriorate into a bloody repeat of Shays' Rebellion. He held two meetings with the rebels' two appointed representatives. Washington reiterated that he would tolerate nothing less than capitulation and would not hesitate to use force if anyone fired on the army. He pushed on with the army toward Pittsburgh for a few more days and, once the final military plans were laid, returned promptly to Philadelphia. With the display of overwhelming military force, the rebellion withered. The army eventually took 150 prisoners. Two men were tried and sentenced to death, but Washington pardoned them. Although the Democratic-Republican Societies predictably criticized his effort, Washington's handling of the Whiskey Rebellion provided an example of how to deal with civil unrest.[102]

Even as calm was restored to the backcountry, it was not restored within Washington's cabinet. Shortly after the Whiskey Rebellion ended, Hamilton tendered his resignation from the treasury and Knox resigned as secretary of war. In the coming months, Washington could not find replacements with the same talent that his first cabinet had. He went through a string of candidates for each post before he found men who were willing to serve, and those who accepted the positions were second-rate. Washington had to confront the added furor over the 1795 Jay Treaty, which the Republicans decried as selling out America to England because it granted England most favored nation status for trade and failed to prevent the Royal Navy from impressing American sailors, and the sting of James Monroe's 473-page condemnation of the administration following his 1796 recall as ambassador to France. Washington's second term did not appear as though it would end on a positive note.[103]

Washington's Collection of Sermons: Voices of Moderation on Popular Issues

Just as he had done during the Revolution, Washington made time to read material on current affairs so that he could be fully informed. With all of the scandals and the negative press coverage, it makes sense that Washington would have turned to other types of print media for a more reassuring appraisal of his administration. He was also inundated with gifts of books, pamphlets, and sermons during his two terms in office. The most interesting of all these gifts are the printed sermons.

Most sermons in the 1790s were political, continuing the trend that had begun in America during the revolutionary era. The sermons had in common certain rhetoric of political discourse, for the clergy interpreted events in terms of a political theology based on philosophical and revelatory learning. The clergy also reflected a population that consistently assimilated the political and constitutional issues of the day based on the insights of philosophical and spiritual traditions. This manner of political theorizing gave shape to the events of the period to the same extent that the newspapers did.[104] As the newspaper war grew in both scale and ferocity during Washington's presidency, it became harder for Washington to find papers that presented nonpartisan accounts.[105] The other barometer available to him at that time was the printed sermon.

Washington collected fifty-seven separate printed sermons during his presidency. While the majority of them were sent to Washington by their authors, there is still a plausible case to be made that he took the time to read at least some of them. The clergymen who wrote them were community leaders who likely thought their sermons reflected the views of their parishioners; so if one of their writings reached the president, then the voice of a community was heard. The sermons offered political opinions without the same degree of biting partisan overtones. It would therefore make sense that Washington would take the time to read them as they came into his possession — regardless of whether he purchased them or the authors sent him complimentary copies — for they offered a different means by which he could gauge how the people viewed his carefully crafted presidential performance.

When examining Washington's sermon collection as a whole, it is important to note that they address all of the major political issues that faced Washington's administration. Washington also kept in his collection copies of sermons that did not necessarily reflect his views, but he did not retain all of his editions of the different opposition newspapers. Some of the sermons were merely celebrations of the new American republic and did not take a strong stand on any of the divisive issues of the day. One example is William Smith's *A Sermon, on Temporal and Spiritual Salvation*. It recounted the saga of the American Revolution cast in theological terms, effectively turning the struggle for independence into a holy war that would allow the New Jerusalem to finally be established on the shores of America.[106] Among Washington's collection of celebratory sermons are five that were preached on February 19, 1795, the day that Washington proclaimed should be set aside as a national day for public thanksgiving and prayer. Jedidiah Morse's *The Present Situation of Other Nations* might have been comforting for Washington to read as Morse urged the people not only to have renewed faith in the federal government but also to properly honor Washington's performance as the nation's father. Given the tumultuous political situations that Washington found himself embroiled in and the fever pitch of the character attacks published in the opposition press, Washington would have been able to read this sermon as a confirmation that his reputation had not been destroyed and that the people in fact appreciated his efforts.[107] Similarly John Mason's *Mercy Remembered in Wrath* offered a defense of Washington's policy of keeping the United States out of foreign wars as well as his handling of the Whiskey Rebellion.[108] Samuel Kendal's *A Sermon, Delivered on the Day of National Thanksgiving, February 19, 1795* uses rhetorical terms similar to Mason's and defends Washington's performance as well while paying special attention to his foreign policy. Kendal also especially mentions the opposition press, condemning the unjust charges leveled at Washington on a daily basis. David Osgood's *A Discourse Delivered* recognized the value of the state constitutions in making laws particular to specific localities; however, he trumpeted the federal government's role of promoting the general welfare.[109]

Washington also kept in his collection sermons that reflected his stance on particular issues including Israel Evans's *A Sermon, Delivered at Concord*. In this sermon, Evans specifically cited Washington's stance on freedom of religion and Hamilton's funding and assumption program. Additionally he stressed the people's duty to elect wise legislators and to obey the laws the legislators passed once in office.[110] Similarly in more overtly theological tones, Samuel Langdon's *A Discourse on the Unity of the Church* also championed freedom of religion.[111] Robert Davidson's

A Sermon, on the Freedom and Happiness of the United States of America championed Washington's handling of the Whiskey Rebellion and general efforts to promote peace and prosperity in the country.[112] These sermons in one way or another discussed all the contentious issues addressed in this chapter. Given that these sermons came from different clergymen of different denominations and in different locations, Washington could read them and gain at least a somewhat broader perspective of how his policies were perceived by those outside the nation's capital, where the partisan press captivated the public's attention.

As stated earlier some of the sermons that Washington collected during this period did not reflect his views. Others, such as Samuel Miller's *A Sermon, Preached in New York*, William Linn's *The Blessings of America*, and Samuel Stillman's *Thoughts on the French Revolution*, expressed much joy over the outbreak of the French Revolution. Unlike the Federalists, they did not regret the toppling of the monarchy and the execution of Louis XVI and Marie Antoinette.[113] What makes these opposition sermons so pertinent to this volume is that with the exception of James Monroe's condemnation of the administration, Washington did not keep any other opposition pieces of any type in his collection. None of his personal copies of the *National Gazette* or the *Aurora* were listed in the estate inventory taken upon his death, so what made these sermons the exception? Most likely he kept them because although the respective authors expressed opinions on the French Revolution that ran counter to Washington's, they did so respectfully. In the high-flown republican theological rhetoric of each of these sermons, no barbs were aimed at Washington personally or at his neutrality proclamation. Indeed, each author pays heed to Washington's position that despite many Americans' feelings of obligation toward the French for their support during the late American Revolution, the United States was not prepared for war; therefore, it made sense for the administration to steer a prudent course in the stormy international waters of the time.

Moreover Washington must have been further gratified in 1796 when William Richards published his *Reflections on French Atheism and on*

English Christianity. Richards addressed the French revolutionaries' decision to disestablish the Catholic Church under the new constitution. He argued that the decision was a positive one, for it would rid the French people of their superstitious obedience to popery and allow them to have freedom of conscience. Richards hoped that this decision would allow the French people, after centuries of persecution and Catholic oppression, to enjoy the same type of religious freedom that Americans had. His opinion was very much in concert with Washington's. Richards further underscored his argument with a challenge to the notion that the French revolutionaries brought atheism to France for the first time. Atheists had been in France before the revolution began, and it was hardly likely that they would turn all people away from God. In other words, Richards urged his congregation to observe the developing French constitution calmly and realistically.

Richards's rational view offered a welcome contrast to the controversy swirling around Thomas Paine's *Age of Reason* and his rebuttal to Edmund Burke's observations on the French Revolution. Washington collected several different critiques of Paine's *Age of Reason* including Miers Fisher's *A Reply to the False Reasoning in the "Age of Reason."* As Fisher was a layman, his critique used a structure and rhetoric that were slightly more direct and not as laden with theological imagery as some of the other sermons in Washington's collection; thus, it would possibly have had a greater appeal to Washington as a reader. It is worth noting that Washington began collecting critiques of Paine at around the same time that Paine began openly attacking Washington's failure to secure his release from a French prison.[114]

The Significance of Washington's Presidential Reading

Having put the sermon collection in context with Washington's habit during his presidency of following the partisan press' development, which occurred after he helped shape the media campaign for ratification, what emerges is that Washington understood how the press could become a political tool. In choosing what material to publish, printers were able to steer public debate and reflect and influence people's views. Observing this process Washington gained useful knowledge not only from reading the texts of periodicals, sermons, and pamphlets but also from witnessing the power of the printed word and how it was used. As noted previously Washington made his best attempt to perform the role of the precedent-setting president, and he constantly sought reviews from the various forms of print media available to him at the time. Although reading the opposition press's attacks was painful, he knew he had to read them nonetheless, because relying only on words of encouragement offered through private correspondents would have given him a false sense of security. When the attacks grew more bitter over time, Washington increasingly looked beyond the newspapers to hear the voice of the people, and the printed sermons fulfilled that purpose.

The view of Washington's presidency through the lens of his reading material and correspondence is mixed. He started down an uncharted path on a high note with his first inauguration; however, it did not take long for his hopes of a harmonious government to be shattered as his best cabinet members squared off against one another in the debate over the correct path for the nation's financial future. The degree of Washington's anxiety is underscored by bearing in mind how carefully he tended his reputation during the confederation period after his resignation from the army. The attention he paid to the literary and historical attempts to chronicle his life and role in the Revolution ultimately paid dividends as Washington entered what would be his final retirement, but during his two terms in office, his status seemed to be on the decline. Washington's post-Revolution career is characterized by his cultivation and careful use of his reputation for the public good, and as this chapter illustrates, he both read and used print media to achieve his ends and monitor his progress. With all of this established, chapter 5 explores how Washington rounded out his library with works intended to secure his legacy.

CHAPTER FIVE

A Legacy Library

March 4, 1797, began like any other day for President Washington. Up before dawn, he devoted time to reading some correspondence that had been unceremoniously dumped on his desk, and he noted the temperature in his diary. He donned a black suit and ate his customary light breakfast. Despite its inauspicious beginning, this day was not, however, a typical day. It was Washington's last morning as president. Just before noon he strode alone to Congress Hall, entering to thunderous applause. He watched as Thomas Jefferson, his former secretary of state and the soon-to-be vice president, wearing a simple blue suit, made his rather unceremonious entrance. Finally the new president John Adams arrived, appearing more than a bit awkward in a pearl-colored suit with wrist ruffles, a powdered wig, and a cocked hat. Adams already looked as though he was not getting any sleep. His appearance must not have been a reassuring sign to those gathered in the chamber to watch the first ever transfer of presidential authority in the brief history of the United States. Adams glanced over at Washington, who by contrast looked positively tranquil, as if the weight of the world had been lifted off his shoulders. Adams later wrote to his wife: "A solemn scene it was indeed, and it was made affecting to me by the presence of the General, whose countenance was as serene and unclouded as the day. He seemed to me to enjoy a triumph over me. Methought I heard him say, 'Ay! I am fairly out and you fairly in! See which of us will be happiest!'"[1] If Washington did not say it, he ought to have, because this day marked the beginning of his longed-for retirement. After decades of public service, Washington was at last taking his final leave of public life and heading back to Mount Vernon.

It is difficult to imagine the immense relief that Washington must have felt upon leaving Congress Hall as a private citizen. He could look forward to returning to Mount Vernon, which once again suffered from his long absences. Additionally as much as Mount Vernon needed Washington's care, Washington needed Mount Vernon's ability to rejuvenate him. His health had declined precipitously over the course of his presidency; the cares of office seemed to have rapidly accelerated the aging process.

The physical toll that the presidency took on Washington was a source of concern for him. During his presidency, his mother had succumbed to breast cancer, and his beloved nephew and estate manager, George Augustine Washington, had passed away. Shortly after he left office, his only surviving sister, Betty, also died.[2] Moreover he knew that Washington men were not typically blessed with longevity, and he had recently celebrated his sixty-fifth birthday. Although he was elated to return home and he did recapture some energy in throwing himself back into the business of managing his estates, Washington seemed to sense that his end was drawing near.[3] With that thought in mind, he focused his time and effort on setting all things right. Getting his financial affairs back on track was merely one aspect of this endeavor. Washington also devoted considerable time to a final attempt at shaping his legacy, and a major part of that undertaking was through building up his library.

As has been established previously, all of Washington's reading was done purposefully with practical intent. Reading was a tool that helped him work through whatever particular circumstance he found himself in, and over the course of a lifetime of such study, he developed a deep appreciation for the power of reading. Chapter 4 illustrated how Washington used different forms of print media both to help craft his reputation and to measure his presidential performance. This chapter shows how in his final retirement Washington added to his library at Mount Vernon those works that would help refine his public image for the ages. This final, short phase of Washington's life is noteworthy not so much because of what he read but because of what he deliberately acquired in order to set the record straight for posterity. Although the presidency exacted a toll on Washington's carefully crafted reputation, he knew that interest in his life would only grow after his death, so he needed to spend whatever time he had left to put his records in order.

This chapter also explores one specific example of how Washington's reading led him to make a momentous decision that would separate him from his fellow southern founders: in his will Washington emancipated his slaves. He was the only founding father to do so.[4] Although the complexities of Virginia law only allowed him to free his own slaves and not those belonging to the Custis estate, Washington's act of setting his slaves free is still immensely significant. His decision to make this provision in his will was not reached quickly or easily; indeed, his views on slavery developed thanks in part to his study of the subject.

Washington's Final Retirement and Homecoming

Upon his return to Mount Vernon, Washington immediately resumed his old routine of rising before dawn, spending several hours in his library before breakfast, then touring his five farms. He quickly found that Mount Vernon needed more extensive repairs than he initially thought. This work left him little time for reading and caused him to fall behind on his correspondence. As he wrote to Secretary of War James McHenry, "I have not looked into a book since I came home, nor shall I be able to do it until I have discharged my workmen; probably not before the nights grow longer, when possibly I may be looking in [the] doomsday book."[5] Still Washington kept up remarkably well with current events by reading newspapers widely. Since he still thought them too biased, he asked Treasury Secretary Oliver Wolcott to tell him the real truth about certain issues.[6] That Washington still set aside the time to keep up with the affairs of the nation through a wide array of printed sources reinforces the argument that Washington was indeed focused on shoring up his legacy for posterity. Given the demands Mount Vernon placed on his time, it would have been perfectly understandable for Washington to turn his attention away from politics and stay informed only through the news brought by the stream of visitors that once again besieged Mount Vernon on a daily basis. For Washington, however, sitting back and ignoring the news accounts simply would not do. He had given up domestic happiness and risked his health and reputation to legitimize the new government. He could not walk away without paying attention to whether the experiment would survive the test of his absence.

Assembling the Record for Posterity

Washington devoted a set amount of time each day to arranging the papers in his vast personal collection. Before departing Philadelphia, he ordered his secretaries to pack up his papers and prepare them for shipment to Mount Vernon, leaving aside only those documents that President Adams required. In addition to arranging his correspondence into a more structured archive, Washington also collected copies of nearly every piece of legislation and every government record that he could get his hands on, from the records of the Continental Congress and the Confederation Congress to copies of the *Congressional Record*, beginning with the convening of the first Congress in 1789. Additionally he obtained copies of the Supreme Court's decisions on major cases.[7] These records from the legislative and judicial branches of the government combined with his archive of presidential and state papers would have constituted the first presidential library in the nation if he had had the chance to complete it. Long before there were such libraries in the United States, Washington seemed to have seriously considered the idea, for records indicate that he was planning to construct a separate building at Mount Vernon to house his voluminous archives. He had even gone so far as to order bookshelves for this new facility, but his death preempted its construction.[8]

To complement the official records of the governments he had both led and served, Washington purchased some of the latest books published on American history, including James Thomson Callender's *The History of the United States for 1796.*[9] Washington also collected separately published commentaries on his different policies, pieces of legislation, and treaties such as Albert Gallatin's *An Examination of the Conduct of the Executive of the United States.*[10] Gallatin's commentary, unlike most tracts Washington collected, was critical of the president's conduct. For example, Gallatin charged that Washington "has interpreted the same parts of the Constitution, variously at different times; and that he has thereby converted the great charter of our country into a thing of chance, liable to the direction of whim, caprice, or design."[11] Gallatin then launched into an attack on Washington's personal handling of foreign affairs from when he took office in order to castigate the 1793 Proclamation of Neutrality and the Jay Treaty.[12] Washington likely felt safe in his decision to keep this assessment in his collection because its stilted argument was balanced by Alexander Addison's refutation, *Observations on the Speech of Albert Gallatin, in the House of Representatives of the United States, on the Foreign Intercourse Bill.*[13] Addison's refutation does not offer a celebratory review of Washington's presidential performance. Instead, Addison provided a point-by-point defense of Washington's conduct according to the parameters set forth in the Constitution. In other words, Addison's work presented a defense of presidential power and Washington's use of it.[14]

War with France? Washington's Recall to Active Duty

The possibility that the United States could be drawn into the ongoing war between Great Britain and France was one diplomatic issue of continued relevance to Washington after he left office. President Adams did his best to sustain Washington's policy of strict neutrality, but fallout at home over the Jay Treaty had not subsided and American shipping was continually menaced on the high seas. Washington's position on the matter remained unchanged, and as he was keenly aware of the ramifications the war would have on the future of the United States, he naturally wanted to stay current on the debate and the latest developments. Washington collected numerous commentaries on the French wars. Some were gifts from their respective authors such as Sir Francis d'Ivernois's *Reflections on the War: In Answer to Reflections on Peace, Addressed to Mr. Pitt, and the French Nation*. Washington also kept from d'Ivernois *A Cursory View of the Assignats and Remaining Resources of French Finance (September 6, 1795): Drawn from the Debates of the Convention* and *State of the Finances and Resources of the French Republic, to the 1st of January 1796: Being a Continuation of the Reflections on the War, and of the Cursory View of the Assignats; and Containing an Answer to the Picture of Europe, by Mr. De Calonne*. Washington also received Baron Thomas Erskine's *A View of the Causes and Consequences of the Present War with France*.[15] Erskine's work was a response to Edmund Burke's *Two Letters Addressed to a Member of the Present Parliament, on the Proposals for Peace with the Regicide Directory of France*. If Washington had not read Burke's work for himself, he almost certainly would have heard of it from his nephew Bushrod Washington, who owned a copy and was often present at Mount Vernon throughout this period.[16] Burke argued that "out of the tomb of the murdered Monarchy in France, has arisen a vast, tremendous, unformed spectre, in a far more terrific guise than any which ever yet have overpowered the imagination . . . going Straight forward to its end, unappalled by peril, unchecked by remorse, despising all common maxims and all common means, that hideous phantom overpowered those who could not believe it was possible she could at all exist."[17] Erskine, by contrast, offered a defense of the French Revolution by illustrating the nature of the oppression that the people endured under the ancien régime. He highlighted the differences between the American and French Revolutions, citing that the Americans rebelled against corruption in the British government that came at a specific point in time whereas the French had overthrown an old order so corrupt in every way that they had no other alternative to rebellion. Erskine used this comparison to justify the excesses of the French Revolution and to explain the causes of the war between Great Britain and France.[18] Both Englishmen took a dark view of the war with France, and their contrasting interpretations of the French Revolution provided Washington with balanced evidence to justify his position that the best course of action for the United States was maintaining its neutrality.

As matters seemed to escalate toward war, Adams solicited Washington's advice on appointing officers for a newly raised army and let it slip that Washington was going to be named its commander in chief. The thought of being pulled back into federal service again demanded Washington's attention. He spent considerable time and effort to becoming apprised of the situation and to determining, first and foremost, how realistic this prospect actually was. He increasingly began to pay particular attention to the defensive posture of the United States and to the readiness of the army. Timothy Pickering sent him nearly every speech and report that government officials produced on the subject of the war including copies of the *Report from the Department of War, Relative to the Fortifications of the Ports and Harbors of the United States* and the *Report of the Committee, Appointed to Enquire into the Actual State of the Naval Equipment Ordered by a Former Law of the United States, and to Report Whether Any and What Further Provision Is Necessary to Be Made on This Subject*.[19] Pickering also purchased a copy for Washington of John Gifford's *A Letter to the Hon. Thomas Erskine: Containing Some Strictures on His View of the Causes and Consequences of the Present War with France*.[20] Pickering had been purchasing various printed works for Washington for quite some time; therefore, he was well aware of what Washington would find particularly useful. In this case Pickering was careful to read the pamphlet before sending it to Washington and commended it as a "very able work." Washington's possession of Erskine's work and his knowledge of Burke's position on the subject would have given him the necessary context to absorb Pickering's latest recommendation. In this pamphlet Gifford pointed out Erskine's defense of the French Revolution and used it to make the argument that the United States should not become involved in the ongoing war.[21] Pickering also sent Washington a copy of a letter he wrote to Mr. Pinckney, the minister plenipotentiary at Paris. Pickering's letter, written during Washington's administration and at his urging, offered a pointed defense of the neutrality policy and responded to specific charges from the French minister that the United States had abandoned its treaty obligations in favor of establishing a more lucrative relationship with Great Britain.[22]

All of this reading in fact became necessary because Adams did commission Washington as the commander in chief of the newly reconstituted United States Army as war fever began to grip the nation. At once Washington was irritated with Adams, who did not seek his permission before ushering the appointment through the Senate. Washington insisted that he would not take the field unless absolutely necessary. Instead of commanding in person, he was confident that he could remain at Mount Vernon and allow a trusted second in command to run the daily administration of the army in his absence.[23] Washington further conditioned his acceptance of the commission on the assertion that he would select the general officers. Adams acquiesced but immediately regretted it because Washington's first choice was none other than Hamilton. Washington's other choices for subordinate generals — Charles Cotesworth Pinckney and Henry Knox, in that order — were also sources of tension for Adams.[24] Adams suggested other men — Daniel Morgan, Horatio Gates, and Benjamin Lincoln — but Secretary of War James McHenry rebuffed all of them. Completely at a loss Adams sent Washington's suggested names to the Senate for confirmation but reversed the order, insisting that Knox had legal precedence over the others and that Pinckney must outrank Hamilton.[25] This maneuver created complete confusion and forever damaged the relationship between Washington and Adams. Eventually Hamilton did get the commission as second in command, and as the plans for the new army began to take shape, Washington appeared more and more to be a figurehead. By 1798 Adams decided to use diplomacy and negotiated a way out of the quasi war with France, and by 1800 the army was disbanded.[26] Washington never had to leave his plantation to take the field again.

Washington Frees His Slaves in His Will

As Washington entered what would be his final year of life and the last thoughts of war faded, he turned his attention to his estate and the question of how to properly arrange his affairs for after his death. In mulling over the complex question of how to dispense his vast amounts of property, Washington's mind kept returning to a dilemma that pricked at his conscience: what should he do with his slaves? Washington was born and raised in a world that ran on the backs of slaves, and over time he had one of the largest slaveholdings in Virginia. His life experiences, however, particularly in the American Revolution, where he saw firsthand that black soldiers were as fully capable as their white counterparts, began to change his mind on slavery. He wrote to Robert Morris in 1786, "There is not a man living who wishes more sincerely than I do, to see a plan adopted for the abolition of it."[27] In fact, the seed for change was apparently in place even before the Revolution began, for he was one of the authors of the Fairfax Resolves that in 1774 called for a ban on the importation of slaves. As this seed grew in the years following the Revolution, Washington knew that the proper way to accomplish the abolition of slavery was through national-level legislation, but as president, he quickly found it to be politically impossible.[28] Now that he approached the end of his life, Washington actively wrestled with the topic on a personal level as he rewrote his will.

Washington's decision to rewrite his will apparently was spurred by a dream he had one night in July 1799 that foreshadowed his death. This story emerged in the nineteenth century from historian Benson Lossing, who was a friend of the Custis family and had heard this piece of family folklore from one of Martha's descendants. Since then more recent historians, who have a healthy distrust for the highly romanticized histories of their nineteenth-century forebearers, have called the story into question. Whether the 1799 anecdote is actually true or not, evidence suggests that Washington began seriously contemplating a manumission project as early as 1794, when he suffered an illness that he mistook for cancer.[29]

At the end of 1793 Washington contacted the renowned British agricultural reformer Arthur Young, asking for assistance in locating "substantial farmers, of wealth and strength," to lease four of the five farms that made up the Mount Vernon estate. In the plan he outlined to Young, Washington intended to only keep the Mansion House farm for his "residence, occupation, and amusement in agriculture." He was even prepared to rent to groups or to further subdivide the four other farms to make the rent more affordable. The main object, however, was to obtain "good farmers" as tenants who would provide Washington with a steady income, fulfilling his "wish to live free from care, and as much at my ease as possible" for the rest of his life.[30] The desire to rest easy in his declining years, however, was just a half-truth. At the same time, Washington instructed Tobias Lear to begin selling off his western lands. He initially gave Lear the same reason he had given to Young for wanting to sell off the real estate, but then he added one other reason that was "more powerful than all the rest": the money obtained from the western land sales would hopefully be enough to allow Washington "to liberate a certain species of property which I possess, very repugnantly to my own feelings."[31] This idea was revolutionary indeed in 1794.

Part of Washington's evolving view that slavery was abhorrent came from his reading on the subject. Beginning in the 1760s when he became a burgess, he began collecting writings on slavery. Some were filled with a strong sense of abolitionism; others simply analyzed cost versus benefit. By the end of his life, Washington had in his library more than twenty works that in one way or another addressed the questions of slavery and emancipation. Among them were Granville Sharp's *An Appendix to the Representation (Printed in 1769) of the Injustice and Dangerous Tendency of Tolerating Slavery*; Anthony Benezet's *The Potent Enemies of America Laid Open: Being Some Account of the Baneful Effects*

Attending the Use of Distilled Spirituous Liquors, and the Slavery of the Negroes; David Cooper's *A Serious Address to the Rulers of America, on the Inconsistency of Their Conduct Respecting Slavery: Forming a Contrast between the Encroachments of England on American Liberty, and American Injustice in Tolerating Slavery*; Joseph Woods's *Thoughts on Slavery: Debates in the British House of Commons, Wednesday, May 13th, 1789, on the Petitions for the Abolition of the Slave Trade*; and August Nordensköld's *A Plan for a Free Community upon the Gold Coast of Africa, under the Protection of Great Britain; but Intirely Independent of All European Laws and Governments*.[32] These publications and the other works in his collection presented Washington with views on slavery from both American and British voices. While some of them, particularly the religious ones by Sharp and Benezet, simply called for the complete abolition of slavery, Nordensköld's work is of particular interest because it proposed a plan for what to do with the slaves once they were set free. Nordensköld proposed returning freed slaves to Africa and establishing a colony on the Gold Coast. The colony would fall under the protection of Great Britain, but the people would enjoy complete self-government. Nordensköld argued that it was the best option for the freed slaves, for absorbing them into white society presented too many challenges.

Such reading must have led Washington to the conclusion that merely emancipating his slaves would not be enough. How could they be expected to support themselves in free society without any training or preparation? Washington churned this question over in his mind for a considerable period before he sat down to rewrite his will. In his particular case whatever plan he devised would be fraught with legal difficulties. First, because he had no biological children, he had no direct heir, and that case itself carried a host of potential issues under Virginia law. Second, from the time that he had married Martha forty years earlier, the Washington and Custis slaves had intermarried and produced children. Under the law Washington could only free the slaves who were his; he had no such power over the Custis slaves. Therefore, if he were to free his slaves, what would the immediate impact be on their spouses and their children? Third, what should he do about the slaves who were too young, too old, or too ill to care for themselves? For these slaves, freedom might actually prove worse than servitude because they would have no guaranteed way of meeting their basic needs.

Washington eventually devised extraordinary answers to all of his questions. In his will he first addressed the matter of ownership. He, in fact, owned only 123 of Mount Vernon's 316 slaves. Of the remainder, 40 were rented, and the rest were the property of the Custis estate and would pass to Martha's heirs upon her death.[33] He acknowledged the legal complexity as follows:

> Upon the decease of my wife, it is my Will & desire that all the Slaves which I hold in my own right, shall receive their freedom. To emancipate them during her life, would, tho' earnestly wished by me, be attended with such insuperable difficulties on account of their intermixture by Marriages with the dower Negroes, as to excite the most painful sensations, if not disagreeable consequences from the latter, while both descriptions are in the occupancy of the same Proprietor; it not being in my power, under the tenure by which the Dower Negroes are held, to manumit them.[34]

The language that Washington used in this passage is intriguing because he is effectively trying to appeal to Martha, or really the Custis heirs, to emancipate the Custis slaves along with his to make the entire process smoother.

Washington next addressed the welfare of the small, sick, and aged slaves who would be unable to care for themselves in free society: "And whereas among those who will receive freedom according to this devise, there may be some, who from old age or bodily infirmities, and others who on account of their infancy, that will be unable to support themselves; it is my Will and desire that all who come under the first and second description shall be comfortably cloathed & fed by my heirs while they live."[35] On the surface this provision might seem unnecessary to those who assume that slave owners were benevolent and always cared for their slaves, even when they were unable to work; however, Washington was well aware that such assumptions were often horrendously incorrect. As such he further stipulated "that a regular and permanent fund be established for their support so long as there are subjects requiring it; not trusting to the uncertain provision to be made by individuals."[36]

The following passage was the most extraordinary aspect of Washington's manumission plan:

> [The children who] have no parents living, or if living are unable, or unwilling to provide for them, shall be bound by the Court until they shall arrive at the age of twenty five years; and in cases where no record can be produced, whereby their ages can be ascertained, the judgment of the Court, upon its own view of the subject, shall be adequate and final. The Negros thus bound, are (by their Masters or Mistresses) to be taught to read & write; and to be brought up to some useful occupation, agreeably to the Laws of the Commonwealth of Virginia, providing for the support of Orphan[s] and other poor Children.[37]

The idea of not only freeing but also educating slaves put Washington's thinking out of step from that of his contemporaries. This clause seems to suggest that Washington did not necessarily believe that blacks were inherently inferior to whites; instead, he appeared to attribute any deficiencies as being the result of enslavement and to believe that with education and employment opportunities, freed slaves could prosper.

What came next implied in no uncertain terms that Washington did not trust his executors: "I do hereby expressly forbid the sale, or transportation out of the said Commonwealth, of any Slave I may die possessed of, under any pretense whatsoever. And I do moreover most pointedly, and most solemnly enjoin it upon my Executors hereafter named, or the Survivors of them, to see that this clause respecting Slaves, and every part thereof be religiously fulfilled at the Epoch at which it is directed to take place; without evasion, neglect, or delay."[38] In being so specific, Washington made it clear that the freed slaves would have a right to live in Virginia and would not or could not be forced to flee somewhere else.

Washington crafted a very particular slave clause for his personal servant, William Lee:

> And to my Mulatto man William (calling himself William Lee) I give immediate freedom; or if he should prefer it (on account of the accidents which have befallen him, and which have rendered him incapable of walking or of any active employment) to remain in the situation he now is, it shall be optional in him to do so. In either case, however, I allow him an annuity of thirty dollars during his natural life, which shall be independent of the victuals and cloaths he has been accustomed to receive, if he chuses the last alternative; but in full, with his freedom, if he prefers the first; & this I give him as a testimony of my sense of his attachment to me, and for his faithful services during the Revolutionary War.[39]

For Washington, this act of justice was in return for the more than thirty years that Lee had served him faithfully as a personal slave. Washington's motive was not likely affection, for no other evidence anywhere in the written records indicates that Washington considered Lee a favorite. Washington maintained different degrees of aloofness from just about everyone except his wife, so it would not make sense that he shared an exceptionally close friendship with a slave. However, almost above friendship, Washington valued loyalty, and by offering Lee immediate freedom or care for life, Washington reciprocated it.

Washington's decision to free his slaves was the final way that he set himself apart from his fellow founders. Although nearly all of them professed at least a theoretical abhorrence of slavery, none of the other southern founders emancipated their slaves. Washington's manumission program brought the ideals of the Revolution home to those who were otherwise excluded from the American dream. On a personal level, in making his will, Washington also made peace with his conscience—the conscience that evidently had been plaguing his mind since he helped pen the Fairfax Resolves decades earlier. There are no records of how his slaves received the news. Typically a wave of terror broke with news of an impending death of a master, but at least for some Mount Vernon slaves, terror likely turned to elation. Washington's executors dutifully followed the letter of the will as far as the law allowed. The executor's ledger of Lawrence Lewis indicates that the estate paid out the final support payment to a former slave named Gabriel in 1839. Unfortunately Virginia law prohibited teaching slaves to read and write (a fact that Washington evidently chose to ignore or assumed would be waived given his uniquely exalted status), so that provision was never honored.[40]

A further examination of Washington's will beyond the passages on slavery reveals another bequest that demonstrates how much he valued reading and how much he lamented that he never had the opportunity to study at a university. In his will he made good on his promise to use Virginia's gift of stock in the Potomac and James River Companies for public education. He bequeathed fifty shares to help establish a national university in the new capital. Washington had long advocated for the establishment of such an institution. He hoped to curtail the practice of sending American youth to be educated in Europe, where they contracted "too frequently not only habits of dissipation & extravagance, but principles unfriendly to Republican Government, and to the true and genuine liberties of mankind."[41] A national university would also bring together students from across the country, thereby breaking them of "local prejudices and habitual jealousies . . . which, when carried to excess, are never failing sources of disquietude to the Public mind, and pregnant of mischievous consequences to this country."[42] Washington also provided a hundred shares of stock in the James River Company to Liberty Hall Academy in Rockbridge, Virginia, and twenty shares of stock in the Bank of Alexandria to Alexandria Academy. Washington could not have known that the bid to establish a national university would never get off the ground. There was little support for it in Congress, and by 1828 the shares of Potomac River stock were worthless. The Alexandria Academy survived, however, eventually becoming a part of the city's public school system. Liberty Hall Academy also survived and has since become known as Washington and Lee University.[43]

Washington's Contribution to the American Future

At the end of his life, Washington looked back and saw all that he was able to achieve by diligently reading carefully selected works. He valued reading and the useful knowledge that could be deduced from the pages of a well-structured piece of writing. Furthermore as the consummate American leader of the time, Washington wanted to see his fellow Americans become intellectually independent from Europe. He thoroughly believed that the country's future success rested on the ability to raise good citizens who could carry the nation forward into the next century and beyond. That ability would be hindered if the best minds were continually exported to Europe, where they risked corruption. America's future depended on a virtuous citizenry educated at home and thus imbued with a strong sense of national identity.

In dispensing with the rest of his personal property, Washington clearly did not intend for Mount Vernon to become a shrine to his memory. He broke up his real estate holdings among his many relatives including the grandchildren whom he and Martha had reared. He gave away many of his cherished personal items and furnishings to trusted friends, relatives, and colleagues. Notably he bequeathed his massive archive and library to his nephew Bushrod Washington, who also inherited Mount Vernon and the Mansion House Farm. Washington's choice of Bushrod as the beneficiary of the home and archive that he had painstakingly built over the course of more than forty years made sense. Washington had a fairly close relationship with Bushrod, who had been appointed an associate justice of the Supreme Court in 1798. He would therefore need a place to live and entertain on an appropriate scale that was close to the new capital. Moreover, since

Bushrod was one of his most educated relatives, Washington likely felt that his library and archive would be in safe hands and would be used appropriately. Washington may have been dismantling his vast estate in his final act; however, he was not about to do the same to his legacy. The evidence that substantiated all that Washington had done was in that library, and he wanted to entrust it to someone who would appreciate and preserve it.

In the last three years of his life, Washington devoted the majority of his time and effort to putting his affairs in order. This endeavor was far more involved than making simple home repairs and minor updates to his will. Washington was intent on both renovating and preserving both his home and his legacy. With respect to his legacy, he dramatically expanded his library to include nearly every official record from his many years of public service in order to complement his vast repository of correspondence. With the exception of his attempt to prepare himself for war with France following Adams's decision to recall him to duty, this phase of Washington's life was not so much punctuated by what he read but by what reading material he collected.

Washington's exceptional decision to free his slaves reflects the impact that his life experience and his long-term reading had on his intellectual development. His manumission plan was the culmination of a personal moral revolution. Washington had grown up with slavery, but over time he had become uncomfortable with the institution. His changing personal convictions were tempered with the considerable amount of reading that he had done over a long period during which he took time to reflect on the knowledge he had gained. Although all the historians who have ever discussed Washington's will remark on the extraordinary nature of this decision, far too little attention has been paid to the fact that it shows how completely Washington inculcated the ideology of the American Revolution. His decision marks a coming together of Washington's intellectual development, his sense of morality, and his life experience to produce the most profound push for abolition by an elite southerner before the Civil War.

Washington's educational endowments signified the degree to which he valued education and believed that the ultimate key to the success of this American republican experiment lay with the next generation of Americans. These bequests mark another merging of Washington's lessons learned with his dreams for a better future. Even though some of Washington's wishes went unfulfilled, as in the examples of the freed slaves not being taught to read and write and his wish for a national university, not even the harshest critic can effectively argue that Washington failed. Washington's former cavalry lieutenant Harry Lee was both sincere and correct when he eulogized Washington as "first in war, first in peace, and first in the hearts of his countrymen."[44]

CHAPTER SIX

A Place for Secluded Study

In the early morning darkness as the clock struck four o'clock retired president George Washington slipped quietly out of bed, taking care to tuck the covers back in around his wife to prevent her from getting cold. Having shared his bed for nearly forty years, Martha Washington had long since become accustomed to her husband's daily routine and thus did not even stir as he stood up and the wood bed frame creaked. He tugged the bed curtains closed, tiptoed out of the room, and descended the private stairway that connected to his library below. No one else in the house was up; it was not yet time for the slaves to make their rounds to each bedroom to stoke the smoldering fires and begin the day. It was a cherished part of Washington's day. During this time the master of Mount Vernon could be alone in his library with his books, papers, and thoughts before he embarked on his daily inspection tours of his farms, before the grandchildren asked to go for horseback rides with their grandpapa, and before the daily onslaught of visitors came to call.

It was during these early morning hours in the solitude of his library that Washington was most productive. Here he did his reading, writing, and planning for the future of his vast estates and the solidification of his legacy. Gen. Henry Lee, a friend and former lieutenant of Washington's, once remarked to his chief, "We are amazed, sir, at the vast amount of work that you accomplish."[1] Washington replied, "Sir, I rise at four o'clock, and a great deal of my work is done while others are asleep."[2] This anecdote is vintage Washington, the old soldier who maintained his characteristically rigid routine until the day he died. The image of the solitary man alone at his desk in the early hours of the morning is one that admiring biographers have long recognized as evidence of his exemplary character, but few have paused this scene long enough to consider the significance of the library for the one who built and worked in it. Indeed, at first glance the study's austere appearance masks the fact that it was designed to be the operations center for Washington's great self-fashioning project. It housed his sizable collection of books, other printed works, and the voluminous correspondence compiled over decades that together cataloged the transformation of an ambitious middle-class boy into the father of his country.

Biographers and scholars have repeatedly glossed over the study's significance for two main reasons. First, of the many labels applied to Washington both during and since his lifetime, "scholar" is not typically among them. He simply cannot be placed in the same academic category with such contemporaries as Jefferson and Adams with their respective university and legal training or even with Franklin, who despite his self-made rise to prominence while lacking a formal education still sought to become a man of letters. Second, Washington's skill as an amateur architect has been largely underappreciated by scholars and critics who cannot move beyond the fact that Mount Vernon's exterior is asymmetrical. Nevertheless, the study's design, its placement within the larger structure of the mansion, and the manner in which it was furnished and used provide keys to understanding how Washington approached the act of reading, for this space in which he engaged in this solitary act was entirely a work of his own creation.

How, where, and what people read reveal a great deal about their attitudes toward the significance of reading as an activity. Do they read in public or otherwise in front of others, thumbing through the materials casually for the sake of entertainment, or do they read in private for the sake of concentrated study? Is there music or other noise that might be distracting? Are they willing to share their materials with others? Do they feel confident enough in their skills as readers to take part in discussions about their reading? What do they read? Why do they choose to read certain types of material and not others? Do they make marginalia or notes? With the extant evidence of how Washington expanded Mount Vernon over the years along with the list of the contents of his private library, it is possible to answer these questions and thus develop a new understanding of Washington's reading and how it contributed to his intellectual development.

Mount Vernon's Exterior: A Powerful First Impression

The layout of the main estate and gardens and the facade of the main mansion house convey a sense of majesty and power not typically found in English manors. In direct contrast to English and European landscape design of the period that typically located the approach road and entrance on a direct axis, Washington created a three-quarter-mile-long axial vista to the house, thereby increasing the dramatic appearance of the mansion from afar. Maximizing the impact by creating a specific physical distance is a technique that Washington also incorporated in meticulously managing his public image. Just as Washington's staged aloofness enhanced his reputation and the mythology surrounding him, the carefully shaped distance between the approach road and the house heightens the mansion's aesthetic appeal to visitors.[3]

A striking reflection of Washington's personality, the resulting design of the mansion house is an architectural manifesto, framing in wood and paint Washington's politics as well as his sense of self. The exterior of the house, with its famed asymmetrical west front that greets visitors upon arriving up the long gravel drive, is deliberately styled in a plainly understated Anglo-American way. It is painted white and free of adornments so as to not detract from the magnificent landscape upon which the house is perched. Although the house is eye-catching and impressive at first sight, upon closer inspection one realizes that what Washington really wanted people to notice was not the house but the land. Washington loved his land and thoroughly believed it was the best piece of real estate in America. Set high above the banks of the Potomac River, the main estate property conveys a masterful sense of dominance. The sheer beauty of this plot of land beside the river is the property's prime asset, and an ostentatious house would have detracted from the impact that the land alone has on the beholder.

A key example of Washington's effort to design an understated exterior to his home that would emphasize the great dramatic landscape is the two-story piazza on the east side of the house. Supported by eight Tuscan columns, the piazza serves as an extension of the central hall, which held family gatherings, and offers a majestic view of the Potomac. The relaxed and intimate scale and the absence of pilasters on the inside wall, as well as the absence of axes, allow visitors to drink in the scene before them, free of architectural distractions. During a visit to Mount Vernon in the 1790s, artist and designer Benjamin Latrobe devoted the longest single section of his travel journal to a description of the piazza:

> Towards the East Nature has lavished magnificence, nor has Art interfered but to exhibit her to advantage. Before the portico a lawn extends on each hand from the front of the house. . . . Down the steep slope trees and shrubs are thickly planted. They are kept so low as to not interrupt the view but merely to furnish an agreeable border to the extensive prospect beyond. The mighty Potowmac runs close under this bank the elevation which must be 250 perhaps feet. The river here is about 1½ miles across and runs parallel with the front of the house for about 3 miles to the left and 4 to the right.[4]

Similarly Julian Niemcewicz, another visitor to Mount Vernon in the late 1790s, noted that from the "immense open portico supported by eight pillars . . . one looks out on perhaps the most beautiful view in the world. . . . It is there that in the evenings the Gl. [General], his family and the gustes [guests] go to sit to enjoy the fine weather and the beautiful view. I enjoyed it more than anyone. . . . What a remembrance!"[5] Abigail Adams also considered the piazza to be Mount Vernon's "greatest ornament."[6] Given that Washington's design for his piazza had the desired effect on his visitors, it makes sense that he designed the rest of his home as deliberately to elicit a certain response from beholders.

Just as he would do when crafting his public persona, when designing the home's exterior, Washington played up its positive attributes to
the fullest while maintaining a sort of dignified simplicity all around.
Presentation was everything to Washington, and given that he viewed
every aspect of his public life as a form of performance, he gave Mount
Vernon a role to play on the grand stage of his landscape. To accentu-
ate the positive attributes of the estate, Washington "dressed up" what
could have been a modest-looking farmhouse to perform the role of
an imposing and powerful structure. As wealthy as Washington was,
procuring enough stone to construct a home on the scale he planned
for was simply financially out of reach. Rather than compromise on
size, Washington chose to use inexpensive wood siding, but he had
the panels rusticated by cutting out grooved panels in each board and
then whitewashing them with a specialized mixture of river sand and
paint that provided the texture and appearance of stone masonry. Thus,
a wood frame house was fitted in a costume of "masonry." According to Washington, this sanding process was "designed to answer two
purposes, durability and presentation of stone."[7] Furthermore, the rustication affected the perceived scale of the house itself. The pronounced
joints in the wide panel boards are emphasized by the shadows cast
on the upper surface and the highlight on the lower surface, so the eye
reads the wall as an incised surface. The sand increases the reflectivity
of each rusticated board and the brilliance of the joint. These different
effects come together to downplay the large expanse of the west facade,
making the house appear smaller than it actually is within the larger
setting of the landscape.[8]

In his travels through Virginia, Washington would have seen several
fine examples of homes and churches constructed with brick walls and
stone coins: the Aquia Church (ca. 1754–57) in Stafford County; the
home of his friend George Mason, Gunston Hall (1755); Thomas Nelson's home (ca. 1710–30) in Yorktown; Cleve (ca. 1750) in King George
County; and the Carlyle House (1751–53) in Alexandria. Through studying the popular architectural books of his day including Batty Langley

and Thomas Langley's *Builder's Jewel, or the Youth's Instructor and Work-man's Remembrancer* and Batty Langley's *The City and Country Builder's and Workman's Treasury of Designs*, Washington learned about more remote sources that he had not visited: Inigo Jones's Banqueting House (1619–22) in Whitehall, London, and Andrea Palladio's Palazzo Thiene (begun ca. 1542) in Vicenza, Italy. Both of these buildings, as well as many of Jones's designs for gateways, had the unusual cut of a V for all horizontal and vertical joints; this design feature is also found in Mount Vernon, Gunston Hall, the Nelson and Carlyle Houses, and the Aquia Church. Additionally a variation of a design feature in the Pantheon, found in plate 75 of Langley's *Builder's Jewel*, that includes upper and intermediate cornices that have the same moldings and unusual form of a block modillion with the cyma recta — or a reverse S-shaped, curved end with associated V-jointed rustication — appears to have inspired Washington. The same details occur at the arcades, dependencies, and exterior cornices of Mount Vernon.[9]

As for the house's layout, Washington took an English style and tailored it to fit American circumstances. Virginians over the course of several generations had honed a method of picking and choosing elements from English plans and styles to fashion homes that suited their slave-holding society as it changed over time. This adaptation included scaling down the hall-parlor English model to produce plans that had few rooms alike in function or size and that were dictated by the owner's attempt to replicate "civic order in a public society." The result was a sort of countryseat, with halls separating the public's entrance from the family's private rooms.[10] Over the course of Washington's various renovations, he took this method and refined it to a higher degree. That Washington molded Mount Vernon into an architectural self-portrait indicates that in some ways he was very much in step with his generation, for during his lifetime, the social, political, economic, and religious conditions in Middle Virginia changed. As Washington reacted to the societal changes happening in his world and his thought process developed, the things he did and the architectural renovations he undertook at Mount Vernon reflected his evolving mind-set.[11] Increasingly Virginians conceived of their society as being a stratified organic whole wherein the social order, distinguishing between the rulers and the ruled, used symbols and trappings to reinforce the notion of hierarchy as natural and ordained by God.[12]

Visitors to Mount Vernon always notice first that the exterior of the house is asymmetrical. The asymmetry of the windows on the west front of the house appears to be a flaw, and indeed it is one of the main reasons why Washington's architectural skills are often critiqued or at the very least underappreciated. The asymmetry of the house's west front exterior has a couple of possible explanations, with the first being that it was simply a mistake. However, given that Washington devoted such attention to detail and that nearly everything he did was somehow loaded with meaning, this explanation seems unlikely. It is even more improbable given that the only effort required to make the exterior symmetrical would have involved moving two windows on the first floor and two on the second, a fairly minor undertaking given the overall complexity of Washington's renovation project.[13] Moreover, the only extant line drawing in Washington's own hand of Mount Vernon's west front provides a glimpse into his thought process. The drawing, most likely completed in 1773 for the construction project that began in 1774, reveals a very different Mount Vernon than the one that was actually constructed. The biggest difference is that the house in the drawing is symmetrical or nearly symmetrical. Although the two windows north of the central doorway are approximately six inches farther from the center of the house than those south of the doorway, the difference is likely attributed to a thick pencil line made in the small drawing or to the fact that, being a study, it did not demand much accuracy. Similar disparities are present in other parts of the drawing as well. Because of the asymmetry in the drawing, the windows of the west parlor and small dining room are in different locations. The small dining room has one window, and the first window to the south side of the center door is in the closet under the staircase. Other differences include wider doors, smaller windows on the first floor with higher sills, and lower second-floor windowsills. The significance of Washington's sketch is that it demonstrates that the asymmetrical reality of Mount Vernon was neither an afterthought nor an oversight.[14]

It is also worth noting that the other three sides of Mount Vernon are also asymmetrical but in different ways. For example, the asymmetry of the north facade seems to juxtapose aristocratic high style with farmhouse practicality. It features Washington's Venetian window, which is the centerpiece of the large dining room addition that was a part of the 1774 expansion. From the exterior, the large, elegant window shares an elevation with the cellar door, which Washington could have either easily moved to some other more discreet part of the building or hidden in a sunken areaway. By opting to leave the cellar door where it was, it seems that Washington sought to communicate to visitors that he saw no incompatibility between the ornamental and the practical being equally visible. Both had functional purposes, and Washington allowed them to exist side by side in his neatly ordered world.[15]

It is possible that Washington chose to incorporate asymmetry as a design theme in order to exploit the visual effect that it has on tricking the eye, thus altering perceptions of the building's scale. Or perhaps despite his perceived preference for formality and aristocratic bearing, Washington did not want to create the perfect English manor house that dominated the landscape. It would seem that he did, in fact, want to preserve and present the fact that Mount Vernon was a farmhouse. He wanted to maintain some sense of the vernacular farmhouse architecture that he both remembered from his childhood and saw firsthand in his extensive travels throughout Virginia.[16]

Mount Vernon's exterior asymmetry was also likely a deliberate by-product of Washington's efforts to expand what had been a somewhat modest farmhouse interior into an elegant countryseat. Part of Washington's extensive renovation (between 1757 and 1760) included raising the roof and expanding the central hall in order to accommodate a larger, grander staircase. This installation naturally impacted the placement of the windows on the south side of the front door.[17] It made perfect sense for Washington to want to improve the appearance of the central hall, for this passage was the most public room in the house. Here he conducted the business transactions of his farms, received visitors, and entertained guests during hot summer days. The wood paneling, finely cut moldings, and wider staircase conveyed a sense of Washington's wealth to any visitor more accustomed to the look of common eighteenth-century homes with plainly plastered interiors or with rude log cabin walls.[18]

Also during this renovation project, Washington enhanced the interior of some of the other existing rooms that were a part of the original structure. What had been Lawrence Washington's red room became the small dining room. The 1757 remodeling of this room included the addition of paneled wainscoting and a second window overlooking the entrance court. Washington also relocated the existing window in the room so that the two windows together were in the same relative position in the room when viewed from the inside. This window realignment had a dual effect: the interior was both balanced and formally enhanced, and the exterior's asymmetry became more pronounced.[19]

Mount Vernon's Expansion

The most ambitious aspect of the 1757–60 renovation was the construction of the west parlor. The room was paneled and two elaborate Ionic door frames were installed. The inspiration for the door frames may have been the "Ionick Entablature" in plate 6 of Langley's *The City and Country Builder's and Workman's Treasury of Designs*. Another possible source is Palladio's rendition of the Ionic order, found in book 1, plate 20 of his *Four Books of Architecture*, but plate 23 of Langley's *Builder's Jewel* is the most likely source.[20] The mantel and overmantel were clearly taken from the designs on plates 50 and 51 in Abraham Swan's handbook *The British Architect*. The chimneypiece, doorframes, and doors were painted with a red mahogany graining, and the walls were covered in a stone-colored paint that contained both ochre and umber pigments mixed with white lead.[21]

The rest of the renovation project consisted of redecorating both rooms on the east side of the house as guest bedchambers, along with the simple bedroom on the north side of the passage that dated from Lawrence Washington's time. Washington also paneled the bedroom on the south side of the passage in 1758; this room would serve as the master bedroom until the next major addition to the house was undertaken in 1774. As a result of the 1757–60 renovation project, the second floor had five bedrooms with plastered rails, cornice moldings, and a chair rail. At this point Washington stopped adding to the house until 1770 so that he could retire some more of his debts to English merchants. Thanks to his willingness to diversify his plantation operations to include such cottage industries as a fishery and livestock trading in addition to his crops, he turned profits that reduced his dependence on imports and drastically changed his way of life. It enabled him to undertake the second phase of the house's expansion, one that would serve as a proclamation of his newfound financial independence and transformation from tobacco planter to diversified farmer.[22]

A Need for Privacy Drives Second Expansion

This second expansion project, begun in 1774, was on a much grander scale than the first. Washington planned to enlarge the house at both ends and to add a two-story piazza facing the river and arcades to connect the dependencies to the house on the west side. He also planned a complete redesign of the west garden to be done simultaneously with the addition. After removing the central driveway, which had been carried over from the English manor tradition, he replaced it with symmetrical parterres and created the bowling green, the serpentine walks, the north and south service lanes, and the flower and vegetable gardens. Also he began an extensive tree-planting program. Construction on the house began on the south end with the addition of Washington's new private study and some storage rooms on the first floor, capped by the master bedroom and two dressing rooms. In this wing of the house, he covered the plaster walls with a simple coat of whitewash, the woodwork in a soft, blue-gray paint, and the doors in burnt umber paint.[23] The master bedroom is modestly decorated with a plain mantel, simple furnishings, and soft, white fabrics on the bed. These choices are probably as much a testament to Martha Washington's taste as to her husband's, for as soon as she arrived at Mount Vernon, she began putting her decorative touches in order and notably found simplicity serene in such a private space as a bedroom.[24]

In designing this wing, Washington constructed buffers to separate these two rooms from the more public side of the house. One must pass through the small dining room and the downstairs bedroom to reach the vestibule that leads to the study and the private stairway up to the master bedroom suite on the second floor. That no hallway directly connects to the library or the staircase speaks to the degree that Washington sought to separate his private life from the public one that he was obliged to lead given his wealth and social standing. As noted previously, beginning with his retirement from the Virginia Regiment and intensifying after the Revolution, staggering numbers of guests — many of whom were complete strangers — poured into Mount Vernon. The beauty of Washington's design of the south wing of the house was that it allowed the Washingtons to entertain the multitudes of visitors with the requisite social graces while sacrificing none of their privacy. Washington bemoaned the burden of his celebrity by comparing his beloved home "to a well resorted tavern," because "scarcely any strangers who are going from north to south, or from south to north do not spend a day or two at it."[25]

During the same phase of construction, Washington added an ornate mantel and overmantel to the small dining room. The ornate design, taken from plate 50 in Swan's *The British Architect*, is unusual for a corner fireplace in a relatively small room.[26] At the same time a French artisan whose name has since been lost created the elaborate plaster ceiling. The work in this room was completed in 1775 while Washington was leading the Continental Army. Remarkably Washington was engaged with nearly every detail of this entire renovation project even though he was many miles away and preoccupied with the business of the Revolution.[27] As noted previously, perfecting Mount Vernon's plans had become necessary for maintaining Washington's sanity. Overseeing the renovations allowed the Continental Army's commander in chief, whose desire for maintaining control was paramount, to mentally escape his daily reality and feel that sense of being in charge. Lund Washington, Washington's cousin and overseer, reported on the finished project in November 1775: "It is I think very Pretty[....] [T]he Stucco man agrees the Cielg [ceiling] is a Handsomeer one than any of Colo[nel] Lewises [Washington's brother-in-law] altho[ugh] not half the work in it[.]"[28]

After constructing the private sanctuary and embellishing the existing public rooms of the house, Washington dramatically added to the public side of the house in 1776. In the most ambitious project of all of Mount Vernon's expansions, Washington designed the two-story dining room as the setting for grand entertainments. Even more remarkable this project began at Washington's urging during the lowest point in the Revolution, after his army had suffered a series of humiliating losses in New York and rapidly had to retreat. He wrote to Lund Washington, urging him to commence work in a "masterly manner."[29] It took nearly twenty years to complete as Washington was away from Mount Vernon from 1775 until 1783 (a period interrupted only by his brief return en route to Yorktown), and following the war he had a difficult time locating the craftsmen needed to complete a project on this scale. Particularly striking are the designs for the dining room's fireplace and its Venetian window, which was taken from Langley's *City and Country Builder's and Workman's Treasury of Designs.*[30] Washington undoubtedly selected such a window for its size, which provides commanding views of the river, for its striking appearance. He also added a marble mantel that was a gift from Samuel Vaughan. The scale and symmetry of this room, when combined with its intricate decoration, convey the sense that Washington was highly attuned to the finest tastes of his times. For example, he had the ceiling embellished with four panels, each with a center motif that incorporates different farming implements to symbolize that he had amassed his wealth by diversifying his agricultural pursuits, and a plaster medallion in the center. This rich detailing contributes to the overall splendor of the room, especially when combined with the added effect of the wallpaper border, which was the latest in interior design accessories and imported from France. In this room, Washington hung some of his finest (and most expensive) paintings.[31]

As a part of the 1774 expansion, Washington had the outbuildings realigned and built the covered walkways connecting the house to the two closest dependencies. In 1777 he had the piazza constructed and in 1778 added the cupola to the roof. In 1785 he began constructing the greenhouse and repainted the small dining room a brilliant verdigris green (an expensive way of dressing up a room given the price of paint at the time). In 1787 he painted the west parlor a bright Prussian blue and added an intricate plaster ceiling. In 1792 he built the slave quarters adjacent to the greenhouse. Four years later, he had Venetian shutters installed to the west front and the shingles on the roofs of both dependencies painted to match the roof of the house. Finally in 1797 he added a wood grain finish to the entry hall that was similar to what he had done in his study in 1786 when he added the unusual built-in, glass-paneled bookcases and refinished the walls.[32]

Given what is known about Washington's lifelong project of shaping his public persona, his layout of the most intimate spaces in his home makes perfect sense. For as much as history remembers him as the majestic, awe-inspiring father of his country, he was also a sensitive man for whom an escape from the public eye was a necessity. To sustain the public face, Washington needed an ultra-private retreat where he could both unburden himself to the one person who knew him best and work out solutions to whatever challenges were before him. Additionally besides the design of this private suite of rooms, Washington went even further to ensure that the master bedroom and the library were indeed secluded by insisting on lighting and maintaining the fire in the master bedroom himself whenever he and Martha were in the room. The slaves who were responsible for lighting the fires in the pre-dawn hours in the other occupied bedrooms of the house did not do so in the master. Furthermore, his step-grandson, George Washington Parke Custis, would later recall that the study was "a place that no one entered without orders."[33]

Having felt the sting of criticism from a young age, he left nothing to chance and therefore sought to protect the two very precious elements that made him who he was — his marriage and his mind. His marriage brought him the love, comfort, and support that he craved. His mind, although sharp, was constantly preoccupied by the fact that unlike so many of the men he led in both the military and political realms, he lacked a formal education. For example, while the highly educated Thomas Jefferson could easily carry on intellectual conversations on any number of subjects with complete strangers, Washington preferred instead to indulge in conversations with women that were light, even flirtatious, and with men only on those subjects that he felt most comfortable with. He engaged in such social activity for short bursts at a time and retired from his company on a rigid schedule, which often precluded the opportunity to become overly familiar with anyone.

A Closer Look at Mount Vernon's Library

Further reinforcing the notion that the library was a private work space were the decor and furnishings in his day: a desk, a dressing table, a small table that held a letterpress, and a large, freestanding globe. Along one side are built-in bookcases with glass doors. The only adornments to the walls were an awkwardly fitted mantelpiece and a portrait of Lawrence Washington, elder half-brother and mentor to young George.[34] There were no other chairs or furnishings that could serve as seating. The austerity of this room is striking when contrasted with the public rooms of the house, including the parlor, entry hall, dining rooms, and music room — all of which are richly paneled, plastered, and accessorized with intricate mantelpieces, ceilings, door frames, chair rails, paint, artwork, furnishings, china, and so forth.[35] Washington laid out and furnished the public rooms to convey to visitors a sense of the family's wealth and prestige while he kept the private rooms simple to eliminate distractions from the reasons for their very existence — a happy marriage and solitary intellectual development.[36] The interior design of Mount Vernon seems to impart Washington's desire to balance pleasure and power, freedom and restraint. Moreover, Mount Vernon is a visual representation of Washington's mental shift from Anglophile to American.[37]

The degree to which Washington's design is unique is further evidenced by the fact that Washington did not have many architectural manuals in his private library.[38] He must have borrowed them from his friends, his neighbors, and the artisans he hired; it would have been fairly easy given the wide availability of these books throughout the colonies.[39] Although, as highlighted throughout this chapter, elements of Mount Vernon's design are taken from some of the most popular building manuals available in the colonies, none of the architectural details from Mount Vernon are exact copies from these various British templates. Just as with nearly everything else in his life, Washington made different choices. From the time he began working on the first expansion of the house, Washington made it clear that he deliberately wanted to avoid reproducing an English manor. His inspiration was British; his design, American. There was nothing accidental about it.

Washington's Mount Vernon Contrasted with Jefferson's Monticello

To place Washington as an architect in a broader context, a brief comparison to Thomas Jefferson and his creation of Monticello can be instructive. In no way can Washington be described as a student of architecture in the same vein as Jefferson, who literally spent decades poring over academic architecture treatises and studying some of the grandest designs in Europe to perfect his vision. However, in placing the two owner-builders' lives side by side, there are several striking similarities and differences that together explain the drive each man had not simply to construct a nice house but also to create a home that was an extension of himself.[40] Furthermore, this comparison reveals that in his design of Mount Vernon Washington was much more creative and thoughtful than previous scholars concluded.

Both Washington and Jefferson lost their fathers as adolescents. Augustine Washington died when George was eleven years old.[41] Peter Jefferson died when Thomas was fourteen.[42] Their fathers' deaths meant that both boys lost the guiding hand that had fostered them, protected them, and steered them onto the path for a successful life at a sensitive age. Washington and Jefferson had cool relationships with their mothers, and they escaped their mothers' homes as early and as often as possible. Later both men sought to make homes for themselves on lands they inherited and deeply loved. They deliberately designed their homes to serve as havens and took decades to complete them. Both Washington and Jefferson carved out distinct public rooms and private rooms within their respective structures. One of the main differences between the two builders was that Washington's project followed a more linear progression of expansion. He started with an existing house and expanded it over several different phases. Furthermore, Washington kept up a program of expansion and redecoration as opposed to renovation. Jefferson began Monticello from scratch and developed a fondness for completely remodeling the structure rather than merely adding to it as his tastes changed.

The difference between Washington's preferences for expansion and Jefferson's penchant for renovation comes down more to their personalities than their finances. Throughout his adult life, Washington sought to present himself to the public as the embodiment of a self-controlled patrician who achieved wealth from hard work and fame through disinterested public service.[43] As a result, Mount Vernon was a work in sequential progress, with Washington expanding when he could afford it; his home was refined rather than revolutionized over time to impress upon visitors a sense of the man who molded it. Conversely Jefferson projected an image of himself as a perpetual Enlightenment student-philosopher who was continually seeking knowledge and experiences that would broaden his mind over a lifetime of development. Monticello therefore was in an almost permanent state of revolution over the course of more than fifty years as Jefferson brought together the series of worlds that he interacted with into the one that he created.[44]

Many scholars and architectural critics credit Jefferson, who pursued a more exactly executed design, as being a better architect than Washington, and they often deride the latter as a mere amateurish home owner who simply managed to produce an oddly asymmetrical wood frame house with pretentiously rusticated siding as a poor substitute for stone. To accept such a critique pays a well-deserved compliment to Jefferson's studied skills in designing his home, but it completely negates Washington's considerable creative skills in shaping his. Jefferson's plans reflect his commitment to architectural orthodoxy while simultaneously bringing together Palladian design with French, Italian, and Chinese elements. Washington's resulting design reflects a no less deliberate effort to use different details of British Palladianism in order to make an amalgamated American structure. If Mount Vernon appears somehow less Palladian and studied than Monticello, then it is because it was intentional on Washington's part and not because it was a mistake or an indication that he was somehow not as gifted as Jefferson was.

Having established the inspiration and deliberateness of Mount Vernon's design and the degree to which Washington relied on his creativity rather than on academic architecture to realize his vision for his dream home, the next question that must be explored is, how did Washington use the house to reinforce the self-image that he worked so continuously to refine and project? Only upon answering this question properly will it then be possible to understand the study as a reading and work space within the larger framework of Washington's life. What must be understood is that Washington was thoroughly a man of his time. After his father's death and having spent the rest of his adolescence under the tutelage of his older half-brothers and powerful patrons, Washington keenly understood that in order to fulfill his ambitions for success in provincial Virginia, he had to act properly in genteel circles. A large part of being cultured thus involved learning how to comport oneself in the social spaces of homes and cultivate the right image. When refined people took to the stage in these social settings to interact, it was possible for the people and the environment to harmonize. That harmony hinged partially on behavior of the human actors and on the ability of the decor, light, furnishings, and the silver to serve their purposes. Only then did the house fulfill its function of projecting its owner's ideal image to his guests.[45]

By the time Washington began his first expansion of Mount Vernon, he had achieved the goals he set out for himself as an ambitious young man. He had made money and powerful connections through his early work as a surveyor, had achieved fame as the commander of the Virginia Regiment during the Seven Years' War, had won elections to be a member of the House of Burgesses, and had married the richest woman in the colony, bringing him both wealth and domestic happiness. He was at the top of Virginia society, and his home needed to reflect the dignity of his station.

The expansion of Mount Vernon's structure was only part of Washington's improvements. He also spent lavishly to decorate the interior to the standard expected among Virginia's elite. As noted, when he married Martha, Washington began to do business with her agent, Robert Cary and Company. The Washingtons were big shoppers and prone to ordering more than their profits could pay for just as so many in their social circle were also accustomed to doing. Washington, a man usually characterized by an extreme degree of calculated restraint, consistently spent so much money on home furnishings, clothing, and accessories for entertaining simply because he was now an upper-class member of a society that was in the midst of a radical transformation itself. When Washington married, Virginians were extending their imaginative horizons beyond the narrowly bound tradition from whence they came. Washington is but one example of a colonist who had undergone a "new birth" by serving in the armies of the empire and who was eager to participate in a wider Anglo-American market.[46] The pace at which the market for consumer goods was expanding picked up rapidly after 1740. Even colonials living three thousand miles from the metropolis of London could take part in consumption.[47] The speed of this transformation coupled with changing fashion trends, which by the mid-eighteenth century were no longer the purview of the aristocracy, are significant to understanding Washington in the broader context of his society during this period.[48]

Although Washington spent lavishly to outfit his house and family, it is curious to note that nearly all of the household accessories he purchased were intended for the more public rooms of Mount Vernon. As stated earlier, the study was comparatively austere in terms of its furnishings and decorations. It thus raises the question why there is such a stark contrast between the adornments of the public rooms of the house and those of the private library. The answer could lie partly in the simple explanation that as he designed his study for his personal use and no one else's, Washington saw little need to embellish the aesthetic appeal of the space. An equally plausible explanation is that Washington intended it to be an efficient study space and operations headquarters for his estates — nothing more. As such he needed to eliminate the potential for distractions, which would not benefit a room designed for constant intellectual activities. Everything about Washington's solitary use of the room, as discussed at the opening of this chapter, supports this interpretation.

Further credence for this efficiency-based interpretation of Washington's study is found in the comparison between Mount Vernon and Monticello. On the one hand, Jefferson also designed his study to be a mostly private room with limited public access; however, he spent years refining and then remodeling the physical design of the overall space to accommodate not just his desk and his bookshelves but also his bedroom and his attached hobby room and greenhouse. In other words, Jefferson created a study that was a personal retreat — a place for rest, reflection, study, and experimentation all in one room.[49] Washington, on the other hand, built a work space. This distinction between the two men's study designs is crucial to defining exactly what kind of an intellectual and reader Washington was. While Jefferson is famously remembered as the darling of the Enlightenment, a constantly evolving intellectual whose academic pursuits changed and expanded dramatically over time, Washington is instead held as the largely self-educated upstart whose own definition of the term "useful knowledge" was information that has a practical application to advancing an individual's wealth and/or place in society. Both men were driven by the need for self-improvement, but their definitions of that term were utterly different. As much as Jefferson was interested in intellectual pursuits that would lead him to practical discoveries and improvements such as inventing a system for recycling rainwater at Monticello, he also had a passion for poetry.[50] Washington, by contrast, read and worked toward specific goals and, from the evidence we have, spent comparatively little time on contemplation.

That the studies at both Monticello and Mount Vernon were reserved for the private use of their owners also says something about each man's attitude toward the pursuit of reading. Both Jefferson and Washington absolutely required solitude. However, Jefferson routinely allowed his daughter Martha access to the room and its contents, and he opened the room to favored visitors to his estate, such as Dr. William Thornton and his wife, Anna Maria.[51] Washington extended no such invitations to enter and peruse his study to either members of his family or any among the visiting hordes that flocked to his doorstep on a daily basis. According to George Washington Parke Custis, books and papers were offered to the ubiquitous guests for their amusement in the sitting rooms.[52]

The lengths that Jefferson and Washington went to in order to keep access to their libraries restricted placed them slightly out of step with many of their contemporaries in the Virginia gentry and in the wider British realm. For example, fellow Virginians such as Speaker of the House of Burgesses Peyton Randolph and George Wythe maintained studies that served as places to entertain male guests and conduct business in their stately Williamsburg homes.[53] Another notable Williamsburg resident who used his private library as a showpiece was Francis Fauquier, the colony's lieutenant governor. Already an accomplished scientist when he moved to Virginia and assumed his post in 1758, he left much of his library in England; however, the partial collection he brought with him revealed a man of engaging personality and high intellect. He frequently invited guests into his library for a mix of intellectual conversation and good food and drink. Moreover, he was frequently willing to loan out books, even his most valuable presentation copies, to interested friends.[54]

Fauquier's frequent use of his library as a space to entertain and exchange ideas and his willingness to lend his books offer a stark contrast to Washington and to a lesser extent to Jefferson, and they further demonstrate that Fauquier was in step with the intellectual trend of mid-eighteenth-century aristocratic England. Over the course of the century, libraries in fashionable English homes had transitioned from private places of study for the homeowners to living and entertaining spaces for entire families and their guests. The homeowners enlarged the rooms, lavishly decorated them with rich artwork and furnishings, and expanded the size and scope of their collections of books. They expanded and repurposed their libraries during this time because attitudes among the aristocracy shifted toward learning and culture. It became increasingly important for the ruling class of Britain to appear worthy, and while uneducated gentlemen could still be found, their peers scorned them.[55]

English-born Fauquier fits neatly into this pattern, and the evidence suggests that this trend had crossed the Atlantic and was reflected in some of the fashionable homes in the colonies. Clearly, however, Washington was not willing to embrace this English fashion. As he did with the rest of Mount Vernon, Washington chose from among English-inspired fashions those that suited his tastes and personality the best. He was not about to turn his study into some sort of living space or salon because in so doing he would risk revealing his Achilles' heel — namely, his "defective education." For a man who was all about carefully fashioning his image so that it projected power, he found it far better to maintain a sense of aloofness in intellectual matters whenever possible, and if that meant being slightly out of fashion with how he managed his private library, so be it. It was better to appear distant than dim. The care and attention to detail that he paid to the design, construction, and decoration of his estate and gardens at Mount Vernon reinforce the notion that Washington deliberately sought to convey a certain message of power, control, and refinement to all who beheld both the home and its owner. How Washington situated and used the study within that setting reveals that he maintained a highly organized and diligent attitude toward his larger life project of self-improvement and zealously guarded his mind at work.

Conclusion

In the fall of 1796, a host of issues plagued President Washington. From a diplomatic standpoint, the United States still faced the threat of being pulled into the war between Great Britain and France. At home Washington could not keep cabinet advisers. After Thomas Jefferson, Alexander Hamilton, and Henry Knox resigned their respective posts, Washington not only found second-rate candidates, but they refused his offers in rapid succession. Meanwhile, the partisan attacks from the Republicans' menacing press grew more vicious. Washington, however, had one headache that eclipsed all of the official ones that came with the burden of his office — his step-grandson George Washington Parke Custis. As a child Washy was a delight to his grandparents, who reared him, but as the boy grew into an adolescent, he began to display the same worrying personality trait toward indolence that his deceased father had exhibited years earlier.

As a grandfather Washington was determined to not make the same mistakes with Washy that he had made with his father, Jacky Custis. When Jacky was a boy, Washington was a new husband and stepfather, who, fearful of offending his wife, deferred to her in the disciplining of her son. Martha doted on the boy, and her spoiling him took its toll. Jacky grew up knowing that one day he would inherit the Custis fortune, so he therefore found no need to apply himself in his studies. Washington did what he could to curb the boy's worst excesses, but he was unable to mold Jacky into the man that he wanted him to be. With Washy, however, he had a second chance.

Washington wanted his grandson to grow into a good citizen of the new republic and not become just another rich young fop. He was determined that the boy should have the best American education possible and decided that when Washy was old enough he would enroll at the College of New Jersey, which was sufficiently conservative without being too puritanical and was far enough away from the diversions of the big cities New York and Philadelphia that could lure the boy from his studies. The College of New Jersey was also an ideal selection for placating Martha, who worried incessantly whenever Washy was away from home. The school was not so far that Washy would be out of reach of the presidential mansion.

Once Washy was enrolled, his grandfather kept in close contact with him and with his tutors to monitor his progress. With regard to study, Washington assured his grandson, "It is yourself who is to derive immediate benefit from these [studies]. Your country may do it hereafter. The more knowledge you acquire, the greater will be the probability of succeeding in both, and the greater will be your thirst for more."[1]

Washy reassured his grandfather that he was working hard, to which Washington replied with a mixture of enthusiasm and relief: "The assurances you give me of applying diligently to your studies, and fulfilling your obligations which are enjoined by your Creator and due to his creatures, are highly pleasing and satisfactory to me. I rejoice in it on two accounts; first, as it is the sure means of laying the foundation of your own happiness, and rendering you, if it should please God to spare your life, a useful member of society hereafter; and secondly, that I may, if I live and enjoy the pleasure, reflect that I have been, in some degree, instrumental in effecting these purposes."[2]

Washington's advice to his grandson captures the meaning that reading had in his own long life. Although Washy did eventually abandon his studies when he found living in his grandfather's shadow too difficult, his grandfather's message did not entirely fall on deaf ears. When Washy published his memoir of life with his grandfather, he included his grandfather's letters, thereby communicating to a wider reading public of young Americans that the father of the nation had placed a premium on education.

Study, in part, made Washington an effective public servant. Moreover, the newly developed concept of republican citizenship mirrored Washington's life. What is most interesting about this fact is that the majority of Washington's admirers, even those who were somewhat close to him, were largely unaware of the extent of his self-directed reading and the significance that it played over the course of his long life in the public spotlight. When considering that Washington consistently occupied positions wherein he was surrounded by individuals who were more qualified than he was, his achievements take on a greater significance. Reading was the way that he compensated for his limited childhood education, and for the most part it served him well.

This book demonstrates the value that Washington placed on reading. Over time Washington absorbed the knowledge that he gleaned from his reading material, and he effectively put it to use. He also learned another lesson from his reading, however, that was equally as important: Washington came to understand the power of the printed word and how that power influenced society and current events.

This book begins with the question of why Washington developed certain reading preferences. Losing his father at age eleven cut short Washington's educational career, and from a young age he had to make his own way. As such, he was careful, especially in his earlier years, to keep this shortcoming hidden from those he was trying to impress. Although Washington could not have known it at the time, his never having had the chance to study abroad the way his older half-brothers did was actually a blessing, for Washington then took a very practically oriented path in terms of his intellectual development that served him well.

Washington was driven. He was always ambitious and was relentless in the pursuit of his goals, a personality trait that never diminished with the passage of time. After his father's death, he set about mastering the knowledge required to become a surveyor so he could earn money and purchase land. His older half-brother Lawrence mentored the young Washington and whetted his appetite for a military career. As a militia officer, Washington turned his intellectual energies briefly toward the rapidly emerging field of the military arts, for he recognized that he was completely unprepared for the rank and position he held. He began reading the books that his British counterparts read; however, when tasked with raising a new Virginia Regiment, Washington turned away from military history and theory in favor of more practical texts on tactics and small unit organization. When it became clear that he was not to get the British commission he had pursued so desperately, Washington abandoned military studies forever, or so he thought.

Instead of military science, Washington developed a keen interest in the science of agriculture, which became one of his great passions. He embarked on a new career as a planter and set his sights on a new goal of making it to the top of provincial Virginian society. After his marriage, he was charged with managing multiple plantations spread throughout Virginia, many of which were not profitable. He therefore studied every available treatise on agriculture with scholarly intensity, making notes and engaging in experiments that would enable him to abandon the unprofitable practice of tobacco cultivation. Washington's goal of ascending to the top of the social ladder was only partly based on economic success. As an elite planter, he was expected to play a role in the public life of the colony. He became a burgess and a vestryman and quickly saw that lawyers and career politicians with considerably more education and experience surrounded him in the House of Burgesses. Washington, who was never comfortable with political power, worked his way up through the ranks of the burgesses by serving on committees on military issues. He took time to do some targeted background reading on some of the major issues of the day, such as the bishop controversy, before speaking up more in the spirited legislative sessions. Eventually he got off the backbench and became one of the more respected burgesses in the assembly.

When tensions began to flare between Great Britain and the colonies,

Washington evolved into a revolutionary ahead of many of his contemporaries. His experiences with the British military bureaucracy and the utterly unregulated system of exchange between planters and their British agents had shown him that the British never considered the colonists as fellow subjects with the same rights as native-born Englishmen. In recognition of his status within Virginia, he was selected a delegate to the Continental Congress in 1774 and again in 1775. When the Second Continental Congress convened in 1775, the colonies clearly were on a collision course for war, and in discussions about raising an army, the delegates debated who should command it. Washington seemed an obvious choice as he was a native-born American with military experience. Other candidates were more qualified, to be sure, but none of them were Americans by birth. Washington was aware of the talk buzzing about him, and the familiar feelings of inadequacy began to build in his mind. He scoured Philadelphia's bookshops, purchased every military treatise he could find, and read them. He would not have long to wait before that useful knowledge was put to the test.

Washington's military reading during the American Revolution is perhaps the most significant because it highlights both his shortcomings and the key to his ultimate success. Always the practical reader, he wasted no time with high-flown military theory and the histories of Europe's greatest wars. He devoted the little spare time he had to reading field manuals and attempting to learn how to raise and maneuver entire armies on wide-open battlefields. His first real attempt to put this knowledge into practice after the British abandoned Boston was in New York, but the battle was a disaster for Washington's fledgling army. This enormous defeat, however, did have a silver lining. The experience of the New York campaign left Washington more than humbled as his glaring shortcomings as a field commander were revealed. In the long term, it was a blessing, for Washington's awareness of his own inadequacies as a tactician kept him from becoming overconfident and risking his precious soldiers in large-scale battles that would have overwhelmed his force. His shortfalls as a commanding general forced him to arrive at what was the correct strategic conclusion: he did not have to win the battles in order to win the war. As Washington was aggressive by nature, he might have been prone to let his fighting spirit rule over his common sense if he had had the European military educational pedigree. The secret to his strategic thinking was that thanks to his lack of a European military education, he was able to evolve into a general who went against the grain of eighteenth-century military convention.

The confederation period saw Washington work to preserve the reputation that he had so carefully constructed over the course of his public life. In this effort, Washington actively sought to become involved in the world of print media, collaborating with historians and biographers who were attempting to generate the first chronicles of the American Revolution. Here Washington did his part to shape the mythology that was already growing up around him. When the time came for him to put his reputation at stake at the Constitutional Convention, Washington was among the first to advocate taking the ratification debate to the newspapers to ensure that the case for the Constitution reached a wider audience. Washington made this suggestion because as a voracious newspaper reader, he understood the power of the press in shaping debates. He never suspected that the same press would one day turn on him.

When he served as the nation's first chief executive, Washington needed to know how the public viewed his presidential performance, for he had no precedent to guide him. He turned first to the newspapers for this information. As an opposition press developed and a fierce newspaper war broke out between the Federalists and Jeffersonians, Washington came under personal attack. Feeling burned, he concluded that he could not trust the papers, so he looked beyond them to printed sermons to ascertain how the people were responding to his policies. The presidency took a significant physical and emotional toll on Washington, who, on entering his final retirement, determined that he had to shore up his legacy for posterity.

One of Washington's chief concerns in his final years was setting the historical record straight. He assembled a massive archive of government documents and records from every phase of his public career. Combined with his voluminous correspondence, this collection would have amounted to the first presidential library had he lived to complete the project. In an extraordinary example of the maturation of his thinking, Washington also decided after years of study, experience, and reflection to emancipate his slaves in his will and support their transition to free society. In this act of manumission he was generations ahead of his time. Washington further sought to make a lasting impact on education by setting up endowments at the primary and university levels so that as he himself had done, future generations would learn to think as Americans.

This book finally explores where Washington did his reading. His library tells us a great deal about his attitude toward the practice of reading and what he expected to derive from it. Understanding Washington's design for his library provides a broader context for examining what he read and how he used the knowledge he gained from it. He sought to gain the most useful information contained in his specially selected reading as rapidly as possible and quickly put it to direct use without distractions. The library at Mount Vernon was Washington's refuge, a place where he could read, think, and plan for the future out of the public eye.

Washington was a practical reader. Previous biographers including Paul Longmore had established that much. The seriousness with which Washington approached the act of reading, however, has been largely overlooked until now. While the purpose of this book is not to remake Washington's image into a sort of closeted scholar, it does argue that reading was a key component behind Washington's success. The real contribution that this volume makes is that it takes one step closer to understanding how Washington's mind worked. While his self-directed reading was not anywhere near that of Jefferson, Franklin, and Adams, Washington outshone them all by combining the knowledge he gained from his reading with his natural talent for leadership into a masterful performance. Washington has always been held up as a shining example of the quintessential American leader. With this book, the understanding of how he rose to that status now has a new dimension. So too does our understanding of how he shaped a new national identity.

SUGGESTIONS FOR FURTHER READING

George Washington is perhaps the most studied man in American history. His first biography was written during his lifetime by David Humphreys, marking the beginning of a continuous influx of new studies that appeared periodically every few years after Washington's death. The American reading public has maintained a healthy interest in Washington to the present day; indeed, there are enough books on Washington currently in print to fill several library shelves. The Washington biographies on sale in bookstores today represent the full spectrum of interpretations of his life and legacy that have swung mercurially back and forth with changing historiographical trends over the years. Similarly while the general public has maintained an interest in both early America and early modern Europe, academic conversations around the question of how best to view and interpret these lost worlds have changed over time. The latest trend that profoundly influenced my work is the emphasis on the Atlantic world and the cultural exchanges that took place between Great Britain and its colonies, as well as the interactions (and often clashes) between the British Empire and its rivals. It's my profound belief that it is not possible to fully understand Washington without properly contextualizing him within his eighteenth-century surroundings. What follows are suggestions for further reading that in my opinion represent the best scholarship and sources available that collectively provide insight into Washington's life and world. For those readers interested in the complete details on the sources I directly consulted in writing this book, please refer to both the endnotes and the bibliography.

Readers interested in traditional "cradle to grave" biographies have several good options. The biggest and newest is Ron Chernow's *Washington: A Life*. The greatest significance of Chernow's work is that he brings to bear the latest primary sources that are still being published through newer editions of edited collections of documents. Still, for all of this new evidence, Chernow does not really depart from the conclusions put forth in the 1960s by the late James Flexner in his sweeping four-volume series on the life of Washington. Moreover, Flexner's view of Washington had largely been shaped by the late Douglas Southall Freeman's seven-volume biography completed in the 1930s. The condensed, single-volume edition of Flexner's work, titled *George Washington: The Indispensable Man* (Boston: Little, Brown, 1974), is a solid introductory biography that is more easily digested than the full four volumes. Likewise, Freeman's magisterial seven volumes are also available in an abbreviated format that is titled simply *Washington*. Joseph Ellis's *His Excellency: George Washington*, John Ferling's *The First of Men*, and Willard Sterne Randall's *George Washington: A Life* also follow Freeman's and Flexner's scholarly lead.

Those readers interested in focusing on Washington as a military officer should refer to the enormous body of scholarship by the late Don Higginbotham. His series of lectures, later published as *George Washington and the American Military Tradition*, offers a highly accessible analysis of Washington's officership and its significance for the development of the American profession of arms. Higginbotham also wrote extensively on the American Revolution; see his *Reconsiderations on the Revolutionary War*. His work greatly informed that of Fred Anderson, whose book *Crucible of War*, in turn, shaped my treatment of Washington's debut as a military officer. For a concise, highly readable evaluation of the quality of Washington's military leadership, see Dave Palmer's *George Washington's Military Genius* and his *George Washington: First in War*. For greater depth on Washington's generalship in the

American Revolution, see John Ferling's *Almost a Miracle* and David Hackett Fischer's *Washington's Crossing*. For a counterbalancing analysis of British leadership in the American Revolution, see Andrew Jackson O'Shaughnessy's *The Men Who Lost America: British Leadership, the American Revolution, and the Fate of the Empire* (New Haven CT: Yale University Press, 2013). For a history of the American Revolution from the British perspective, see Piers Mackesy's *The War for America, 1775–1783*.

For readers interested in exploring Washington's career in politics, the best study of his entry into the House of Burgesses is still Charles Sydnor's *Gentlemen Freeholders*. For studies that focus on Washington's political legacy, see Paul Longmore's *The Invention of George Washington*, John Ferling's *The Ascent of George Washington*, Barry Schwartz's *George Washington*, and Garry Wills's *Cincinnatus*. Finally to underscore the significance of Washington's performance as a political actor on the public stage, see Clifford Geertz's "Centers, Kings, and Charisma" in his *Local Knowledge*.

As noted earlier, before even attempting to assess his legacy I cannot emphasize enough the need to contextualize Washington in his world in order to properly understand him. To that end, for readers interested in learning more about colonial Virginia, see T. H. Breen's *Tobacco Culture*, Rhys Isaac's *The Transformation of Virginia*, and Lorena Walsh's *Motives of Honor, Pleasure, and Profit*. To understand how colonial Virginia's material culture compared with that of the rest of the colonies as well as with England, see Richard Bushman's excellent book *The Refinement of America* and Mark Girouard's *Life in the English Country House*. To gain insight into how Washington and his contemporaries developed their sense of identity within the context of the evolving British identity, see Linda Colley's fascinating study *Britons: Forging the Nation, 1707–1837*, Paul Langford's *Englishness Identified*, and Gerald Newman's *The Rise of English Nationalism*.

For readers looking to broaden their understanding of the changing political circumstances that surrounded American independence and the establishment of the United States, see Bernard Bailyn's classic work *The Ideological Origins of the American Revolution* and the late Pauline Maier's tremendous scholarship including *From Resistance to Revolution* and *Ratification*. See also Brendan McConville's *The King's Three Faces* and Jack Rakove's *The Beginning of National Politics*. Moreover, Gordon Wood's *The Radicalism of the American Revolution* and *The Creation of the American Republic* build off Bailyn's work and have become necessary footnotes for students of early America. Stanley Elkins and Eric McKitrick's *The Age of Federalism* and James Roger Sharp's *American Politics in the Early Republic* are both classic studies that represent the dueling Federalist and Republican interpretations of the political development of the early United States. Following on their heels, a new wave of histories of the political culture of the early republic shed both an important and different sort of light on a well-worn political narrative. Among the best are David Waldstreicher's *In the Midst of Perpetual Fetes*, Douglas Bradburn's *The Citizenship Revolution*, Jay Fleigelman's *Prodigals and Pilgrims*, and Eran Shalev's *Rome Reborn on Western Shores*.

In my work I stress the importance of the religious writings that Washington collected over time. To fully appreciate them, it is essential to understand the religious landscape of eighteenth-century America and the arguments that have been made about the role that religion played in Washington's life. Patricia Bonomi's *Under the Cope of Heaven* is a nice, concise survey of colonial religious life and movements. John Butler's *Awash in a Sea of Faith* is a similar survey that covers the period from the Great Awakening in the 1740s through the Second Great Awakening in the early nineteenth century. It can be complemented with Alan Heimert's classic *Religion and the American Mind*, Thomas S. Kidd's *God of Liberty*, and Mark Noll's *America's God*. Washington's faith has been the subject of much speculation because during his lifetime he never made his precise beliefs explicitly known to anyone. As such, so many poorly structured arguments are perilously anchored on sweeping assumptions made on the basis of circumstantial evidence. That said, two excellent books on the subject are Frank Grizzard Jr.'s *The Ways of Providence* and Mary Thompson's *"In the Hands of a Good Providence."*

In order to fully appreciate the significance of Washington's reading, I delved extensively in the burgeoning fields of the histories of the book and of reading. In graduate school I was introduced to Kevin Sharpe's *Reading Revolutions*, which makes powerful arguments about reading and politics in early modern England based on the extensive marginal notes of Sir William Drake. Sharpe's book planted the seed in my mind to take a closer look at how Washington approached reading as a developmental activity. For an in-depth examination of the history of the book and language in early America, see Hugh Amory and David Hall's *The Colonial Book in the Atlantic World*, Richard Beale Davis's *A Colonial Southern Bookshelf* and his *Intellectual Life in the Colonial South*, Robert Ferguson's *Law and Letters in American Culture* and his *Reading in the Early Republic*, Jay Fliegelman's *Declaring Independence*, Kevin Hayes's *The Road to Monticello*, Michael Kramer's *Imagining Language in America*, Scott Liell's *46 Pages*, Christopher Looby's *Voicing America*, and Jeffrey Pasley's *The Tyranny of Printers*.

An integral part of understanding Washington's approach to reading was to dissect his design for the library at Mount Vernon and specifically to discover how and why he maintained this space as a private sanctuary to which outsiders were not invited. Mount Vernon is very much an architectural self-portrait, and for those interested in learning more about the mansion's design, see Robert F. Dalzell Jr. and Lee Baldwin Dalzell's *George Washington's Mount Vernon* and Alan Greenberg's *George Washington, Architect*. In order to contextualize Washington's Mount Vernon on the wider spectrum of eighteenth-century owner-builders, see Susan Stein's *The Worlds of Thomas Jefferson at Monticello* and Jack McLaughlin's *Jefferson and Monticello*. For broader studies of eighteenth-century English and American architecture, see Henry Glassie's *Folk Housing in Middle Virginia*, John Harris's *The Palladians*, William Kelso's *Kingsmill Plantation, 1619–1800*, and Marcus Whiffen's *The Eighteenth-Century Houses of Williamsburg*.

The advent of electronic databases has significantly enhanced archival research capabilities on topics pertaining to early America and early modern England. Accessing the collections of the edited papers belonging to entire families is now possible with a few clicks of a mouse, and nearly the entire range of printed material from the colonial period is at a researcher's fingertips in the blink of an eye. Washington's papers and diaries, along with those belonging to several of the other founders, are available by digital subscription through the University of Virginia Press and the Library of Congress. Most college and university libraries maintain subscriptions, as do many public libraries and historic archives. These collections are also available in printed volumes; however, that they are still being updated as new documents surface is a powerful inducement to rely instead on the databases whenever possible. Additionally *Eighteenth-Century Collections Online* and *Early American Imprints* are two treasure troves that contain scanned copies of nearly everything that was printed on both sides of the Atlantic during the seventeenth and eighteenth centuries. Approximately 80 to 90 percent of the works contained in Washington's library can be viewed in their original form through these two digital archives. These databases are similarly available by subscriptions. It is beyond question that the breathtakingly fast pace of technological innovation has enriched the study of history by throwing open the archives to all those seeking the same useful knowledge our forefathers themselves once coveted.

NOTES

INTRODUCTION

1. John Adams to Benjamin Rush, March 19, 1812, in Adams, Jefferson, and Rush, *Old Family Letters*, 1:372–73; and John Adams to Benjamin Rush, April 22, 1812, in Adams, Jefferson, and Rush, *Old Family Letters*, 1:377.
2. John Adams quoted in Ferling, *John Adams*, 127.
3. Gordon-Reed, *The Hemingses of Monticello*, 24.
4. Isaacson, *Benjamin Franklin*, 2.
5. Grant, *John Adams*, 1–13.
6. See Freeman's *George Washington*, the seven-volume biography that was long considered the most comprehensive biography on Washington ever written.
7. Freeman, *Washington*, 516.
8. Freeman, *George Washington*.
9. Longmore, *Invention of George Washington*, ix–x.
10. Longmore, *Invention of George Washington*, 217. See also "A List of Books at Mount Vernon, July 23, 1783." The original copy of this list is in the collection of the George Washington Papers at the Library of Congress, Washington DC, and has been made digitally available. It is also reproduced as an appendix in Carroll and Meacham, *Library at Mount Vernon*, 162–63.
11. Sharpe, *Reading Revolutions*, 27.
12. Sharpe, *Reading Revolutions*, 36.
13. Weintraub, *George Washington's Christmas Farewell*; and Wills, *Cincinnatus*.
14. Adams, *Diary and Autobiography*, 1:45–48. Each quotation remains true to the original text. I refrained from updating spelling and grammar throughout the manuscript. Apostrophes are frequently missing, random words tend to be capitalized for no apparent reason, and spelling is nonstandard, especially when Anglicizing names. Modern historians are often dismissive of Washington's intellect simply because of these types of editorial inconsistencies, but I dispute that assumption. To do so fairly, I have kept all quotations in

their original forms throughout, regardless of whom the author was, to show these errors were the norm in eighteenth-century writing.

15. Washington used the word "defective" to describe his education on several occasions throughout his life in correspondence with his closest friends and associates. For one such example, see Washington to David Humphreys, July 25, 1785, in Washington, *Papers of George Washington*, digital ed. Additionally Washington was a keen supporter of the further development of American universities. See Washington to George Chapman, December 15, 1784, in Washington, *Papers of George Washington*, digital ed.; and Washington to the President and Professors of the College of William and Mary, October 27, 1781, in Washington, *Writings*, 23:276–77. See Washington's "First Annual Message to Congress," January 8, 1790, in Washington, *Papers of George Washington*, digital ed. These sentiments, when combined, reflect both that Washington was conscious of the limits of his own education and that he placed a premium on education as the means to developing a prosperous American society.

1. PURSUING USEFUL KNOWLEDGE

1. The notebook that contained Washington's manuscript of *The Rules of Civility* went unnoticed for nearly a century until his papers were purchased for the Library of Congress in 1849. By then, reverent biographers began to explore the manuscript and its possibilities. Jared Sparks misused the manuscript first in his biography. Later Washington Irving sensationalized it in order to create a homespun origin for Washington's *Rules of Civility*. By the 1880s an interest in the study of the subject of etiquette had developed, and the *Rules of Civility* was reprinted both in England and the United States. American publishers began to use Washington's manuscript as a way to boost sales, rather than simply selling the French translation that Washington used. Dr. J. M. Toner's 1888 work, *George Washington's Rules of Civility*, revealed the full extent of Washington's writing, including his abbreviations, capitalization, and nonstandard spelling. Toner also left gaps where mice had eaten away dozens of the rules on several pages. See Washington, *George Washington's Rules of Civility* (2005), 13.

2. Flexner, *George Washington*, 1:17.

3. Flexner, *George Washington*, 1:19–25; and Custis, *Recollections and Private Memoirs*, 130. Much of what is known about Mary Ball Washington comes from anecdotal evidence. Her few surviving letters are littered with errors, well beyond what was considered normal in the eighteenth century, indicating that she was not well educated. Given her middling social status, it

is likely that she was taught to read and write passably, was given ample religious instruction (it was a mother's responsibility to teach religion to her children in Virginia), and was trained in the necessary female tasks of running a home and rearing children. See Chernow, *Washington*, 5–6. Girls' education in Virginia had not changed greatly by the time Martha Washington was born, so she would have been instructed in the same things that Mary Ball Washington had been. Evidence, however, suggests that she was more highly educated. See Brady, *Martha Washington*, 23–25.

4. Washington, *Quotations of George Washington*, 7.

5. Lawrence Washington cited in Custis, *Recollections and Private Memoirs*, 131.

6. Humphreys, *Life of General Washington*, 6–7.

7. Humphreys, *Life of General Washington*.

8. Humphreys, *Life of General Washington*.

9. Custis, *Recollections and Private Memoirs*, 141; and Thompson, *"In the Hands,"* 16–20.

10. Griffin, *Catalogue*, 497–503.

11. Flexner, *George Washington*, 1:20.

12. Washington's fear of criticism is borne out in his correspondence over the course of his public life. From his first days in the Virginia Regiment, he developed a bad habit of deflecting blame onto others whenever possible when reporting a defeat or some other unfortunate event. He maintained this habit throughout the Revolution. For example, in his official report to Congress on the losses of Forts Washington and Lee he squarely blamed his subordinate commanders, including Nathanael Greene, while completely neglecting to note the decisions he made that contributed to the defeat. During his presidency when the partisan press began to attack him, he vented his frustration and anger to his close associates in a more outward manner than he had in his younger years.

13. Flexner, *George Washington*, 1:23. In his young adulthood Washington also read Henry Fielding's *Tom Jones* and Tobias Smollett's *The Adventures of Peregrine Pickle*. These novels are among those listed on the 1764 inventory of the books at Mount Vernon that Washington compiled. See the list in Washington, *Papers of George Washington*, digital ed.

14. See the George Washington Papers at the Library of Congress (reel 1, Washington Papers Microfilm), Washington DC. The source can also be found in John C. Fitzpatrick, *George Washington Himself* (Indianapolis: Bobbs-Merrill, 133), 28.

15. Flexner, *George Washington*, 1:23.

16. There is evidence in Washington's surviving papers that he largely taught himself to survey through trial and error. He ran his first lines at his childhood home, Ferry Farm. His sketches and calculations survive in his notebooks. Biographers Freeman, Flexner, and Chernow all attest that Washington had an aptitude for surveying and before long was being paid by neighbors for his work. His first earnings were three pounds and two shillings. Surveyors in Virginia were officially licensed through the College of William and Mary after making an application and presumably submitting a sample of their work to prove competency. It was possible to apprentice to an experienced surveyor; however, this practice did not appear to be as long or as formal as apprenticeships for other skilled trades, which often required more than seven years of training. There is insufficient evidence to support the claim that Washington was ever formally apprenticed to any surveyor. What is documented is that he conducted his first extensive surveying trip with George William Fairfax and several others from March to April 13, 1748, to chart and subdivide Lord Fairfax's land grant from the crown. See Washington, "A Journal of My Journey over the Mountains Began Fryday the 11th of March 1747/8," in Washington, *Papers of George Washington*, digital ed.

17. Humphreys, *Life of General Washington*, 7.

18. Custis, *Recollections and Private Memoirs*, 155; and Ferling, *First of Men*, 10.

19. Ferling, *First of Men*, 52. The particular details of Lawrence Washington's will can also be found in more extensive detail in Freeman, *George Washington*, 1:325.

20. Flexner, *George Washington*, 1:53.

21. Freeman, *George Washington*, 1:275.

22. Washington, *Journal of Major George Washington*, 21.

23. Washington, *Journal of Major George Washington*, 2.

24. Washington, *Journal of Major George Washington*. See also Dorothy Twohig's editor's note in Washington, *Diaries of George Washington* (1999), 33. The journal was printed in various colonial newspapers, including the *Md. Gazette*, March 21 and March 28, 1754; and *Boston Gazette*, April 16–May 21, 1754. On February 15, 1754, the journal was delivered to the House of Burgesses, and the members voted to award Washington £50 for his efforts.

25. Gruber, *Books and the British Army*, 1–53.

26. See the correspondence between Washington and William Fairfax in 1754 in Washington, *Papers of George Washington*, digital ed.

27. Freeman, *George Washington*, 1:354.

28. Washington, "Letter to Governor Horatio Sharpe, April 24, 1754," in Washington, *Papers of George Washington*, Colonial series, 1:86.

29. Anderson, *Crucible of War*, 60.

30. Anderson, *Crucible of War*, 52–53.

31. Washington, diary entry, May 27, 1754, in Washington, *Diaries, 1748–1799*, 1:87.

32. Anderson, *Crucible of War*, 53–57.

33. Anderson, *Crucible of War*, 53–57. Anderson traced the other accounts of the events at Jumonville's glen, some of which supported Washington's version while others contradicted it. Contrecoeur, a French soldier who escaped the glen before the massacre was complete, wrote the French account, which was published in Europe at the beginning of the European phase of the Seven Years' War. It was reprinted first in London as *Memorial Containing a Summary View* and then again in New York in 1757. For the original see Grenier, *Papiers Contrecoeur*. Contrecoeur insisted that the French party had been asleep or had only recently woken up at the time of the British attack, thereby making the point that the attack was unprovoked — a direct challenge to Washington's claim that he was acting in self-defense. This account would seem to indicate that Contrecoeur escaped without putting his shoes on first. Contrecoeur's evidence is corroborated by an Indian messenger who came to Washington at Great Meadows on June 5 and reported having "met a Frenchman who had made his Escape in the Time of M. de Jumonville's Action, he was without Shoes or Stockings, and scarce able to walk; however, we let him pass, not knowing they had been attacked" (Washington, *Diaries of George Washington* [1976–79], 1:91).

34. Lengel, *General George Washington*, 39–41.

35. Gruber, *Books and the British Army*, 147–49; Bernard, *Remarks on the Modern Fortification*; and Bisset, *Theory and Construction*.

36. Humphreys, *Life of General Washington*, 12–13.

37. Humphreys, *Life of General Washington*, 42–46; and Anderson, *Crucible of War*, 63–64.

38. "Articles of Capitulation, July 3, 1754," in Washington, *Papers of George Washington*, Colonial series, 1:165–66. The description of the circumstances of the British surrender are taken from the "Point of Woods" account by George Washington and James Mackay, "The Capitulation of Fort Necessity, July 19, 1754," in Washington, *Papers of George Washington*, Colonial series, 1:160. For the French description of the events, see Contrecoeur, *Memorial Containing a Summary View*, 99–100.

39. Humphreys, *Life of General Washington*, 13.

40. Anderson, *Crucible of War*, 64.

41. George Washington, Letter to William Fitzhugh, November 15, 1754, in *Papers of George Washington*, Colonial series, 1:226.

42. Longmore, *Invention of George Washington*, 27. See also Lengel, *General George Washington*, 49–62; and Anderson, *Crucible of War*, 94–107.

43. Anderson, *Crucible of War*, 94–107. For further evidence of Braddock's dislike for colonials, see Pargellis, *Military Affairs in North America*. For further evidence of Braddock and Washington's senior-subordinate relationship, see Washington, *Papers of George Washington*, Colonial series, 1:267, 272, 278, 312, 320–23; Washington, *Papers of George Washington*, Colonial series, 4:89; and Freeman, *George Washington*, 2:52–53.

44. Humphreys, *Life of General Washington*, 19.

45. Longmore, *Invention of George Washington*, 29. See also Washington, *Papers of George Washington*, Colonial series, for the following: congratulatory letters from Dinwiddie, July 26, 1755, 1:344–45; from William Fairfax, July 26, 1755, 1:345–46; from Sally Fairfax, Ann Spearing, and Elizabeth Dent, July 26, 1755, 1:346; from Charles Lewis, August 9, 1755, 1:357–58; from Philip Ludwell, August 8, 1755, 1:356–57; from John Martin, August 30, 1755, 2:12; and from Christopher Gist, October 15, 1755, 2:115. Congratulations from England came first from Washington's uncle John Ball in a letter dated September 5, 1755, in Washington, *Papers of George Washington*, Colonial series, 2:15. All of these documents from *Papers of George Washington* are also available in the digital edition.

46. Longmore, *Invention of George Washington*, 36. See also Washington, *Papers of George Washington*, Colonial series, for Washington to Andrew Lewis, September 6, 1755, 2:23–24; to Adam Stephen, September 11, 1755, 2:27; Memorandum, September 11, 1755, 2:28; and Address, January 8, 1756, 2:257. And see Instructions to Company Captains, July 29, 1757, Washington, *Papers of George Washington*, Colonial series, 4:344. Washington must have anticipated the need to train himself for future service, for during the Braddock campaign he took the time to copy out general orders for his personal reference. See Washington, Letter to Robert Orme, July 28, 1755, in *Papers of George Washington*, Colonial series, 1:347, 348n7; and Enclosure of invoice to Richard Washington, December 6, 1755, placing an order for a copy of Bland's *Treatise of Military Discipline*, in Washington, *Papers of George Washington*, Colonial series, 2:209. He most likely also read *Julius Caesar's Commentaries* and other works from ancient military writers and

theorists on the suggestion of his mentor William Fairfax. For the refer-
ence, see the letter from William Fairfax, May 13–14, 1756, in Washington,
Papers of George Washington, Colonial series, 3:125. These documents from
Papers of George Washington are also available in the digital edition. Bland's
Treatise was considered to be the bible of the British army, and *Caesar's
Commentaries* was required reading for any British officer aspiring to high
command. See Gruber, *Books and the British Army*.

47. Bland, *Treatise of Military Discipline*, 144.

48. Monck, Duke of Albemarle, *Observations*.

49. Machiavelli, *Libro della Arte della Guerra*. See also Peter Withorne's 1573
English translation of the book, which was reprinted several times in the
eighteenth century. The most recent edition that Washington's contemporaries would likely have read was published in 1732. See Gruber, *Books and
the British Army*, 194.

50. Gruber, *Books and the British Army*, 225.

51. Gruber, *Books and the British Army*, 3.

52. Gruber, *Books and the British Army*, 163.

53. Gruber, *Books and the British Army*, 34–45.

54. Lengel, *General George Washington*, 77.

55. Longmore, *Invention of George Washington*, 39.

56. Longmore, *Invention of George Washington*, 41.

57. For Washington's opinions on the decision to reinforce Fort Cumberland
at the expense of other frontier positions, see Washington, *Papers of George
Washington*, Colonial series, for the letter to Dinwiddie, September 23, 1756,
3:414–15; to Lt. Col. Adam Stephen, October 23, 1756, 3:440–42; Remarks on
the Council of War, November 5, 1756, 3:450–52; to Dinwiddie, November
24, 1756, 4:32; from Dinwiddie, September 30, 1756, 3:424; from Dinwiddie,
October 26, 1756, 3:443; from Dinwiddie, November 16, 1756, 4:26; Minutes
of Council, November 15, 1756, 4:27–28; from Dinwiddie, December 10, 1756,
4:50–55; to Capt. William Bronaugh, December 17, 1756, 4:59; and to Dinwiddie, December 19, 1756, 4:62–63. All of these documents are also available in
the digital edition.

58. For Washington's requests for leave, in Washington, *Papers of George Washington*, Colonial series, see his letter to Dinwiddie, December 19, 1756, 4:64–65;
from Dinwiddie, December 27, 1756, 4:72; and from Dinwiddie, February 2,
1757, 4:107. The documents are also available in the digital edition.

59. Washington to John Campbell, Earl of Loudon, January 10, 1757, 4:79–93; to
Capt. James Cunningham, January 28, 1757, 4:105–7; and from Cunningham,

February 27, 1757, 4:111–12, in Washington, *Papers of George Washington*, Colonial series. The documents are also available in the digital edition.

60. Washington to John Campbell, Earl of Loudon, January 10, 1757, in Washington, *Papers of George Washington*, Colonial series, 4:79–93. The document is also available in the digital edition.

61. Washington to Dinwiddie, March 10, 1757, in Washington, *Papers of George Washington*, Colonial series, 4:112–15. It can now be found in the digital edition as well. The document is also available in the digital edition.

62. Dinwiddie, *Official Records*, 2:184,191; and Flexner, *George Washington*, 1:174–75. After the meeting with Washington, Loudoun sent a curtly written letter back to Dinwiddie that communicated the orders issued during the meeting and made clear to the lieutenant governor in no uncertain terms that none of Washington's wishes were granted. This communiqué is noteworthy because it exemplifies the increasingly negative attitudes some British imperial officials harbored toward colonials during the Seven Years' War.

63. Longmore, *Invention of George Washington*, 49.

64. Washington to Francis Fauquier, December 9, 1758, in Fauquier and Reese, *Official Papers*, 130–31. For more on Washington's career as a burgess, see Sydnor, *Gentlemen Freeholders*, 19–25, 41–58, 68–70, 73.

65. Thomas Jefferson to William Jones, January 2, 1814, in Jefferson, *Writings of Thomas Jefferson*, 14:48.

66. McConville, *King's Three Faces*, 7, 82, 86. See also Bushman, *King and People*, 5; Langford, *Englishness Identified*, 2, 19, 268, 315; Wilson, *Sense of the People*, 23; Wilson, "Empire, Trade, and Popular Politics," 94–95; and Newman, *Rise of English Nationalism*, 161.

67. Humphreys, *Life of General Washington*, 6. Humphreys provides an overview of Washington's education, and since this biography was written with Washington's cooperation and heavy editing, it can be safely concluded that the reference to Washington's study of history is true. While his surviving schoolbooks do not provide a wealth of evidence as to which history books he read, a reasonable assumption can be made based on the knowledge of what histories were the most popular in Virginia at the time. The study of ancient Greek and Roman history as well as British history was popular from the seventeenth century on. Among the favored British history books during Washington's youth were Sir Walter Raleigh's *History of the World*, William Camden's *Britannia*, Sir Richard Baker's *Chronicle of the Kings of England*, and Bishop White Kennett's *Complete History of England*. See Davis, *Colonial Southern Bookshelf*, 35–37. Given the enduring popularity of these books, it

is entirely probable that either Washington would have been assigned or directed to read at least one if not more of them or he would have heard about these books (and British history in general) from his older half-brothers, who had been educated in England and oversaw young Washington's education for a time. It is also likely that as a teenager he was schooled in British history from William Fairfax and Thomas, Sixth Lord Fairfax, who was the first member of the aristocracy with whom Washington became acquainted.

68. See Colley, *Britons*, 1, 5, for the argument that nationalism is partially contingent on the ability to define oneself against another. This argument explains to some extent the surge of patriotic sentiment that fueled the American colonists before, during, and immediately after the Seven Years' War. T. H. Breen builds on this idea and applies it directly to Washington and his fellow Virginians in *Tobacco Culture*, xiv.

69. The average colonial library in seventeenth-century Virginia had fewer than ten books. The most common titles were the Bible, *The Book of Common Prayer, The Whole Duty of Man, The Compleat Lawyer, History of England, The Young Secretary's Guide*, and *The Family Physician and the House Apothecary*. See Davis, *Colonial Southern Bookshelf*, 24.

70. For the best comprehensive works that analyze and compare education and private libraries in seventeenth- and eighteenth-century Virginia, see Wright, *First Gentlemen of Virginia*, 95–155; and Davis, *Intellectual Life in the Colonial South*, 1:257–386, 2:489–627, and 3:1307–1507.

71. Thomas Jefferson quoted in McLaughlin, *Jefferson and Monticello*, 43. Herein also is a description of the types of entertainments Fauquier hosted and the people he included in those events. Not entirely surprising, Washington was not among those who engaged with Fauquier in academically oriented conversations.

72. Franklin, *Autobiography of Benjamin Franklin*, 13–36.

73. Franklin, *Autobiography of Benjamin Franklin*, 13–36. See also Isaacson, *Benjamin Franklin*, 126; and Wood, *Americanization of Benjamin Franklin*, 41.

74. See Isaacson, *Benjamin Franklin*, 122–47; and Wood, *Radicalism of the American Revolution* (1991), 77, 85–86, 199.

75. Girouard, *Life in the English Country House*, 178–80, 234–36.

76. Isaacson, *Benjamin Franklin*, 134–39; *The Gentleman's Magazine* (London), January and May 1750; Franklin, *Experiments and Observations on Electricity*; Abbé Guillaume Mazéas to Stephen Hales, May 20, 1752, in Franklin, *Papers of Benjamin Franklin*, 4:315; and Franklin, *Autobiography*, 132–35.

77. Franklin, *Autobiography*, 149–50.

78. Isaacson, *Benjamin Franklin*, 222–32.

79. Benjamin Franklin to Joseph Galloway, August 22, 1772, in Franklin, *Papers of Benjamin Franklin*, 19:275.

80. Wood, *Americanization of Benjamin Franklin*, 141. See also "The Hutchinson Letters, 1768–1769," in Franklin, *Papers of Benjamin Franklin*, 20:550.

81. Benjamin Franklin to Thomas Cushing, December 2, 1772, in Franklin, *Papers of Benjamin Franklin*, 19:411–13.

82. Benjamin Franklin to Thomas Cushing, December 2, 1772, in Franklin, *Papers of Benjamin Franklin*, 19:411–13. See also Wood, *Americanization of Benjamin Franklin*, 142; and Bailyn, *Ordeal of Thomas Hutchinson*, 237. See also Benjamin Franklin to William Franklin, October 6, 1773, in Franklin, *Papers of Benjamin Franklin*, 20:437, 439.

83. Wood, *Americanization of Benjamin Franklin*, 146; and "The Final Hearing before the Privy Council, January 29, 1774," in Franklin, *Papers of Benjamin Franklin*, 20:60, 47–49.

84. Wood, *Americanization of Benjamin Franklin*, 147–50.

85. Wood, *Americanization of Benjamin Franklin*, 172–73.

86. "Birth" was the term used during the period. Social standing was determined more by place and circumstances of birth than simply ancestral roots because of the cross-border mixing that occurred after the Act of Union officially created Great Britain. Additionally, it became increasingly possible in both Britain and America to overcome one's circumstances and climb the social ladder through the gentry classes. Birth determined where one started on the ladder and how much he or she would have to climb.

87. Custis, *Recollections and Private Memoirs*, 171.

88. Davis, *Intellectual Life*, 2:555–60.

2. PROVINCIAL READING

1. Invoice to Robert Cary and Company, Williamsburg, May 1, 1759, in Washington, *Papers of George Washington*, digital ed.

2. Invoice to Robert Cary and Company, Williamsburg, May 1, 1759; and George Washington to Robert Cary and Company, Virginia, June 12, 1759, in Washington, *Papers of George Washington*, digital ed.

3. Griffin, *Catalogue*, 544.

4. Duhamel du Monceau, *Practical Treatise of Husbandry*. Washington's copy with the marginalia is housed at the Virginia Historical Society, Richmond.

5. For a broader context as to the economic realities and their social ramifications facing Virginia's elite planters throughout the eighteenth century,

see Evans, *A "Topping People,"* 90–176; and Walsh, *Motives of Honor,* 472–538. According to the evidence Walsh cites, Washington seemed to set a trend for diversification that his fellow planters started to follow. The other prominent planter family that came closest to mirroring what Washington was doing at Mount Vernon was that of the Carters, who interestingly also engrossed themselves in the study of agriculture. They struggled more with grain cultivation, probably because of the quality of the soil at their plantations and because they were trying to exactly replicate the latest English practices, which did not always work in North America. Here Washington differs from the Carters because he worked through European agriculture books and experimented to develop the necessary adaptations that had to be made because of the geographic and climate-related differences between America and Europe.

6. Griffin, *Catalogue,* 522, 544.

7. Custis, *Recollections and Private,* 167.

8. For an example of Washington's use of a direct quote from Shakespeare, see Washington to George Washington Parke Custis, November 28, 1796, in Custis, *Recollections and Private,* 76. Washington used biblical allusions in both public and private writings throughout his adult life. They are explored more completely later in this chapter and chapters 3 and 4.

9. The original list as compiled by Washington's executors — Tobias Lear, Thomson Mason, Thomas Peter, and William H. Foote — was deposited with his will and the schedule of his property at the Fairfax, Virginia, Court House. The original will is still there; however, the additional documents, including the book list, were scattered during the Civil War. John A. Washington, the last private owner of Mount Vernon, had a copy of the original list, which he shared with Edward Everett, who printed it in his *Life of George Washington* in 1860. All subsequent printings of Washington's book list stem from Everett's reproduction. The list contains numerous spelling errors and abbreviated titles, and it is impossible to know whether the appraisers or the various historians who have reproduced the list since 1860 committed those errors. After Everett, Benson J. Lossing was the next historian to publish the list, which he claimed to have obtained from the Fairfax Court House, but most likely it was based on Everett's work. Lossing's list has several inconsistencies in spelling and abbreviation from both Everett's list and Griffin's list. Neither Everett nor Lossing detail whether each book bears Washington's autograph, bookplate, or any other significant signatures or markings. That information was added by Griffin, who personally studied both the portion

of Washington's collection that is now at the Boston Athenaeum and the various auction lists' detailed descriptions of the rest of Washington's books that were sold off intermittently throughout the 1870s. Presumably the auctioneers wanted to advertise which books had either Washington's signature or that of other members of his family in order to raise prices. Griffin additionally cross-referenced the list with Washington's expense accounts and correspondence to determine which books were purchased by Washington, which ones were gifts, and what if any additional pertinent information could be gleaned. As only a third of Washington's library is housed at the Boston Athenaeum and a few volumes are in Mount Vernon's special collections, with the rest having been sold to private collectors at auction, Griffin's work is the most accurate complete listing that we have to work from. See also Lossing, *Home of Washington*, 376–92; and Everett, *Life of George Washington*, 286–317.

10. Griffin, *Catalogue*, 498–500.
11. See Fischer, *Albion's Seed*, 334; Davis, *Colonial Southern Bookshelf*, 65–90; Davis, *Intellectual Life*, 580–84; Wright, *First Gentlemen*, 134; and Thompson, "In the Hands," 17–18.
12. Grizzard, *Ways of Providence*, 1. Of all the work done on the subject of Washington and religion, Grizzard's offers the most concise and plausible argument by stripping away the Parson Weems–inspired myths and arguing that while Washington was a practicing Episcopalian, there is simply not enough evidence to suggest that he was either a Diest or a deeply spiritual Christian. Furthermore, Grizzard argues, it is beyond doubt that Washington believed that religion was good for society, and inherent in that belief was toleration.
13. Fischer, *Albion's Seed*, 336.
14. Blackall, *Sufficiency of a Standing Revelation*, 18.
15. Comber, *Short Discourses*, 2.
16. Sheffling and Shattuck, *Oxford Guide*, 1.
17. Evidence exists that Washington read at least some issues of *The Spectator* while a schoolboy, as notes in his early hand in his commonplace books attest. Those commonplace books are currently in the archives of the Library of Congress and are available on microfilm. Washington's copy of the seventh edition of Chevalier Ramsay's *Travels of Cyrus* is in the Boston Athenaeum and bears Washington's youthful signature on the title page. It makes sense that he would have read this book on the ancient world while a schoolboy, for as an adolescent he would have been beginning the typical classical education before his father's death brought his education to an abrupt end. It further makes sense that Washington would have been exposed to and encouraged

to read Lord Anson's *Voyage Round the World* when it looked as if he might actually embark on a career in the Royal Navy, for the book catalogs the 1739 expedition against the Spanish in their ports. Washington's copy, a sixth edition of the book, is in the Boston Athenaeum and bears his autograph in a youthful hand. This popular book was published in fifteen editions. Travel narratives had captured the attention of Englishmen since the days of Richard Hakluyt's promotional efforts in Elizabeth I's court. See Mancall, *Hakluyt's Promise*, 86–92.

18. Brown, *Knowledge Is Power*, 62.

19. Flexner, *George Washington*, 1:30–31.

20. The surname Schomberg is the Anglicized version of the original, von Schönberg. The umlaut was dropped from the spelling of the name in the panegyric's title when it was published. In English sources, the name most commonly appears as Schomberg.

21. Email exchange with Ted Crackel, March 8, 2011; and de Luzancy, *Panegyrick*.

22. Panegyrics commemorating the lives of great men were popular on both sides of the Atlantic in both the seventeenth and eighteenth centuries. However, by the early 1800s, critics complained that such works obscured the true character of the subject in the interest of gaining patronage and increasing sales. See Casper, *Constructing American Lives*, 35.

23. Griffin, *Catalogue*, 550. According to Griffin's catalogue and the 1764 list of books at Mount Vernon, the fact that this book belonged first to William Fairfax was confirmed by his autograph, along with that of Edward Washborne, on the title page. The book was sold at auction to private buyers twice in 1876 and February 1891; so Griffin's account, which is based on the auction records, is the best evidence available.

24. Gruber, *Books and the British Army*, 149–50. See also Houlding, *Fit for Service*, 182. Houlding declares Bland's book was "the best known of all eighteenth-century military treatises in the English language."

25. Hamilton, *Letters to Washington*, 1:231–32, 256; and Gruber, *Books and the British Army*, 154–55.

26. Flexner, *George Washington*, 1:185–87.

27. During his final months in command of the Virginia Regiment in 1758, Mount Vernon was undergoing a major renovation that Washington had designed personally. In his absence, Washington asked George William Fairfax to supervise the project. Washington sent Fairfax repeated letters asking numerous, detailed questions on its progress. Fairfax, for his part, faithfully answered them. See the exchange of letters between Washington and George

William Fairfax during the summer and early fall of 1758 in Washington, *Papers of George Washington*, digital ed.

28. Flexner, *George Washington*, 1:193.
29. Park, *List of Architectural Books*, 49–75.
30. "Appendix D: Inventory of the Books in the Estate c. 1759," in Washington, *Papers of George Washington*. This list includes all the books in the Custis estate that Washington had transported to Mount Vernon for Jacky. Almost all of the books belonging to Daniel Parke Custis had been inherited from his father, John Custis. The list is in Washington's own hand. He most likely made the list at the Custis townhouse in Williamsburg. The appraisers valued the books in the townhouse as being worth £25 and the books at White House in New Kent County at £4. Jacky Custis took possession of the books when he came of age. It is not known precisely how many he read or used at King's College throughout the course of his studies, which he abandoned. When Jacky died of typhoid in 1781, his executors wrote to Washington on March 20, 1782, asking him if he wanted to keep the books or to sell them. Washington replied on April 20, "I had no particular reasons for keeping and handing down to his Son the Books of the late Colo. [Daniel Parke] Custis, saving that I thought it would be taking the advantage of a low appraisement to make them my own property at it; and that to sell them was not an object, as they might be useful to him [young Custis]." Nearly all of the books listed in the probate records of Jacky Custis's will were subsequently listed in the catalog of Washington's books made after his death in 1799. With the exception of two Custis books that bore both Daniel Parke Custis's signature and Washington's underneath, there is no indication that Washington read any of them. Washington encountered multiple problems with the management of the Custis estate. There were thorny legal problems, and the actions of inefficient plantation overseers negatively impacted the quality of the crops being produced on the Custis plantations. See Walsh, *Motives of Honor*, 447–48; and Washington to Bartholomew Dandridge, April 20, 1782, *George Washington Papers at the Library of Congress, 1741–1799*, Series 3, Varick Transcripts, Library of Congress, Washington DC, http://memory.loc.gov/cgi-bin/ampage?collId=mgw3&file Name=mgw3h/gwpage002.db&recNum=298&tempFile=./temp/~ammem _4tqk&filecode=mgw&next_filecode=mgw&prev_filecode=mgw&item num=19&ndocs=100.
31. Thompson, *"In the Hands,"* 40.
32. Breen, *Tobacco Culture*, 80.

33. Invoice to Robert Cary and Company, Williamsburg, May 1, 1759, in Washington, *Papers of George Washington*, digital ed.

34. Washington to Robert Cary and Company, Virginia, June 12, 1759, in Washington, *Papers of George Washington*, digital ed.

35. In Washington, *Papers of George Washington*, digital ed., see Washington to Robert Cary and Company, Virginia, October 24, 1760; and Invoice from Robert Cary and Company, March 31, 1761.

36. Breen, *Tobacco Culture*, 82–83; and Longmore, *Invention of George Washington*, 68–72.

37. Washington, *Diaries*, 1:211–344, 2:49–172.

38. Dorothy Twohig, introduction, in Washington, *Diaries of George Washington* (1999), xi.

39. Dorothy Twohig, introduction, in Washington, *Diaries of George Washington* (1999), i.

40. See Washington's diary entry, August 3, 1771, in Washington, *Diaries, 1748–1799*, 31.

41. See Washington's diary entry for June 19, 1773, in Washington, *Diaries, 1748–1799*, 115.

42. Washington to Burwell Bassett, June 20, 1773, in Washington, *Papers of George Washington*, digital ed.

43. Griffin, *Catalogue*, 544.

44. Duhamel, *Practical Treatise*, 110.

45. Duhamel, *Practical Treatise*, iii.

46. Washington to Robert Cary and Company, Williamsburg, May 1, 1759, in Washington, *Papers of George Washington*, digital ed. It is but one example of Washington's excessive spending, which began shortly after his marriage. An examination of most of his orders with Cary and Company reveals that sinking deeper into debt irritated Washington greatly but did not curtail his shopping sprees. He was too much a man of his social world to abandon the consumption of luxury goods on a grand scale. Instead, as a typical Virginian, he blamed Cary and Company along with British taxation policies for his mounting bills.

47. In today's money, £2,000 would be equivalent to $323,043.02.

48. Washington to Robert Stewart, April 27, 1763, in Washington, *Papers of George Washington*, digital ed.

49. Sydnor, *Gentlemen Freeholders*, 3–9.

50. Wright, *First Gentlemen*, 152–53; and for a more complete treatment of the preponderance of books by genre in private colonial libraries, see Davis,

Intellectual Life, 579–84. Concentrating on the seventeenth and early eighteenth centuries, Wright argues that Virginians at that time placed a greater premium on utilitarian books than on belles lettres. Typically Virginians preferred books on religion, law, and statecraft. Wright also highlights that Virginians relied on older books that had already been tested by time. As the eighteenth century dawned and the elite planters were established on profitable estates with inherited wealth, they were able to devote more of their time and attention to education and refining their reading tastes. The result was a much greater emphasis in the eighteenth century on the classics, languages, history, the study of English common law, natural philosophy, and belles lettres. Davis picks up on Wright's argument and examines the contents of private libraries and the developing trends in education in the South much more thoroughly. The larger private libraries belonged to such men as William Fitzhugh, Richard Lee II, and Richard Wormley II, each of whom owned more than three hundred volumes. The largest library in Virginia belonged to William Byrd II of Westover, who amassed a library of more than three thousand volumes.

51. Wright, *First Gentlemen*, 117; and McMurtrie, *Beginnings of the Printing Press*, 7–9.

52. Resolution of the House of Burgesses, February 26, 1759, in Washington, *Papers of George Washington*, digital ed.; Flexner, *George Washington*, 1:227; and Ferling, *Ascent of George Washington*, 51.

53. For a discussion of the expectation for members of Virginia's social and economic elite to serve in politics, see Evans, *A "Topping People,"* 23–89.

54. Capt. Robert Stewart to Washington, two letters on March 12, 1761, in Hamilton, *Letters to Washington*, 3:203, 204–10. The first letter records Washington's request for information from Stewart on the status of the Virginia Regiment; the second letter contains that information. Stewart's letter of April 6 mentions the information that Washington sent him on March 27 regarding the expectation that the bill would pass (in Hamilton, *Letters to Washington*). See also Longmore, *Invention of George Washington*, 62–63. Longmore points out that these letters contradict Douglas Southall Freeman's argument that at this point Washington was apathetic in military matters. Freeman does not even mention these letters in his discussion of the 1761 legislative sessions. It is unusual as they would have been available to him at the time he was completing his biography.

55. Kennedy and McIlwane, *Journals of the House of Burgesses, 1761–65*:45, 92, 94, 97, 100–101, 111, 117, 140.

56. Toland, *Oceana of James Harrington*, 183.
57. Adams, Diary, August 1, 1761, in *Works of John Adams*, 2:131.
58. Although Washington was initially elected to the House of Burgesses before his resignation from the Virginia Regiment and his marriage to Martha Custis, he was not a very active member because his military duties mostly kept him away from Williamsburg during his final campaign in the Seven Years' War. It was only after his resignation and his marriage that he began attending sessions with greater frequency. His increased presence would no doubt have required him to develop a greater knowledge of the political issues of the day grounded in historical context.
59. In Washington, *Papers of George Washington*, digital ed., see the order from Washington to Robert Cary and Company, November 15, 1762; and the invoice of goods shipped from Cary and Company, April 13, 1763.
60. In Adams, *Adams-Jefferson Letters*, see John Adams to Thomas Jefferson, December 25 and July 15, 1813, 2:410, 357.
61. Fabel, "The Patriotic Briton," 100.
62. Colburn, *Lamp of Experience*, 205, 208, 210, 211, 216, 222, 229.
63. Smollett, *Complete History of England*, 1:228.
64. Smollett, *Complete History of England*, 1:257–59.
65. Pocock, *Ancient Constitution*, 31, 33.
66. "A List of Books at Mount Vernon, 1764," in Washington, *Papers of George Washington*, digital ed.
67. "A List of Books at Mount Vernon, 1764," in Washington, *Papers of George Washington*, digital ed. See also Griffin, *Catalogue*, 527–31. After Washington's death, Washington's law books passed to his nephew Supreme Court justice Bushrod Washington. Although the copies of *The Landlord's Law* and the *Attorney's Pocket Book* do not bear Washington's autograph, Bushrod and Lawrence Washington certified that they did in fact belong to their uncle. Moreover, a comparison of Washington's 1764 list to the one he made of the Custis books in 1759 indicates that he obtained his copies of Pearce's and Meriton's books from the Custis estate. It is interesting to consider that Washington declined to keep the entire extensive Custis library for himself; rather he selected the volumes that had immediate, practical use. It is possible that he began referring to them when he was entangled in the lengthy probation of Daniel Parke Custis's estate and therefore felt entitled to use them as opposed to the rest, which he set aside for Jacky Custis's future education.
68. Kidd, *God of Liberty*, 50–51.
69. Kidd, *God of Liberty*, 52.

70. Isaac, *Transformation of Virginia*, 148–50. In his analysis of the long-term impact of the Great Awakening on Virginia, Isaac argues that the reactions of the ruling elite were more concerned with the social rather than the religious ramifications. This argument is plausible given that Virginians, although devout Christians for the most part, are not associated with the same degree of piety that characterized New England life, where the Great Awakening had a profound effect.

71. Kidd, *God of Liberty*, 63–64; and Isaac, *Transformation of Virginia*, 198–204.

72. Griffin, *Catalogue*, 39. See also the invoice of goods sent by Robert Cary and Company, March 1766, in Washington, *Papers of George Washington*, digital ed.

73. Griffin, *Catalogue*, 501.

74. See Washington's ledger for April 16, 1764, in Washington, *Papers of George Washington*, digital ed. Washington had these pamphlets bound into the volume "Poems on Several Occasions." Additional copies were also bound into a separate volume, "Poems, &c." Both are now in the Washington collection at the Boston Athenaeum. See also Longmore, *Invention of George Washington*, 73. Longmore argues that the controversy surrounding the Two Penny Act marked the beginning of Washington's active conversion to the emerging patriot cause as it was taking place while Washington was sinking further into debt and feeling increasingly hamstrung in his dealings with Robert Cary and Company. According to Longmore, Washington saw his personal financial struggles in a parallel vein to the emerging colonial struggle against the increasingly heavy-handed British rule. I disagree with Longmore on this point and argue again that Washington's intellectual break with Britain had begun several years earlier in the Seven Years' War.

75. Longmore, *Invention of George Washington*, 73.

76. Washington to Robert Cary and Company, September 20, 1765, in Washington, *Writings*, 2:427–31.

77. Washington, *Writings*, 2:427–31. See also Washington's letter to Francis Dandridge, September 20, 1765, in Washington, *Writings*, 2:425–26.

78. Washington's letter to Francis Dandridge, September 20, 1765, in Washington, *Writings*, 2:425–26.

79. Kennedy and McIlwane, *Journals of the House of Burgesses, 1766–69*: 211, 228.

80. For the significance of the Chiswell murder case and the Robinson scandal, see Greene, "Virtus et Libertas," in Crow and Tise, *Southern Experience*, 55–108. For an analysis of the continued rise of dissenters, see Beeman and Isaac,

"Cultural Conflict," 525–50; Isaac, "Evangelical Revolt," 348–65; and Isaac, "Religion and Authority," 3–36.

3. REVOLUTIONARY READING

1. The best description of the events surrounding the battles of Lexington and Concord is Fischer, *Paul Revere's Ride*. Fischer retraced the steps of both the British and American key players in the days leading up to the battles and the conduct of the battles themselves to such a painstaking degree that the old familiar mythologies are set aside, leaving behind an unbiased depiction of the outbreak of the war.

2. Washington to George William Fairfax, May 31, 1775, in Washington, *Papers of George Washington*, digital ed.

3. Washington's motive for wearing his uniform to the daily congressional sessions has been a matter of heated debate among historians. Those sympathetic to Washington highlight it as an example of his extreme patriotism while those with a more suspicious nature argue that his actions were a rather artless effort to secure the command of the Continental Army for himself. See Ellis, *His Excellency George Washington*, 66–70; and Flexner, *George Washington in the American Revolution*, 9–14.

4. "Address to the Continental Congress," June 16, 1775, in Washington, *Papers of George Washington*, digital ed.

5. In Washington, *Papers of George Washington*, digital ed., see Washington to Martha Washington, June 18, 1775, and Washington to John Augustine Washington, 1775.

6. Washington to Burwell Bassett, June 19, 1775, in Washington, *Papers of George Washington*, digital ed.

7. See Washington's expense accounts for June 1775 in Washington, *Papers of George Washington*, digital ed.

8. See also in Washington, *Papers of George Washington*, digital ed.: letter from the Richmond County Independent Company to Washington, March 17, 1775; letter from the Prince William Independent Company to Washington, April 26, 1775; letter from the Fairfax Independent Company to Washington, April 25, 1775; letter from the Spotsylvania Independent Company to Washington, April 26, 1775; and letter from the Albemarle Independent Company, April 29, 1775.

9. Griffin, *Catalogue*, 541. See also Washington's expense account for November 1774 in Washington, *Papers of George Washington*, digital ed.

10. Webb, *Military Treatise*, 1–110.

11. Griffin, *Catalogue*, 538.

12. Harvey, *New Manual*, 3.

13. Griffin, *Catalogue*, 539. Washington's preparedness for command has been the subject of considerable debate among biographers and military historians. See Higginbotham, *George Washington*, 43. Higginbotham argues that "too much has been made of Washington's military limitations" and that "Caesar and Cromwell, like Washington, were in their forties when they began their most serious soldiering. The duties of Grant and Lee as aides to Mexican War generals scarcely qualified them to direct hosts in the Civil War. Dwight Eisenhower, supreme allied commander in Europe during World War II, had never seen combat in a career that extended back to 1915." I disagree with Higginbotham's argument at several points. Although I understand and sympathize with Higginbotham's advocacy for Washington's natural talent for leadership, he ignores Washington's lack of a military education as a limiting factor at the outset of the Revolution. Washington's comparative age with Caesar and Cromwell is irrelevant. Moreover, the really problematic aspect of Higginbotham's argument is his comparison of Washington's lack of high command experience at the outset of the Revolution to that of Grant, Lee, and Eisenhower. It's true that Grant, Lee, and Eisenhower had not previously worn stars on their collars prior to the outbreak of the Civil War and World War II, but all three had the benefit of a West Point education and had served for years as regular army officers. They were well schooled in the military profession and were therefore more academically equipped for the exalted positions they would occupy. Washington had no such training to lean on.

14. *Essay on the Art of War*, vi.

15. *Essay on the Art of War*, 99.

16. Lengel, *General George Washington*, 106.

17. Lengel, *General George Washington*, 106–8. See also Washington to Lund Washington, August 20, 1775, in Washington, *Papers of George Washington*, Revolutionary War series, 1:336. The document is also available in the digital edition.

18. Washington, "General Orders," July 4, 1775, in Washington, *Papers of George Washington*, digital ed.

19. Lengel, *General George Washington*, 108–11; and Ellis, *His Excellency George Washington*, 81–82.

20. Washington to Richard Henry Lee, August 29, 1775, in Washington, *Papers of George Washington*, Revolutionary War series, 1:372. The document is also available in the digital edition.

21. Washington's many biographers have largely given him credit for imposing much-needed discipline on the Continental Army. While it is true that
Washington was committed to imposing discipline above any other task,
and to his credit his unceasing attention to detail enabled his success in this
endeavor, he was not the first to recognize the need to maintain respect for
civilians and their property. An independent company of volunteers under
Benedict Arnold from New Haven, Connecticut, adopted a code of conduct
on April 24, 1775, that echoed the same sentiment that Washington would
impart to the Continental Army en masse less than three months later. For
this, see Maier, *From Resistance to Revolution*, 286.

22. Washington to William Woodford, November 10, 1775, in Washington, *Papers
of George Washington*, Revolutionary War series, 2:346–47. The document is
also available in the digital edition.

23. Muller, *Treatise of Artillery*, xxxviii, 148–214.

24. See Lengel, *General George Washington*, 115; Griffith, *War for American Independence*, 212–13; and Ellis, *His Excellency George Washington*, 84–85.

25. Ellis, *His Excellency George Washington*, 84–85.

26. Washington to John A. Washington, July 22, 1776, in Washington, *Papers of
George Washington*, digital ed.

27. Muller, *Treatise Containing the Practical Part*.

28. Young, *Manoeuvres*, 26.

29. Fischer, *Washington's Crossing*, 90–98; and Lengel, *General George Washington*,
140–47. Fischer and Lengel differ somewhat on their willingness to place the
majority of the blame on Washington for the defeat on Long Island. Fischer
places nearly all of it, even those mistakes made by subordinate commanders,
on Washington because he replaced his subordinates so many times that none
of them had any real situational awareness going into the battle. Lengel is a bit
gentler on Washington, conceding that he "stumbled a bit" but that his real
mistake was in giving Putnam too much latitude. Major General Sullivan and
Brigadier General Stirling clearly had no idea what they were doing, nor did
they have control over their men. See also William Smallwood to Maryland
Convention, October 12, 1776, in Force, *American Archives*, 5th ser., 2:1011;
and Washington, "General Orders," October 25, 1776, in Washington, *Papers
of George Washington*, digital ed.

30. John Morin Scott, Brigadier General from New York, to John Jay, Member
of the Congress from New York, September 6, 1776, and "Account by Col.
Benjamin Tallmadge of Connecticut," in Commager and Morris, *Spirit of
Seventy-Six*, 444–46.

31. "Account by Col. Benjamin Tallmadge of Connecticut," in Commager and Morris, *Spirit of Seventy-Six*, 444–46. See also Washington, "General Orders," August 31, 1776, in Lengel, *Glorious Struggle*, 60–62.

32. Washington, "General Orders," August 31, 1776, in Lengel, *Glorious Struggle*, 60–62.

33. Washington to the Continental Congress, September 8, 1776, in Washington, *Papers of George Washington*, digital ed. Military historians have repeatedly praised Washington's strategic thinking. One of the most recent is Dave R. Palmer in his latest book on Washington, *George Washington's Military Genius*. In this book, Palmer characterizes the 1776 strategy as "masterpiece of strategic thought, a brilliant blueprint permitting a weak force to combat a powerful opponent" (136).

34. Washington owned a copy of Paine's *Common Sense*, which is now in the collection at the Boston Athenaeum. He obtained a copy as soon as it was released in print and thought highly of the pamphlet as being the catalyst that pushed many reluctant Americans toward embracing independence. See Griffin, *Catalogue*, 156–57. See also Washington to Joseph Reed, April 1, 1776, in Washington, *Papers of George Washington*, digital ed.

35. Paine, *American Crisis*, 1.

36. Washington was actively contemplating a major action at least a week before Christmas. The first indication of his planning was that he wrote to John Hancock and specifically asked for an extension of his decision-making authority. He normally maintained a great respect for civilian authority and remained committed to the notion of civil control over the military; however, with his soldiers' enlistments due to expire at the end of the year, he did not have the time to devise a plan, call a council of war to deliberate, and then petition Congress for a final decision. See Washington to John Hancock, December 20, 1776, in Washington, *Papers of George Washington*, digital ed.

37. In Washington, *Papers of George Washington*, digital ed., see Washington to Joseph Reed, December 23, 1776; and Washington, "General Orders," December 25, 1776. See also "Memoirs of Elisha Bostwick," partially reprinted in Commager and Morris, *The Spirit of 1776*, 511–12. See also Fischer, *Washington's Crossing*, 206–62; and Ferling, *Almost a Miracle*, 173–86.

38. Ferling, *Almost a Miracle*, 173–86.

39. Washington, "General Orders," December 27, 1776; and Washington to John Hancock, December 27, 1776, in Washington, *Papers of George Washington*, digital ed.

40. In Commager and Morris, *Spirit of Seventy-Six*, 519–23: "Account of Princeton"; "An Account of the Battle of Princeton Completed on April 18, 1777, by an Eighty-five-Year-Old Resident, Name Unknown"; and "Journal of Captain Thomas Rodney, 3 January 1777."

41. Lt. Col. Allan Maclean to Alexander Cummings, February 19, 1777, in Commager and Morris, *Spirit of Seventy-Six*, 523.

42. Fischer, *Washington's Crossing*, 206–62; and Ferling, *Almost a Miracle*, 173–86.

43. Palmer, *George Washington*, 43. Palmer argues that the campaigns of 1776 were the culminating events in Washington's military education. This argument fits nicely with mine in that Palmer suggests that Washington's tactical knowledge gained from his limited reading on the subject was put to the test in these campaigns. Just as Washington had with every other endeavor in his life, he brought knowledge to bear with experience, learning as he went along.

44. Looby, *Voicing America*, 15.

45. John Adams to Hezekiah Niles, February 13, 1818, in Adams, *Adams-Jefferson Letters*, 2:455.

46. Looby, *Voicing America*, 31.

47. Looby, *Voicing America*, 48.

48. Clark, *Language of Liberty*, 12.

49. Clark, *Language of Liberty*, 10.

50. Ball and Pocock, *Conceptual Change*, 2–3.

51. Historians have long debated the significance of the role that religion played in the American Revolution. See Berthold, *American Colonial Printing*; Bloch, "Religion and Ideological Change," in Noll, *Religion and American Politics*, 41–61; Heimert, *Religion and the American Mind*; and Bailyn, *Ideological Origins*. Many other historians since have sensed the connection between the Great Awakening and the Revolution, but they reject the notion of any direct ideological connections between the two events. See Strout, *New Heavens and New Earth*; Bonomi, *Under the Cope*; and Hatch, *Sacred Cause of Liberty*. More recently Jon Butler, in *Awash in a Sea of Faith*, cast significant doubt on any interpretation that stressed the influence of the Great Awakening on the Revolution. After Butler's more secular interpretation of the origins of revolutionary ideology, others seemed to follow in rapid succession, but they were not without their critics. See Harry Stout, "Religion, Communications, and the Career of George Whitefield," in Sweet, *Communication and Change*, 109; and Miller, "From the Covenant," in Smith and Jamison, *Shaping of American Religion*, 1:340. Much more recent is the work of Mark Noll, who in *America's God* delineated many of the connections between republican thought and

the disparate theologies of the colonials. Looby, in *Voicing America*, and Fliegelman, in *Declaring Independence*, support Noll's arguments about how the ambiguity of the colonial vocabulary enabled politics and religion to be talked about in interchangeable terms and the impact that had on audiences who listened to this rhetoric. For an even more enthusiastic interpretation of the impact of evangelical preaching on the coming of the Revolution, see Mahaffey, *Preaching Politics*.

52. Smith, *Sermon on the Present Situation*.

53. Coombe, *Sermon Preached*.

54. Kidd, *God of Liberty*, 115–30.

55. Griffin, *Catalogue*, 106.

56. Washington, "General Orders," July 9, 1776, in Washington, *Papers of George Washington*, digital ed. See also Kidd, *God of Liberty*, 118.

57. Kidd, *God of Liberty*, 118. See also Washington to Governor John Trumbull, December 15, 1775, in Washington, *Papers of George Washington*, digital ed.

58. Price, *Observations on the Nature*; and Griffin, *Catalogue*, 168–69.

59. Uzal Ogden and his family were patriots during the Revolution. Although offered various posts at southern Anglican parishes, Ogden chose to remain in New Jersey and, unlike the majority of Anglican clergy, did not become a loyalist when the war broke out. In a more multidenominational, war-torn colony, he found himself having to minister to people from various denominational affiliations, and he was comfortable borrowing some practices and ideals from them. He also was a prolific pamphleteer. The sermons cited in note 61 by Ogden pre-date the correspondence between Ogden and Washington. See the *Journals of the Diocese* and *Journals of the General Convention* at the archives of the Diocese of New Jersey, Trenton.

60. Griffin, *Catalogue*, 153–54.

61. Ogden, *Sermon on Practical Religion* (1779); and Ogden, *Sermon on Practical Religion* (1782).

62. Ogden, *Sermon Delivered at Roxbury*.

63. Griffin, *Catalogue*, 179–82.

64. Richard Henry Lee to Washington, September 26, 1775, in Washington, *Papers of George Washington*, digital ed.

65. Griffin, *Catalogue*, 59. See also William Milnor to Washington, November 29, 1774, in Washington, *Papers of George Washington*, digital ed.

66. Chandler, *Friendly Address*, 5.

67. Lee, *Strictures on a Pamphlet*, 1–4.

68. Lee, *Strictures on a Pamphlet*.

69. Griffin, *Catalogue*, 59.

70. Griffin, *Catalogue*, 57. See also Washington to George William Fairfax, July 25, 1775, in Washington, *Papers of George Washington*, digital ed.

71. Washington to George William Fairfax, July 25, 1775, in Washington, *Papers of George Washington*, digital ed. See also the editorial notes attached to the letter.

72. Griffin, *Catalogue*, 122.

73. Griffin, *Catalogue*, 156–57. Refer also to this chapter's note 51. For an analysis of *Common Sense* and its significance, see Liell, *46 Pages*.

74. These periodicals offered reprints of political essays from both sides of the Atlantic. Although the preponderance of the articles was of British origin, the periodicals featured a fair number of American authors. Over time, as tensions intensified between Great Britain and the colonies, the overall representation of American writers increased.

4. PRESIDENTIAL READING

1. "Extract of a letter from New-York, May 2," *Massachusetts Centinel* (Boston), May 23, 1789. Washington's act of kissing the Bible upon completing the oath of office has been a subject of some debate since the event took place. Four eyewitness accounts, including this anonymous newspaper account, positively attest to Washington's actions. The other three are from Samuel Otis, William A. Duer, and Eliza S. M. Quincy. Secretary of the Senate Otis's account is entered in the "Journal of the Secretary of the Senate, 1789–1813," in RG46, Records of the United States Senate [8E2/22/15/1], 187, National Archives, Washington DC. William A. Duer witnessed the ceremony from a rooftop of one of the nearest buildings to Federal Hall and claimed to have a direct line of sight to where Washington stood. "William A. Duer's Description of the Inauguration" is entered in the record of the First Federal Congress, in Bickford et al., eds., *Documentary History*, 15:396. Eliza S. M. Quincy witnessed the ceremony from the rooftop of the house on Broadway that was nearest to Federal Hall and claimed to be close enough not only to see Washington but also to hear him speak. Her account is included in her *Memoir of the Life of Eliza S. M. Quincy* (Boston: Printed by J. Wilson and Son, 1861), 52.

2. Chernow, *Washington*, 568.

3. George Washington, "First Inaugural Address, April 30, 1789," in Washington, *Writings of George Washington*, digital ed. Available from the George Washington Papers, 1741–99, Library of Congress (database online).

4. Ellis, *His Excellency George Washington*, 185–86. See also the editorial note, April 30, 1789, in Washington, *Papers of George Washington*, digital ed.

5. Alexander Hamilton, Benjamin Lincoln, Thomas Johnson, and Gouverneur Morris were among those who urged Washington to accept the presidency after the Constitution was ratified. See Leibiger, *Founding Friendship*, 100–101. See also in Hamilton, *Papers of Alexander Hamilton*: Alexander Hamilton to Washington, August 13, 1788, 5:201–2; Alexander Hamilton to Washington, September 13, 1788, 5:220–23; Washington to Alexander Hamilton, August 28, 1788, 207–8; and Washington to Alexander Hamilton, October 3, 1788, 222–24. See also Washington, *Papers of George Washington*, Presidential series: Benjamin Lincoln to Washington, September 24, 1788, 1:6–7; Thomas Johnson to Washington, October 10, 1788, 1:42; Gouverneur Morris to Washington, December 6, 1788, 1:165–66; Washington to Benjamin Lincoln, October 26, 1788, 1:71–73; Washington to Jonathan Trumbull Jr., December 4, 1788, 1:136; Washington to Lewis Morris, December 13, 1788, 1:159; and Washington to William Gordon, December 23, 1788, 1:178, 200. The documents from the *Papers of George Washington* are also available in the digital edition.

6. For one of the most recent interpretations of the impact of Roman history on the American revolutionaries, see Shalev, *Rome Reborn*. Shalev argues that Americans relied heavily on the classical world in order to articulate their attitudes toward their own history as well as the future. For an examination of how the Dutch perceived their republic in their golden age, see Schama, *Embarrassment of Riches*, 51–93. For an examination of Cromwell's protectorate in the context of the Glorious Revolution, see Pincus, *1688*, 382.

7. See this chapter's note 5, specifically Washington's responses to those who urged him to accept the presidency.

8. See notes 48–51 for chapter 3.

9. Smollett, *Complete History of England*, 1:326.

10. Washington to Fielding Lewis, February 24, 1784, in Washington, *Papers of George Washington*, digital ed.

11. Washington to Henry Knox, January 5, 1785, in Washington, *Papers of George Washington*, digital ed.

12. Washington, *Diaries of George Washington* (1976–79), 4:255. See also Walsh, *Motives of Honor*, 507. Walsh includes a criticism of Washington's plantation management in her discussion of Richard Corbin's efficiency, citing that Washington did not emplace such rigid tracking mechanisms until the 1790s. I disagree with Walsh's characterization of Washington because she neglects

the enormous fact that Washington was away from his estates for so many years during his public service.

13. In Washington, *Papers of George Washington*, digital ed., see Arthur Young to Washington, January 7, 1786; Arthur Young to Washington, February 1, 1787; Washington to Young, August 6, 1786; and Washington to Young, November 1, 1787. See also Washington's diaries from 1786 in *Papers of George Washington*, digital ed., for specific notes about how he applied Young's information to his plantations. Additionally see Griffin, *Catalogue*, 231; and Maier, *Ratification*, 8–9.

14. For the complete details of Washington's agricultural activities during this period, see his diaries from the Confederation series beginning March 11, 1786, in Washington, *Papers of George Washington*, digital ed. His daily entries record the manner in which he evaluated his estate's situation and exactly how he set about to rectify it. He noted precise quantities of crops planted by type on each of his different farms and chronicled the progress of his different agricultural experiments and renovation projects.

15. Washington, diary entry, June 30, 1785, in Washington, *Papers of George Washington*, digital ed.

16. Thompson, *"In the Hands,"* 80. See also Chernow, *Washington*, 469–70.

17. Washington to Benjamin Harrison, January 22, 1785, in Washington, *Papers of George Washington*, digital ed.

18. Washington to Benjamin Harrison, January 22, 1785, in Washington, *Papers of George Washington*, digital ed.

19. Washington to Benjamin Harrison, January 22, 1785, in Washington, *Papers of George Washington*, digital ed.

20. Washington to Henry Knox, February 28, 1785, in Washington, *Papers of George Washington*, digital ed. Washington naturally did not want people to know that he was cash poor.

21. Washington to Henry Knox, February 28, 1785, in Washington, *Papers of George Washington*, digital ed. See also Washington to Edmund Randolph, July 30, 1785, in Washington, *Papers of George Washington*, digital ed.

22. Griffin, *Catalogue*, 149, 510, 553.

23. Griffin, *Catalogue*, 506.

24. Chernow, *Washington*, 470.

25. Washington to Henry Knox, June 18, 1785, in Washington, *Papers of George Washington*, digital ed.

26. Washington to Richard Henry Lee, June 22, 1785, in Washington, *Papers of George Washington*, digital ed.

27. Washington, *George Washington's Diaries* (1999), 280.

28. Washington to Lafayette, May 28, 1788, in Washington, *Papers of George Washington*, digital ed.

29. Washington to Lt. Bezaleel Howe, November 9, 1783, in Washington, *Writings of George Washington*, 27:238.

30. Washington expressed his misgivings about Bowie's proposition in a letter to Dr. James Craik, March 25, 1784, in Washington, *Papers of George Washington*, Confederation series, 1:235. The document is also available in the digital edition.

31. In Washington, *Papers of George Washington*, digital ed., see the exchange of letters between Washington and Gordon on November 2, 1785; July 13, 1786; February 16, 1789; and February 25, 1791. See also Chernow, *Washington*, 472.

32. Washington to James Craik, March 25, 1784; and letter between Dr. William Gordon to Horatio Gates in Washington, *Papers of George Washington*, digital ed.

33. Washington to David Humphreys, July 25, 1785, in Washington, *Papers of George Washington*, digital ed.

34. Humphreys, *Life of General Washington*.

35. In Madison, *Papers of James Madison*, see the letters from James Madison to Washington for December 7, 1786, 9:200; December 24, 1786, 9:284; and February 21, 1787, 9:286.

36. In Washington, *Papers of George Washington*, digital ed., see Washington to David Humphreys, December 26, 1786; Washington to Knox, December 26, 1786; Washington to Benjamin Lincoln, February 24, 1787; and Washington to Lafayette, March 25, 1787.

37. Wood, "Interests and Disinterestedness," in Beeman, Botein, and Carter, *Beyond Confederation*, 73. See also Bradburn, *Citizenship Revolution*, 65. Perhaps the best summary of the weaknesses of the Confederation Congress is in Rakove, *Beginnings of National Politics*, 331–59.

38. Washington made his opinions on the need for a much stronger central government very plain to his like-minded friends and former associates in his many postwar letters. One such example is Washington to Henry Knox, December 5, 1784, in Washington, *Papers of George Washington*, digital ed. Further examples are in the exchange of letters between Washington and Madison. Madison first sought Washington's opinions and then sought to garner Washington's support for a convention of delegates from all the states to revise if not overhaul the Articles of Confederation, for he knew that any

such meeting would be meaningless without Washington's presence and, more important, his prestige. Ellis, *American Creation*, 92.

39. Ellis, *American Creation*, 98.

40. See Madison's letters to Washington in Washington, *Papers of James Madison*, 9:115–56, 166–67, 170–71, 199–200, 224–25; they can also be found in Washington, *Papers of George Washington*, digital ed. For Washington's reaction to his selection for Virginia's delegation, see also in Washington's *Papers of George Washington*, digital ed.: Washington to Madison, November 18, 1786; Washington to David Stuart, November 19, 1786; Washington to David Humphreys, December 26, 1786; and Washington to Henry Knox, February 3, 1787. Washington and Madison actually became close friends in the years between 1784 and 1797. For a detailed analysis of this friendship and its significance to the careers of both men and their impact on the new nation, see Leibiger, *Founding Friendship*. See also Banning, *Sacred Fire*; McCoy, *Last of the Fathers*; McDonald, *Presidency of George Washington*; Charles, *Origins of the American Party System*; Elkins and McKitrick, *Age of Federalism*; and Phelps, *George Washington*.

41. Washington to James Madison, March 31, 1787, in Washington, *Papers of George Washington*, digital ed.

42. Chernow, *Washington*, 529.

43. Chernow, *Washington*, 529.

44. George Mason quoted in Brookhiser, *Founding Father*, 66.

45. See Washington's diary entries from March through September 1787, in Washington, *Papers of George Washington*, digital ed.

46. Griffin, *Catalogue*, 516, 491–95. With regard to the periodicals specifically, Washington received *The Columbian Magazine* as a gift from the publishers. After Washington received it, he wrote back to them on January 9, 1787, in Washington, *Papers of George Washington*, digital ed., acknowledging receipt and asked to be considered to be a regular subscriber "as I conceive a publication of that kind may be the means of conveying much useful knowledge to the community which might otherwise be lost, and when it is properly conducted, it should, in my opinion be properly encouraged." Washington wrote to Mathew Carey on June 25, 1788, in Washington, *Papers of George Washington*, digital ed. In the letter, Washington commended Carey for publishing a work that was "eminently calculated to disseminate political, agricultural, philosophical and other valuable information; but that it has been uniformly conducted with taste, attention, and propriety. If to these important objects be superadded the more immediate design of rescuing

public documents from oblivion, I will venture to pronounce, as my sentiment, that a more useful literary plan has never been undertaken in America, or one more deserving public."

47. In Washington, *Papers of George Washington*, digital ed., see Washington to Marquis de Lafayette, February 7 and April 28, 1788; Washington to John Cowper, May 25, 1788; Washington to Adrian Ven Der Kemp, May 28, 1788; and Washington to Thomas Jefferson, August 31, 1788.

48. Leibiger, *Founding Friendship*, 85.

49. James Madison to Edward Everett, June 3, 1827, in Farrand, *Records of the Federal Convention*, 3:476.

50. See George Mason, "Objections to This Constitution of Government," in *Papers of George Mason*, 3:991–93.

51. See Washington to James Madison, October 10, 1787; and James Madison to Washington, October 18, 1787, in Washington, *Papers of George Washington*, digital ed.

52. In Washington, *Papers of George Washington*, digital ed., see Washington to Henry Knox, October 15, 1787; Washington to Bushrod Washington, November 10, 1787; Washington to James Wilson, April 4, 1788; and Washington to Benjamin Lincoln, April 2, 1788.

53. Washington to David Stuart, November 30, 1787, in Washington, *Papers of George Washington*, digital ed.

54. Leibiger, *Founding Friendship*, 89. For the impact that the Federalists' newspaper campaign had on the ratification in Virginia, as well as in the other states that reprinted *The Federalist* and other essays, see Maier's *Ratification*. This book offers a comprehensive examination of the ratification conventions as they played out in the different states and offers the best and most extensive review of the subject.

55. Maier, *Ratification*, 436–37.

56. See the fragments of the first inaugural address and the corresponding editorial note in Washington, *Papers of George Washington*, digital ed. The inaugural address exists now only in fragmentary form because Jared Sparks, one of the first compilers of Washington's papers in the early nineteenth century, judged the draft to be of no historical value and cut it to pieces to distribute to friends who wanted samples of Washington's handwriting.

57. James Madison to Washington, May 30, 1789, in Washington, *Papers of George Washington*, digital ed.

58. James Madison to Jared Sparks, May 30, 1827, in Sparks and Adams, *Life and Writings*, 2:211–13.

59. Washington, "First Inaugural Address: Final Version," in Washington, *Papers of George Washington*, digital ed.

60. Leibiger, *Founding Friendship*, 108.

61. Washington to Catharine Sawbridge Macaulay Graham, January 9, 1790, in Washington, *Papers of George Washington*, digital ed.

62. Elkins and McKitrick, *Age of Federalism*, 93.

63. Tench Coxe to Alexander Hamilton, March 5, 1790, in Hamilton, *Papers of Alexander Hamilton*, 8:291.

64. Ferguson, "State Assumption of Federal Debt," 406.

65. For the text of the speech, see James Madison, "Assumption of State Debts," in *Papers of James Madison*, 13:164. See also the corresponding editor's note for details regarding the speech's publication. Madison worked closely with his political mentor, Thomas Jefferson, to formulate a response to Hamilton's argument that establishing and maintaining a national debt was good for the nation's future. See Sloan, *Principle and Interest*, 133–40.

66. Ketcham, *Framed for Posterity*, 132.

67. Sharp, *American Politics*, 38–39.

68. Sharp, *American Politics*, 38–39.

69. Morgan, "George Washington," in Higginbotham, *George Washington Reconsidered*, 302.

70. Washington to Henry Lee, September 22, 1788, in Washington, *Papers of George Washington*, digital ed.

71. See Washington's diaries in Washington, *Papers of George Washington*, digital ed.

72. Waldstreicher, *In the Midst*, 121. For detailed information on the specific receptions staged for Washington during his tours, see Washington's diaries in Washington, *Papers of George Washington*, digital ed.; Griswold, *Republican Court*, 113–36, 183–202, 329–40; Henderson, *Washington's Southern Tour*; and Smith, *Patriarch*, 87–107.

73. See Washington to Alexander Hamilton, Thomas Jefferson, and Henry Knox, April 4, 1791, in Hamilton, *Papers of Alexander Hamilton*, 8:242–43.

74. See the editorial note for Washington's letters to inhabitants of the different southern cities he visited in April 1791 in Washington, *Papers of George Washington*, digital ed.

75. Washington to the inhabitants of New Bern, North Carolina, April 20–21, 1791, in Washington, *Papers of George Washington*, digital ed.

76. Washington to the inhabitants of Wilmington, North Carolina, April 25, 1791, in Washington, *Papers of George Washington*, digital ed.

77. Washington to the inhabitants of Fayetteville, North Carolina, April 26, 1791, in Washington, *Papers of George Washington*, digital ed.

78. Washington to the officials of Charleston, South Carolina, May 3, 1791, in Washington, *Papers of George Washington*, digital ed.

79. Washington to the officials of Savannah, Georgia, May 13–14, 1791, in Washington, *Papers of George Washington*, digital ed.

80. Many studies analyze the changes that took place in American language during the Revolutionary War and Early Republican eras. See Ferguson, *Reading the Early Republic*; Kramer, *Imagining Language*; Clark, *Language of Liberty*; Ball, *Transforming Political Discourse*, 47–79; Gilmore, "Letters of the Early Republic," in Bercovitch, *Cambridge History*, 541–58; Gilmore, "Magazines, Criticism, and Essays," in Bercovitch, *Cambridge History*, 558–72; Looby, *Voicing America*; and Ferguson, *Law and Letters*, 3–96.

81. Flexner, *George Washington and the New Nation*, 229; Sydnor, *Gentlemen Freeholders*, 10; and Waldstreicher, *In the Midst*, 117–26. For the impact that the cult of Washington had on American culture and politics at the end of the eighteenth century, see Albanese, *Sons of the Fathers*, 143–81; Friedman, *Inventors of the Promised Land*, 41–77; Fliegelman, *Prodigals and Pilgrims*, chap. 7; Wills, *Cincinnatus*; Schwartz, *George Washington*; Longmore, *Invention of George Washington*; and Newman, "Principles or Men?," 477–507. For the emergence of the sentimental monarchy and its parallels to popular patriotism and the making of American nationalism, see Bushman, *King and People*; Colley, *Britons*, 195–236; Schama, *Citizens*, 155–56; Hunt, *Family Romance*, chap. 4; and Wood, *Radicalism of the American Revolution* (1992), 95–100. For the art of performing power, see Geertz, "Centers, Kings, and Charisma," in *Local Knowledge*, 124.

82. One notable critic of the argument that Washington and his fellow founders deliberately had considered the elements of monarchy when infusing symbolism into the presidency is Pocock, "States, Republics, and Empires," in Ball and Pocock, *Conceptual Change*, 73–74.

83. See the quote from the *Daily Advertiser* in Unger, *Unexpected George Washington*, 245. See also Chernow, *Washington*, 579.

84. Chernow, *Washington*, 579. See also Decatur, *Private Affairs*, 68.

85. Washington to David Stuart, June 15, 1790, in Washington, *Papers of George Washington*, digital ed.

86. Thomas Jefferson's conversation with Washington, October 1, 1792, in Washington, *Papers of George Washington*, digital ed.

87. Thomas Jefferson's notes on a conversation with Washington, February 7, 1793, in Washington, *Papers of George Washington*, digital ed.

88. See the editorial note on the origins of the *National Gazette* in Madison, *Papers of James Madison*, digital ed.

89. Chernow, *Washington*, 671–74; Leibiger, *Founding Friendship*, 153–55; and Ferling, *Leap in the Dark*, 327–44.

90. Philip Freneau, "On the Funding System," *National Gazette*, no. 40 (Philadelphia: March 15, 1792): 158, in America's Historical Newspapers database online.

91. Chernow, *Alexander Hamilton*, 403.

92. See the editorial note for Madison's *National Gazette* essays, November 19, 1791–December 20, 1792, and the text of the eighteen separate essays in Madison, *Papers of James Madison*, digital ed.

93. See in Washington, *Papers of George Washington*, digital ed.: Washington to Thomas Jefferson, August 23, 1792; Washington to Alexander Hamilton, August 26, 1792; Alexander Hamilton to Washington, September 9, 1792; Thomas Jefferson to Washington, September 9, 1792; and Thomas Jefferson's Conversation with Washington, October 1, 1792. For the draft of Hamilton's fourteen-thousand-word defense, which was enclosed in his letter to Washington dated September 9, 1792, see Hamilton, *Papers of Alexander Hamilton*, 12:229–58.

94. Elizabeth Willing Powell to Washington, November 17, 1792, in Washington, *Papers of George Washington*, digital ed.

95. Chernow, *Washington*, 686.

96. See the letter from Veritas to Washington, May 30, 1793, in Washington, *Papers of George Washington*, digital ed.

97. See the letter from Veritas to Washington, June 3, 1793, in Washington, *Papers of George Washington*, digital ed.

98. Chernow, *Washington*, 698; and Ferling, *Leap in the Dark*, 360–65.

99. Griffin, *Catalogue*, 91–95.

100. Washington, "Proclamation," September 25, 1794, in Washington, *Writings of George Washington*, 33:507–8. This document is also found in Washington, *Papers of George Washington*, digital ed.

101. Washington, "Proclamation," September 25, 1794, in Washington, *Writings of George Washington*, 33:507–8. This document is also found in Washington, *Papers of George Washington*, digital ed.

102. For a comprehensive examination of the Whiskey Rebellion, see Slaughter, *Whiskey Rebellion*.

103. Washington appointed Monroe as minister to France in 1794 in a move that he hoped would placate Republicans. However, the evidence indicated that once in France, Monroe did not uphold the administration's policy of neutrality and displayed a blatant favoritism toward the French. He made matters worse when he leaked some of the details of the Jay Treaty to a French official, inciting anger. Washington recalled him and replaced him with Charles Cotesworth Pinckney in July 1796. Monroe was seething by the time he returned to Philadelphia and published his defense, *A View of the Conduct of the Executive in the Foreign Affairs of the United States*. Washington obtained a copy of the book and was enraged. He filled more than sixty pages of the book's margins with bluntly worded remarks: "Self-importance appears here," "insanity to the extreme," and "curious and laughable." Jared Sparks printed Washington's comments in part in his edition of Washington's papers; Ford printed them in full in his edition of Washington's writing, *The Writings of George Washington*, 13:452–90. Of note Monroe's book is the only example of biting criticism that Washington retained in his library.

104. Sandoz, foreword to *Political Sermons*, 1:xii. See also Noll, *America's God*, 56–57.

105. Pasley, *Tyranny of Printers*, 24–78.

106. Smith, *A Sermon, on Temporal and Spiritual Salvation*.

107. Morse, *Present Situation of Other Nations*.

108. Mason, *Mercy Remembered*, 1.

109. Kendal, *Sermon*; and Osgood, *Discourse Delivered*.

110. Evans, *Sermon, Delivered at Concord*.

111. Langdon, *Discourse on the Unity*.

112. Davidson, *Sermon, on the Freedom*.

113. Miller, *Sermon, Preached in New York*; Linn, *Blessings of America*; and Stillman, *Thoughts on the French Revolution*.

114. Fisher, *Reply to the False Reasoning*. See also Washington to David Stuart, June 8, 1797, in Washington, *Papers of George Washington*, digital ed. In this letter, Washington commented on Paine's attack, which was printed by Benjamin Franklin Bache, the *Aurora*'s publisher. What is so interesting about the timing of Paine's attack on Washington is that after Paine was released from prison, he went to live with James Monroe, who was then serving his brief stint as the American minister in Paris. It is assumed that Monroe composed his savage attack on Washington's administration while Paine was in residence. Having been stung by both Paine and Monroe, Washington seemed to make a point of collecting at least some of the works by Paine's most vociferous critics.

5. A LEGACY LIBRARY

1. John Adams to Abigail Adams, March 16, 1797, quoted in Freeman, *George Washington*, 7:437. See also Ferling, *John Adams*, 334–35.

2. Washington was notified of his mother's death by Burgess Ball, who was married to George Augustine Washington's sister Frances. See Ball's letter, August 25, 1789, in Washington, *Papers of George Washington*, digital ed. George Augustine Washington died on February 5, 1793; see Bryan Fairfax to Washington, February 17, 1793, in Washington, *Papers of George Washington*, digital ed. Betty Washington Lewis died on March 31, 1797; see Washington's reference to her death in a letter to his nephew, George Lewis, April 9, 1797, and the corresponding editorial note in Washington, *Papers of George Washington*, digital ed.

3. Washington's last sibling, Charles, died on September 16, 1799. Washington was notified by Burgess Ball, and Washington replied that he "was the first, and now am the last, of my fathers Children by the second marriage who remain. When I shall be called upon to follow them, is known only to the giver of life. When the summons comes I shall endeavor to obey it with a good grace." The death of his mother, brothers, sister, and nephew within a few years of each other evidently affected Washington, making him aware of his own advancing age and declining health and faculties. See Washington to Burgess Ball, September 22, 1799, in Washington, *Papers of George Washington*, digital ed.

4. With regard to the other southern founders not freeing their slaves, see Sloan, *Principle and Interest*, 11–12. Sloan seems to hint that Jefferson felt conflicted over the status and future of his slaves but effectively was unable to emancipate them because he was so deeply in debt. Sloan, however, tempers this point by highlighting that in all of Jefferson's writings that chronicle his thoughts on his unceasing problems with personal debt, Jefferson is silent about the ramifications that this debt had on his slaves.

5. Washington to James McHenry, May 29, 1797, in Washington, *Papers of George Washington*, digital ed.

6. Washington to Oliver Wolcott, Jr., May 15, 1797, in Washington, *Papers of George Washington*, digital ed.

7. Griffin, *Catalogue*, 202–12.

8. Chernow, *Washington*, 777.

9. Washington to Clement Biddle, September 15, 1797, in Washington, *Papers of George Washington*, digital ed. Washington's letter makes it clear that he wanted this specific book and not just any available history, for in his order he

specified that Biddle should "send me the History of the United States . . . the one which contains No's 5 and 6 alluded to in Col'o Hamilton's late Pamphlet." This request indicates that in his final retirement Washington was keeping current not only with political affairs but also with what was being written about them. He maintained an interest in history books as useful devices for shaping public opinion. See also Griffin, *Catalogue*, 40.

10. Griffin, *Catalogue*, 84.

11. Gallatin, *Examination of the Conduct*, 2.

12. Gallatin, *Examination of the Conduct*, 2–72.

13. Gallatin, *Examination of the Conduct*, 2–72. See also Washington to Alexander Addison, June 3, 1798, in Washington, *Papers of George Washington*, digital ed. Washington wrote that he had read both Gallatin's and Addison's respective works "with equal attention & satisfaction; and although it has been justly observed in one of them that to offer conviction to a person convinced before . . . is labor lost, yet, much good may & I am persuaded will result, from the investigation of political heresies."

14. Addison, *Observations on the Speech*, 1–52.

15. Griffin, *Catalogue*, 107, 75.

16. Griffin, *Catalogue*, 75.

17. Burke, *Two Letters*, 5.

18. Thomas Erskine, *A View of the Causes and Consequences of the Present War with France*, 5th ed. (Boston: Printed for Adams and Larkin, Court-Street, and E. Larkin, no. 47 Cornhill, 1797), 1–100.

19. Griffin, *Catalogue*, 207. For further details on the extent to which Pickering kept Washington informed and supplied with publications pertaining to government affairs, see the correspondence between Washington and Pickering between April 5, 1797, and October 24, 1799, in Washington, *Papers of George Washington*, digital ed.

20. Timothy Pickering to Washington, January 20, 1798, in Washington, *Papers of George Washington*, digital ed.

21. John Gifford, *A Letter to the Honorable Thomas Erskine, Containing Some Strictures on His View of the Causes and Consequences of the Present War with France* (Philadelphia: Published by William Cobbett, Opposite Christ-Church, 1797), 1–128.

22. Timothy Pickering, *A Letter from Mr. Pickering, a Secretary for the Department of State of the United States — to Mr. Pinckney, Minister Plenipotentiary of the United States of America, at Paris* (Stockbridge MA: Printed by Rosseter and Willard, 1797), 6.

23. Washington to John Adams, July 13, 1798, in Washington, *Papers of George Washington*, digital ed.

24. Washington to John Adams, September 25, 1798, in Washington, *Papers of George Washington*, digital ed.

25. John Adams to Washington, October 9, 1798, in Washington, *Papers of George Washington*, digital ed.

26. Chernow, *Washington*, 783–93; Ferling, *John Adams*, 348–71; Ferling, *Leap in the Dark*, 410–27; and Elkins and McKitrick, *Age of Federalism*, 601–5.

27. Washington to Robert Morris, April 12, 1786, in Washington, *Papers of George Washington*, Confederation series, 4:16. The document is also available in the digital ed.

28. Dalzell and Dalzell, *George Washington's Mount Vernon*, 211. See also Washington to Lawrence Lewis, August 4, 1797, in Washington, *Papers of George Washington*, digital ed.

29. Wiencek, *Imperfect God*, 353–54. Wiencek accepts the validity of the story of Washington's dream foreshadowing his 1799 death. Its authenticity has most recently been challenged by Peter Henriques, who called into question several inconsistencies in the story. See Henriques, *Death of George Washington*, 77. If there is any truth in the 1799 story, it was likely passed orally from Martha Washington to her descendants, who in turn told Lossing. See also Fields, *"Worthy Partner,"* 272–73, 321–22; and Flexner, *George Washington*, 4:149.

30. Washington to Arthur Young, December 12, 1793, in Washington, *Papers of George Washington*, digital ed.

31. Washington to Tobias Lear, May 6, 1794, in Washington, *Writings of George Washington*, 33:367–60.

32. Griffin, *Catalogue*, 557.

33. Wiencek, *Imperfect God*, 354.

34. See George Washington's "Last Will and Testament" in Washington, *Papers of George Washington*, digital ed.

35. Washington, "Last Will and Testament," in Washington, *Papers of George Washington*, digital ed.

36. Washington, "Last Will and Testament," in Washington, *Papers of George Washington*, digital ed.

37. Washington, "Last Will and Testament," in Washington, *Papers of George Washington*, digital ed.

38. Washington, "Last Will and Testament," in Washington, *Papers of George Washington*, digital ed.

39. Washington, "Last Will and Testament," in Washington, *Papers of George Washington*, digital ed.

40. Dalzell and Dalzell, *George Washington's Mount Vernon*, 217.

41. Dalzell and Dalzell, *George Washington's Mount Vernon*, 219. See also Washington, "Last Will and Testament," in Washington, *Papers of George Washington*, digital ed.

42. Washington, "Last Will and Testament," in Washington, *Papers of George Washington*, digital ed.

43. Dalzell and Dalzell, *George Washington's Mount Vernon*, 219.

44. Lee, *Funeral Oration*.

6. A PLACE FOR SECLUDED STUDY

1. Conversation between Gen. Henry Lee and George Washington recorded by George Washington Parke Custis and cited in his *Recollections and Private Memoirs*, 454.

2. Custis, *Recollections and Private Memoirs*, 454.

3. Greenberg, *George Washington, Architect*, 12. Greenberg is a former classical architecture professor at Yale University and Law School, Columbia University, and the University of Pennsylvania who works on architectural commissions. His book focuses on the aesthetics of Mount Vernon without providing a great deal of historical context, but Greenberg makes an important connection between Washington's design of the estate and his mental world. It is important to further develop Greenberg's allusion in the historical context, for it helps to inform the discussion of precisely how Washington engaged in the act of reading.

4. Latrobe, *Virginia Journals*, 165–66.

5. Niemcewicz, *Under Their Vine*, 97.

6. Abigail Adams to Mrs. Richard Cranch, December 21, 1800, cited in Mount Vernon Ladies Association, *Annual Report* (1957). The original letter is in the collections at the Massachusetts Historical Society, Boston.

7. George Washington to William Thornton, October 1, 1799, in Washington, *Writings of George Washington*, 37:387. The document is also available in Washington, *Papers of George Washington*, digital ed. See also George Washington, "Memorandum," dated November 5, 1796, in Washington, *Writings of George Washington*, 35:263–64, in which Washington discusses how to prepare the sand and apply it to the paint; and "Restoration Painting," in Mount Vernon Ladies Association, *Annual Report* (1956), 15.

8. Greenberg, *George Washington, Architect*, 67–69.

9. Greenberg, *George Washington, Architect*, 32. For a further explanation of the architectural details listed, see also Harris and Higgot, *Inigo Jones*, 129–35; Harris, *The Palladians*, 48–49; Langley, *Builder's Jewel*, plate 75; and Mosca, "The House and Its Restoration," 464.

10. Mosca, "The House and Its Restoration," 464. See also Kelso, *Kingsmill Plantations*, 23–25; Waterman, *Mansions of Virginia*; Whiffen, *Eighteenth-Century Houses*; and Upton, "Vernacular Architecture," 197.

11. Glassie, *Folk Housing*, 189–90. See also Isaac, *Transformation of Virginia*, 36–37.

12. Longmore, *Invention of George Washington*, 3.

13. Greenberg, *George Washington, Architect*, 24. See also Charles E. Brownell, "Mount Vernon," in Brownell et al., *Making of Virginia Architecture*, 206.

14. Greenberg, *George Washington, Architect*, 22–24.

15. Greenberg, *George Washington, Architect*, 24.

16. Greenberg, *George Washington, Architect*, 27. See also Deetz, *In Small Things Forgotten*, 126. See also George Washington to George Augustine Washington, June 3, 1787, in Washington, *Papers of George Washington*, 29:228. The document is also available in the digital edition.

17. Greenberg, *George Washington, Architect*, 62.

18. Bushman, *Refinement of America*, 114.

19. Mesick, Cohen, Waite, Architects, *Historic Structure Report*, 2:297, 302.

20. Greenberg, *George Washington, Architect*, 65; Langley, *City and Country Builder's*, plate 6; Palladio, *Four Books of Architecture*, book 1, plate 20; and Langley, *Builder's Jewel*, plate 23.

21. Mosca, "House and Its Restoration," 468; and Swan, *British Architect*, plates 50 and 51.

22. Greenberg, *George Washington, Architect*, 65. To enrich the context for Washington's diversification of his plantation operations, see Walsh, *Motives of Honor*, 472–538. Walsh makes the point that only the most daring planters risked planting wheat. Washington was one of the first to attempt large-scale wheat production and struggled. This point is discussed more fully in chapter 4.

23. Greenberg, *George Washington, Architect*, 65–67.

24. Brady, *Martha Washington*, 68.

25. George Washington to Mary Ball Washington, February 15, 1787, in Washington, *Papers of George Washington*, Confederation series, 5:35. The document is also available in the digital edition.

26. Swan, *British Architect*, plate 50.

27. See the series of letters between George Washington and Lund Washington between August and November 1775, in Washington, *Papers of George*

Washington, digital ed. The letter he wrote to Lund Washington that specifically gets to the heart of Washington's need to mentally escape to Mount Vernon and maintain a sense that he had control over it is dated August 20, 1775. He provides a summary of his position in Cambridge and resorts to making a lengthy list of instructions for Lund for paying and assigning millers and carpenters, safekeeping the crops harvested from the fields, procuring certain cloth, putting pressure on the craftsmen working on the dining room chimney piece, repairing the rustication of the both the new and old kitchens, boarding up a well, seeing to the painter's accounts, sowing wheat in the ground, and determining which horses were to be used to accomplish the work. That this letter swings back and forth between a discussion of the litany of problems with the army and detailed instructions for activities at home suggests that Washington was exasperated under the weight of the immense pressure on him and that he needed to have a firm grip on the things that were within his ability to control. Lund Washington's reply, dated October 15, 1775, painstakingly answers each point raised in the previous letter. He is remarkably deferential. He makes recommendations on how to proceed with various projects but awaits further instructions before acting, even though as the on-site overseer he is in a much better position to decide how best to handle construction matters. Such issues are separate from those concerning decorative taste, which is the purview of the owner alone.

28. Lund Washington to George Washington, November 12, 1775, in Washington, *Papers of George Washington*, Revolutionary War series, 2:356. The document is also available in the digital edition.

29. George Washington to Lund Washington, September 30, 1776, in Washington, *Papers of George Washington*, Revolutionary War series, 6:442. The document is also available in the digital edition.

30. Langley, *City and Country Builder's*, plate 51. The text that explains the proper placement and use of the design is on page 18.

31. Greenberg, *George Washington, Architect*, 70.

32. Greenberg, *George Washington, Architect*, 77.

33. Custis, *Recollections and Private Memoirs*, 527–28.

34. Dalzell and Dalzell, *George Washington's Mount Vernon*, 15–16.

35. Dalzell and Dalzell, *George Washington's Mount Vernon*, 15–16.

36. Email exchange with Ted Crackel, August 21, 2012, regarding Washington's use of his study as a refuge from the many people in and around Mount Vernon on a daily basis. See also Washington to Lawrence Lewis, August 4, 1797,

in Washington, *Papers of George Washington*, digital ed. Washington asked Lewis to live with him at Mount Vernon and assume some of Washington's hospitality responsibilities. Washington wrote that constant company was troublesome given that "it is my inclination to retire . . . either to bed, or to my study, soon after candlelight."

37. Dalzell and Dalzell, *George Washington's Mount Vernon*, 98.

38. Griffin, *Catalogue*, 482–566.

39. Park, *List of Architectural Books*. Park not only lists both the architectural books that were available in the colonies from Britain but also includes the cities in which reprint editions were produced in subsequent years. The considerable list of titles, along with the numerous editions available up and down the Eastern Seaboard, supports the assumption that Washington would have had no problem gaining access to copies of the different manuals from which he gleaned inspiration. Since he did not intend to assiduously copy any design, it seems logical that he would leaf through the books that he could access and simply take the few details that he wanted to incorporate in Mount Vernon's design. For a discussion of the particular books that Park identifies as being most prevalent in Virginia, see Whiffen, *Eighteenth-Century Houses*, 58–65.

40. Refer to the argument that Deetz made about the significance of vernacular architecture in his book *In Small Things Forgotten*: "Vernacular structures are the immediate product of their users and form a sensitive indicator of these persons' inner feelings, their ideas of what is or is not suitable to them. Consequently, changes in attitude, values, and worldview are very likely to be reflected in changes in vernacular architectural forms" (126). The circumstances of both Washington and Jefferson losing their fathers at a young age and having cool relationships with their mothers led each man to make new homes that were their own. The development of Washington's worldview, although certainly inspired by Britain, was a sort of progression away from embracing a British identity and toward developing a new, distinct American one. Jefferson's worldview was conversely shaped by his embrace of European and Enlightenment ideas gleaned from his extensive formal education through the College of William and Mary; his legal studies under George Wythe, who introduced him to Virginia's other educated and erudite men; his travel to Europe and his long residence there; and above all his desire to cultivate and train his mind in the classical European tradition.

41. Flexner, *George Washington*, 1:17.

42. McLaughlin, *Jefferson and Monticello*, 33.

43. The term "disinterested" is commonly used in reference to the founders and

their political careers, and it refers to their not seeking financial gain from public service. One sees the term used quite a bit in the political language of the day. The idea was that the people only wanted virtuous men who were financially self-sufficient in public offices; they assumed the men served because they genuinely wanted to support the public good and were not in it for the money.

44. Stein, *Worlds of Thomas Jefferson*, 12. Stein argues that "Jefferson's Monticello is woven out of both American self-confidence and absorption with the arts of eighteenth-century France; of both untutored innocence of taste and a remarkable sophistication. It is, in short, not the story of a single world but of the series of worlds that Jefferson made at Monticello."

45. Bushman, *Refinement of America*, 127.

46. Breen, "Meaning of Things," in Brewer and Porter, *Consumption*, 250.

47. Dalzell and Dalzell, *George Washington's Mount Vernon*, 53–54; and Breen, "Meaning of Things," in Brewer and Porter, *Consumption*, 251.

48. Breen, "Meaning of Things," in Brewer and Porter, *Consumption*, 257.

49. Stein, *Worlds of Thomas Jefferson*, 103–10.

50. McLaughlin, *Jefferson and Monticello*, 157.

51. McLaughlin, *Jefferson and Monticello*, 20.

52. Custis, *Recollections and Private Memoirs*, 167.

53. Whiffen, *Eighteenth-Century Houses*, 174, 193.

54. Hayes, *Road to Monticello*, 60–61.

55. Girouard, *Life in the English Country House*, 166–70, 178–80.

CONCLUSION

1. Washington to George Washington Parke Custis, November 15, 1796, in Custis, *Recollections and Private Memoirs*, 73.

2. Washington to George Washington Parke Custis, November 28, 1796, in Custis, *Recollections and Private Memoirs*, 73.

SELECTED BIBLIOGRAPHY

Adams, John. *The Adams-Jefferson Letters: The Complete Correspondence between Thomas Jefferson and Abigail and John Adams.* Edited by Lester J. Cappon. Chapel Hill: University of North Carolina Press, 1988.

———. *The Diary and Autobiography of John Adams.* Edited by L. H. Butterfield, Leonard C. Faber, and Wendell D. Garrett. Cambridge MA: Belknap Press of Harvard University Press, 1961.

———. *The Works of John Adams.* 10 vols. Boston: Little, Brown, 1856.

Adams, John, Thomas Jefferson, and Benjamin Rush. *Old Family Letters: Contains Letters of John Adams, All but the First Two Addressed to Dr. Benjamin Rush; One Letter from Samuel Adams, One from John . . . Dr. Rush.* Philadelphia: J. B. Lippincott, 1892.

Addison, Alexander. *Observations on the Speech of Albert Gallatin, in the House of Representatives of the United States, on the Foreign Intercourse Bill.* Washington PA: Printed by John Colerick, 1798.

Albanese, Catherine L. *Sons of the Fathers: The Civil Religion of the American Revolution.* Philadelphia: Temple University Press, 1976.

Amory, Hugh, and David D. Hall, eds., *A History of the Book in America.* Vol. 1, *The Colonial Book in the Atlantic World.* New York: Cambridge University Press, 1999.

Anderson, Fred. *Crucible of War: The Seven Years' War and the Fate of Empire in British North America, 1754–1766.* New York: Vintage, 2001.

Anson, George. *A Voyage Round the World in the Years MDCCXL, I, II, III, IV, by George Anson, Esq; Afterwards Lord Anson . . . Compiled from His Papers and Materials, by Richard Walter.* 6th ed. London: n.p., 1746.

Bailyn, Bernard. *The Ideological Origins of the American Revolution.* Cambridge MA: Harvard University Press, 1992.

———. *The Ordeal of Thomas Hutchinson.* Cambridge MA: Belknap Press of Harvard University Press, 1974.

Ball, Terence. *Transforming Political Discourse: Political Theory and Critical Conceptual History.* New York: Basil Blackwell, 1988.

Ball, Terence, and J. G. A. Pocock. *Conceptual Change and the Constitution.* Lawrence: University Press of Kansas, 1988.

Banning, Lance. *Sacred Fire: James Madison and the Founding of the Federal Republic.* Ithaca NY: Cornell University Press, 1978.

Beeman, Richard, and Rhys Isaac. "Cultural Conflict and Social Change in the Revolutionary South: Lunenburg County, Virginia." *Journal of Southern History* 46 (1980): 525–50.

Bernard, Jean-François. *Remarks on the Modern Fortification, to Which Is Added the Easiest and Most Reasonable Manner of Constructing All Sorts of Works. . . .* Translated by William Horneck. London: J. and R. Tonson, 1738.

Berthold, Arthur Benedict. *American Colonial Printing as Determined by Contemporary Cultural Forces, 1639–1763.* New York: Burt Franklin, 1934.

Bickford, Charlene Bangs, Kenneth R. Bowling, William Charles diGiacomantonio, and Helen E. Veit, eds. *Correspondence: First Session, March–May 1789.* Vol. 15 of *Documentary History of the First Federal Congress of the United States of America, March 4, 1789–March 3, 1791.* Baltimore: Johns Hopkins University Press, 2004.

Bisset, Charles. *The Theory and Construction of Fortification.* London: S. Buckley, 1727.

Blackall, Offspring. *The Sufficiency of a Standing Revelation in General, and of the Scripture Revelation in Particular. Both as to the Matter of It, and as to the Proof of It; . . . In Eight Sermons. . . . by Offspring Blackall.* London: H. Hills, 1769.

Bland, Humphrey. *A Treatise of Military Discipline: In Which Is Laid Down and Explained the Duty of the Officer and Soldier, thro' the Several Branches of the Service.* London: S. Buckley, 1727.

Bloch, Ruth. "Religion and Ideological Change in the American Revolution." In *Religion and American Politics: From the Colonial Period to the 1980s,* edited by Mark A. Noll, 41–61. New York: Oxford University Press, 1989.

Bonomi, Patricia. *Under the Cope of Heaven: Religion, Society, and Politics in Colonial America.* New York: Oxford University Press, 1986.

Bradburn, Douglas. *The Citizenship Revolution: Politics and the Creation of the American Union, 1774–1804.* Charlottesville: University of Virginia Press, 2009.

Brady, Patricia. *Martha Washington: An American Life.* New York: Viking, 2005.

Breen, T. H. "The Meaning of Things: Interpreting the Consumer Economy in the Eighteenth Century." In *Consumption and the World of Goods*, edited by John Brewer and Roy Porter, 249–60. New York: Routledge, 1994.

———. *Tobacco Culture: The Mentality of the Great Tidewater Planters on the Eve of Revolution*. 2nd pbk. ed. Princeton NJ: Princeton University Press, 2001.

Brookhiser, Richard. *Founding Father: Rediscovering George Washington*. New York: Free Press, 1997.

Brown, Richard D. *Knowledge Is Power: The Diffusion of Information in Early America, 1700–1865*. New York: Oxford University Press, 1989.

Brownell, Charles E., Calder Loth, William M. S. Rasmussen, and Richard Guy Wilson. *The Making of Virginia Architecture*. Charlottesville: University Press of Virginia, 1992.

Burke, Edmund. *Two Letters Addressed to a Member of the Present Parliament, on the Proposals for Peace with the Regicide Directory of France*. Philadelphia: Printed for William Cobbett, in Second Street, Opposite Christ-Church, and J. Ormrod, no. 41, Chestnut Street, by Bioren and Madan, 1797.

Bushman, Richard L. *King and People in Provincial Massachusetts*. Chapel Hill: University of North Carolina Press for the Institute of Early American History and Culture, 1985.

———. *The Refinement of America: Persons, Houses, Cities*. New York: Vintage, 1993.

Butler, Jon. *Awash in a Sea of Faith: Christianizing the American People*. Cambridge MA: Harvard University Press, 1990.

Caesar, Julius. *Julius Caesar's Commentaries of His Wars in Gaul, and Civil War with Pompey. To which Is Added, a Supplement to His Commentary of His Wars in Gaul; as also, Commentaries of the Alexandrian, African, and Spanish Wars, by Aulus Hirtius or Oppius, &c. With the Author's Life. Adorn'd with Sculptures from the Designs of the Famous Palladio*. Translated by Col. Martin Bladen. London: Printed by T. Wood for J. & J. Knapton, 1732.

Callender, James Thomson. *The History of the United States for 1796; Including a Variety of Interesting Particulars Relative to the Federal Government Previous to That Period*. Philadelphia: Press of Snowden & M'Corkle, 1797.

Carroll, Frances Laverne, and Mary Meacham. *The Library at Mount Vernon*. Pittsburgh PA: Beta Phi Mu, 1977.

Casper, Scott E. *Constructing American Lives: Biography and Culture in Nineteenth-Century America*. Chapel Hill: University of North Carolina Press, 1999.

———. *Sarah Johnson's Mount Vernon: The Forgotten History of an American Shrine*. New York: Hill and Wang, 2009.

Chandler, Thomas Bradbury. *A Friendly Address to All Reasonable Americans, on the Subject of Our Political Confusions in Which the Necessary Consequences of Violently Opposing the King's Troops, and of a General Non-Importation Are Fairly Stated.* New York: n.p., 1774.

Chaplin, Joyce. *The First Scientific American: Benjamin Franklin and the Pursuit of Genius.* New York: Basic Books, 2007.

Charles, Joseph. *The Origins of the American Party System: Three Essays.* Chapel Hill: University of North Carolina Press, 1956.

Chernow, Ron. *Alexander Hamilton.* New York: Penguin Press, 2004.

———. *Washington: A Life.* New York: Penguin Press, 2010.

Clark, J. C. D. The Language of Liberty Political Discourse and Social Dynamics in the Anglo-American World, 1660–1832. Cambridge: Cambridge University Press, 1994.

———. *The Language of Liberty, 1660–1832: Political Discourse and Social Dynamics in the Anglo-American World.* New York: Cambridge University Press, 1994.

Colburn, H. Trevor. *The Lamp of Experience: Whig History and the Intellectual Origins of the American Revolution.* Chapel Hill: University of North Carolina Press, 1965.

Colley, Linda. "Britishness and Otherness: An Argument." *Journal of British Studies* 31, no. 4 (October 1992): 309–29.

———. *Britons: Forging the Nation, 1707–1837.* New Haven CT: Yale University Press, 1992.

Comber, Thomas. *Short Discourses upon the Whole Common-Prayer: Designed to Inform the Judgment, and Excite the Devotion as Such as Daily Use the Same.* 4th ed. London: J. Nicholson, 1712.

Commager, Henry Steele, and Richard B. Morris, eds. *The Spirit of Seventy-Six: The Story of the American Revolution as Told by Its Participants.* New York: Harper Collins, 2002.

Contrecoeur. *A Memorial Containing a Summary View of Facts, with Their Authorities, in Answer to the Observations Sent by the English Ministry to the Courts of Europe.* New York: H. Gaine, 1757.

Coombe, Thomas. *A Sermon Preached before the Congregations of Christ-Church and St. Peter's, Philadelphia, on Thursday, July 20, 1775. Being the Day Recommended by the Honorable Continental Congress for a General Fast throughout the Twelve United Colonies of North-America. By Thomas Coombe, M.a. Chaplain to the Most Noble the Marquis of Rockingham.* Philadelphia: n.p., 1775.

Custis, George Washington Parke. *Recollections and Private Memoirs of George Washington*. 1860. Reprint, Bridgewater VA: American Foundation Publications, 1999.

Dalzell, Robert F., Jr., and Lee Baldwin Dalzell. *George Washington's Mount Vernon: At Home in Revolutionary America*. New York: Oxford University Press, 2000.

Dann, John C., ed. *The Revolution Remembered: Eyewitness Accounts of the War for Independence*. Chicago: University of Chicago Press, 1983.

Darnton, Robert. *The Great Cat Massacre and Other Episodes in French Cultural History*. New York: Vintage Books, 1985.

Davidson, Robert. *Sermon on the Freedom and Happiness of the United States of America, Preached in Carlisle, on the 5th October 1794, and Published at the Request of the Officers of the Philadelphia and Lancaster Troops of Light Horse*. Philadelphia: Samuel Harrison Smith, 1794.

Davis, Richard Beale. *A Colonial Southern Bookshelf: Reading in the Eighteenth Century*. Athens: University of Georgia Press, 1979.

———. *Intellectual Life in the Colonial South, 1585–1763*. 3 vols. Knoxville: University of Tennessee Press, 1978.

Decatur, Stephen, Jr. *Affairs of George Washington: From the Records and Accounts of Tobias Lear, Esquire, His Secretary*. Boston: Houghton Mifflin, 1933.

Deetz, James. *In Small Things Forgotten: An Archaeology of Early American Life*. Expanded and rev. ed. New York: Anchor Books, 1996.

De Fonblanque, Edward B. *Political and Military Episodes . . . from the Life and Correspondence of John Burgoyne, General*. London: n.p., 1876.

de Luzancy, H. *A Panegyrick to the Memory of His Grace Frederick, Late Duke of Schonberg*. London: R. Bentley, 1690.

Dinwiddie, Robert. *The Official Records of Robert Dinwiddie: Lieutenant-Governor of the Colony of Virginia, 1751–1758*. 2 vols. Richmond: Virginia Historical Society, 1933–34.

Diocese of New Jersey. *Journals of the Diocese of New Jersey, 1785–Present*. Trenton: Diocese of New Jersey, 1785–.

———. *Journals of the General Convention, 1785–Present*. Trenton: Diocese of New Jersey, 1785–.

Duhamel du Monceau, Henri-Louis. *A Practical Treatise of Husbandry: Wherein Are Contained, Many Useful and Valuable Experiments and Observations in the New Husbandry, Etc. . . .* 2nd ed. London: C. Hitch and L. Hawes, et al., 1762.

Elkins, Stanley, and Eric McKitrick. *The Age of Federalism: The Early American Republic, 1788–1800*. New York: Oxford University Press, 1993.

Ellis, Joseph J. *American Creation: Triumphs.* New York: Alfred A. Knopf, 2007.

———. *His Excellency: George Washington.* New York: Alfred A. Knopf, 2004.

Essay on the Art of War: In Which the General Principles of All the Operations of War in the Field Are Fully Explained; the Whole Collected from the Opinions of the Best Authors. London: Printed for A. Millar, 1761.

Evans, Emory G. *A "Topping People": The Rise and Decline of Virginia's Old Political Elite, 1680–1790.* Charlottesville: University of Virginia Press, 2009.

Evans, Israel. *A Sermon, Delivered at Concord, before the Honorable General Court of the State of New Hampshire, at the Annual Election, Holden on the First Wednesday in June, M.DCC.XCI.* Concord NH: George Hough, 1791.

Everett, Edward. *The Life of George Washington.* New York: Sheldon, 1860.

Ewald, Johann. *Diary of the American War: A Hessian Journal.* Edited by Joseph P. Tustin. New Haven CT: Yale University Press, 1979.

Fabel, Robin. "The Patriotic Briton: Tobias Smollett and English Politics, 1756–1771." *Eighteenth Century Studies* 8, no. 1 (Autumn 1974): 100–114.

Farrand, Max, ed. *The Records of the Federal Convention of 1787.* Rev. ed. 4 vols. New Haven CT: Yale University Press, 1974.

Fauquier, Francis, and George Henkle Reese. *The Official Papers of Francis Fauquier, Lieutenant Governor of Virginia, 1758–1768.* Edited by George Reese. Charlottesville: University of Virginia Press, 1981.

Ferguson, E. James. "State Assumption of Federal Debt during the Confederation." *The Mississippi Valley Historical Review* 38, no. 3 (December 1951): 403–24.

Ferguson, Robert A. *Law and Letters in American Culture.* Cambridge MA: Harvard University Press, 1984.

———. *Reading the Early Republic.* Cambridge MA: Harvard University Press, 2004.

Ferling, John. *Almost a Miracle: The American Victory in the War of Independence.* New York: Oxford University Press, 2007.

———. *The Ascent of George Washington: The Hidden Political Genius of an American Icon.* New York: Bloomsbury Press, 2009.

———. *The First of Men: A Life of George Washington.* New York: Oxford University Press, 2010.

———. *John Adams: A Life.* New York: Henry Holt, 1996.

———. *A Leap in the Dark: The Struggle to Create the American Republic.* New York: Oxford University Press, 2003.

Fields, Joseph, ed. *"Worthy Partner": The Papers of Martha Washington.* Westport CT: Greenwood Press, 1994.

Fischer, David Hackett. *Albion's Seed: Four British Folkways in America.* Vol. 1 of *America: A Cultural History.* New York: Oxford University Press, 1989.

———. *Paul Revere's Ride.* New York: Oxford University Press, 1995.

———. *Washington's Crossing.* New York: Oxford University Press, 2004.

Fisher, Miers. *A Reply to the False Reasoning in the "Age of Reason": To Which Are Added, Some Thoughts on Idolatry; on the Devil; and the Origin of Moral Evil; on Educating Young Men for the Gospel Ministry; and on What Is "the Word of God"; All Which Refer, More or Less, to Opinions Advanced in Thomas Paine's "Investigation of True and Fabulous Theology," by a Layman.* Philadelphia: Henry Tuckniss, 1796.

Flexner, James Thomas. *George Washington and the New Nation: 1783–1793.* Vol. 3. New York: Little, Brown, 1970.

———. *George Washington in the American Revolution (1775–1783).* Vol. 2. New York: Little, Brown, 1968.

———. *George Washington: Anguish and Farewell (1793–1799).* Vol. 4. Boston: Little, Brown, 1972.

———. *George Washington: The Forge of Experience, 1732–1775.* Vol. 1. New York: Little, Brown, 1965.

Fliegelman, Jay. *Declaring Independence: Jefferson, Natural Language and the Culture of Performance.* Stanford CA: Stanford University Press, 1993.

———. *Prodigals and Pilgrims: The American Revolution against Patriarchal Authority, 1750–1800.* New York: Cambridge University Press, 1982.

Force, Peter. *American Archives: Fifth Series, Containing a Documentary History of the United States of America from the Declaration of Independence, July 4, 1776, to the Definitive Treaty of Peace with Great Britain, September 3, 1783.* 3 vols. Washington DC: M. St. Clair Clarke and Peter Force, 1848–53.

Ford, Worthington C., ed. *Journals of the Continental Congress.* 24 vols. Washington DC: Government Printing Office, 1904–37.

Franklin, Benjamin. *The Autobiography of Benjamin Franklin.* 1788. Reprint, New York: Tribeca Books, 2011.

———. *Experiments and Observations on Electricity: Made at Philadelphia in America, by Mr. Benjamin Franklin, and Communicated in Several Letters to Mr. P. Collinson of London, F.R.S.* 1750. Reprint, Farmington Hills MI: Gale Ecco, Sabin Americana, 2012.

———. *The Papers of Benjamin Franklin.* Edited by Leonard W. Labaree. 37 vols. New Haven CT: Yale University Press, 1959–.

Freeman, Douglas Southall. *George Washington: A Biography.* 7 vols. New York: Charles Scribner's Sons, 1948–57.

————. *Washington*. New York: Scribner, 1968.

Friedman, Lawrence J., *Inventors of the Promised Land*. New York: Alfred A. Knopf, 1975.

Gallatin, Albert. *An Examination of the Conduct of the Executive of the United States, towards the French Republic; Likewise an Analysis of the Explanatory Article of the British Treaty — in a Series of Letters, by a Citizen of Pennsylvania*. Philadelphia: Printed by Francis and Robert Bailey, 1797.

Geertz, Clifford. "Centers, Kings, and Charisma: Reflections on the Symbolics of Power." In *Local Knowledge: Further Essays in Interpretive Anthropology*, 121–46. New York: Basic Books, 1983.

Gilmore, Michael T. "Letters of the Early Republic." In *The Cambridge History of American Literature*, vol. 1, *1590–1820*, edited by Sacvan Bercovitch, 541–58. New York: Cambridge University Press, 1994.

————. "Magazines, Criticism, and Essays." In *The Cambridge History of American Literature*, vol. 1, *1590–1820*, edited by Sacvan Bercovitch, 558–72. New York: Cambridge University Press, 1994.

Girouard, Mark. *Life in the English Country House: A Social and Architectural History*. New Haven CT: Yale University Press, 1994.

Glassie, Henry. *Folk Housing in Middle Virginia: A Structural Analysis of Historic Artifacts*. Knoxville: University of Tennessee Press, 1976.

Gordon-Reed, Annette. *The Hemingses of Monticello: An American Family*. Reprint, New York: W. W. Norton, 2009.

Grant, James. *John Adams: Party of One*. New York: Farrar, Straus and Giroux, 2005.

Greenberg, Allan. *George Washington, Architect*. London: Andreas Papadakis, 1999.

Greene, Jack P. "Virtus et Libertas: Political Culture, Social Change, and the Origins of the American Revolution in Virginia, 1763–1776." In *The Southern Experience in the American Revolution*, edited by Jeffrey J. Crow and Larry E. Tise, 55–65. Chapel Hill: University of North Carolina Press, 1979.

Grenier, Fernand, ed. *Papiers Contrecoeur et autres documents concernant le conflit anglo-français sur l'Ohio de 1745 à 1756*. Quebec: Presses universitaires Laval, 1952.

Griffin, Appleton P. C. *A Catalogue of the Washington Collection in the Boston Athenæum*; 1897. Reprint, Ithaca: Cornell University Library, 2009.

Griffith, Samuel B., II. *The War for American Independence: From 1760 to the Surrender at Yorktown in 1781*. Urbana: University of Illinois Press, 2002.

Griswold, Rufus Wilmot. *The Republican Court; or American Society in the Days of Washington*. 2nd ed. New York: D. Appleton, 1867.

Grizzard, Frank E., Jr. *The Ways of Providence: Religion and George Washington*. Buena Vista VA: Mariner, 2005.

Gruber, Ira D. *Books and the British Army in the Age of the American Revolution.* Chapel Hill: University of North Carolina Press, 2010.

Habermas, Jürgen. *The Structural Transformation of the Public Sphere: An Inquiry into a Category of Bourgeois Society.* Studies in Contemporary German Social Thought. Translated by Thomas Burger. Cambridge MA: Harvard University Press, 1989.

Hamilton, Stanislaus Murray, ed. *Letters to Washington and Accompanying Papers.* 1898. 5 vols. Reprint, Ithaca: Cornell University Library, 2009.

Harris, John. *The Palladians.* London: Trefoil Books, 1981.

Harris, John, and Gordon Higgot. *Inigo Jones: Complete Architectural Drawing.* New York: Harper & Row, 1989.

Harvey, Edward. *A New Manual, and Platoon Exercise: With an Explanation.* London: 1764.

Hatch, Nathan O. *The Sacred Cause of Liberty: Republican Thought and the Millennium in Revolutionary New England.* New Haven CT: Yale University Press, 1977.

Hayes, Kevin J. *The Road to Monticello: The Life and Mind of Thomas Jefferson.* New York: Oxford University Press, 2008.

Heimert, Alan. *Religion and the American Mind: From the Great Awakening to the Revolution.* Cambridge MA: Harvard University Press, 1966.

Henderson, Archibald. *Washington's Southern Tour, 1791.* Boston: Houghton Mifflin, 1923.

Henriques, Peter R. *The Death of George Washington: He Died as He Lived.* Mount Vernon: Mount Vernon Ladies Association, 2000.

Higginbotham, Don. *George Washington and the American Military Tradition.* Lamar Memorial Lectures, No 27. Athens: University of Georgia Press, 1987.

————. *Reconsiderations on the Revolutionary War: Selected Essays.* Westport CT: Greenwood Press, 1978.

Houlding, John. *Fit for Service: The Training of the British Army, 1715–1795.* New York: Oxford University Press, 1981.

Humphreys, David. *Life of General Washington: With George Washington's Remarks.* Edited by Rosemarie Zagarri. Athens: University of Georgia Press, 2006.

Hunt, Lynn. *The Family Romance of the French Revolution.* Berkeley: University of California Press, 1992.

Isaac, Rhys. "Evangelical Revolt: The Nature of the Baptists' Challenge to the Traditional Order in Virginia, 1774–1776." *William and Mary Quarterly* 31 (1974): 348–65.

————. "Religion and Authority: Problems of the Anglican Establishment in Virginia in the Era of the Great Awakening and the Parsons' Cause." *William and Mary Quarterly* 30 (1973): 3–36.

———. *The Transformation of Virginia, 1740–1790*. Chapel Hill: University of North Carolina Press, 1999.

Isaacson, Walter. *Benjamin Franklin: An American Life*. New York: Simon & Schuster, 2003.

Jefferson, Thomas. *The Writings of Thomas Jefferson*. Edited by Albert Ellery Bergh and Andrew A. (Adgate) Lipscomb. 20 vols. Washington DC: Issued under the auspices of the Thomas Jefferson Memorial Association of the United States, 1903.

Kelso, William M. *Kingsmill Plantations, 1619–1800: Archaeology of Country Life in Colonial Virginia*. Studies in Historical Archaeology. Charlottesville: University of Virginia Press, 2004.

Kendal, Samuel. *A Sermon, Delivered on the Day of National Thanksgiving, February 19, 1795*. Boston: Samuel Hall, 1795.

Kennedy, John Pendleton, and H. R. McIlwane, eds. *Journals of the House of Burgesses of Virginia*. 13 vols. Richmond: Colonial Press, 1905–15.

Ketcham, Ralph. *Framed for Posterity: The Enduring Philosophy of the Constitution*. Lawrence: University Press of Kansas, 1993.

Kidd, Thomas S. *God of Liberty: A Religious History of the American Revolution*. New York: Basic Books, 2010.

Kramer, Michael P. *Imagining Language in America: From the Revolution to the Civil War*. Princeton NJ: Princeton University Press, 1992.

Langdon, Samuel. *A Discourse on the Unity of the Church as a Monumental Pillar of the Truth; Designed to Reconcile Christians of All Parties and Denominations in Charity and Fellowship, as One Body in Christ; Delivered before an Association of Ministers Convened at Portsmouth, October 12, 1791, and in Substance Repeated at a Lecture in Hampton Falls, January 26, 1792*. Exeter NH: Henry Ranlet, 1791.

Langford, Paul. *Englishness Identified: Manners and Character, 1650–1850*. Oxford: Oxford University Press, 2002.

Langley, Batty. *The Builder's Jewel: Or the Youth's Instructor, and Workman's Remembrancer: Explaining Short and Easy Rules, Made Familiar to the Meanest Capacity, for Drawing and Working*, 12th ed. Edinburgh: Printed for R. Clark, Bookseller in the Parliament-house, 1768.

———. *The City and Country Builder's and Workman's Treasury of Designs: Or the Art of Drawing and Working the Ornamental Parts of Architecture*. London: By S. Harding, 1745.

Latrobe, Benjamin Henry. *The Virginia Journals of Benjamin Henry Latrobe, 1795–1798*. Vol. 2, *1797–1798*. Edited by Edward C. Carter II. New Haven CT: Yale University Press, 1977.

Lee, Charles. *Strictures on a Pamphlet, Entitled, "A Friendly Address to All Reasonable Americans, on the Subject of Our Political Confusions in Which the Necessary Consequences of Violently Opposing the King's Troops, and of a General Non-importation Are Fairly Stated": Addressed to the People of America*. Philadelphia: William and Thomas Bradford, 1774.

Lee, Henry. *Funeral Oration on the Death of George Washington*. Philadelphia: John Hoff, 1800.

Leibiger, Stuart. *Founding Friendship: George Washington, James Madison, and the Creation of the American Republic*. Constitutionalism and Democracy Series. Charlottesville: University of Virginia Press, 1999.

Lengel, Edward G. *General George Washington: A Military Life*. New York: Random House, 2005.

———. *This Glorious Struggle: George Washington's Revolutionary War Letters*. New York: Harper Collins, 2007.

Liell, Scott. *46 Pages: Thomas Paine, Common Sense, and the Turning Point to American Independence*. Philadelphia: Running Press, 2003.

Linn, William. *The Blessings of America: A Sermon Preached at the Middle Dutch Church, on the Fourth July 1791, Being the Anniversary of the Independence of America at the Request of the Tammany Society, or Columbian Order*. New York: Thomas Greenleaf, 1791.

Longmore, Paul K. *The Invention of George Washington*. Charlottesville: University of Virginia Press, 1999.

Looby, Christopher. *Voicing America: Language, Literary Form, and the Origins of the United States*. Chicago: University Of Chicago Press, 1996.

Lossing, Benson J. *The Home of Washington, or Mount Vernon and Its Associations, Historical, Biographical, and Pictorial*. New York: Virtue & Yorston, 1870.

Machiavelli, Niccolò. *Libro della Arte della Guerra*. Florence, 1519.

Mackesy, Piers. *The War for America, 1775–1783*. Lincoln: University of Nebraska Press, 1993.

Madison, James. *The Papers of James Madison*. Edited by William T. Hutchinson, Robert A. Rutland, and John C. A. Stagg. 34 vols. Charlottesville: University Press of Virginia, 1962–.

———. *The Papers of James Madison*. Edited by John C. A. Stagg. Digital ed. Charlottesville: University Press of Virginia, 2010–15.

Mahaffey, Jerome D. *Preaching Politics: The Religious Rhetoric of George Whitefield and the Founding of a New Nation*. Waco TX: Baylor University Press, 2007.

Maier, Pauline. *From Resistance to Revolution: Colonial Radicals and the Development of American Opposition to Britain, 1765–1776*. New York: W. W. Norton, 1991.

————. *Ratification: The People Debate the Constitution, 1787–1788.* New York: Simon & Schuster, 2010.

Mancall, Peter C. *Hakluyt's Promise: An Elizabethan's Obsession for an English America.* New Haven CT: Yale University Press, 2007.

Mason, George. *The Papers of George Mason, 1725–1792.* Edited by Robert A. Rutland. 3 vols. Chapel Hill: University of North Carolina Press, 1970.

Mason, John M. *Mercy Remembered in Wrath: A Sermon, the Substance of Which Was Preached on the 19th of February, 1795, Observed throughout the United States as a Day of Thanksgiving and Prayer.* New York: John Buel, 1795.

McConville, Brendan. *The King's Three Faces: The Rise and Fall of Royal America, 1688–1776.* Chapel Hill: University of North Carolina Press, 2007.

McCoy, Drew R. *The Last of the Fathers: James Madison and the Republican Legacy.* Cambridge MA: Harvard University Press, 1989.

McDonald, Forrest. *The Presidency of George Washington.* Lawrence: University Press of Kansas, 1974.

McLaughlin, Jack. *Jefferson and Monticello: The Biography of a Builder.* Reprint, New York: Holt Paperbacks, 1990.

McMurtrie, Douglas C. *The Beginnings of the Printing Press in Virginia.* Lexington VA: Printed in the Journalism laboratory of Washington and Lee University, 1935.

Mesick, Cohen, and Waite Architects. *Historic Structure Report.* 3 vols. Mount Vernon: Mount Vernon Ladies Association, 1993.

Miller, Perry. "From the Covenant to the Revival." In *The Shaping of American Religion.* Vol. 1 of *Religion in American Life,* edited by James W. Smith and A. Leland Jamison, 340–61. Princeton NJ: Princeton University Press, 1961.

Miller, Samuel. *A Sermon, Preached in New York, July 4th 1793; Being the Anniversary of the Independence of America: At the Request of the Tammany Society, or Columbian Order.* New York: Thomas Greenleaf, 1793.

Monck, George. *Observations upon Military and Political Affairs . . .* London: Printed by A. C. for Henry Mortlocke and James Collins, 1671.

Monroe, James. *A View of the Conduct of the Executive in the Foreign Affairs of the United States.* Philadelphia: Printed by and for Benjamin Franklin Bache, 1797.

Morgan, Edmund S. "George Washington: The Aloof American." In *George Washington Reconsidered,* edited by Don Higginbotham, 287–308. Charlottesville: University Press of Virginia, 2001.

Morse, Jedidiah. *The Present Situation of Other Nations of the World, Contrasted with Our Own: A Sermon, Delivered at Charlestown, in the Commonwealth of Massachusetts, February 19, 1795; Being the Day Recommended by George Washington,*

President of the United States of America, for Publick Thanksgiving and Prayer.
Boston: Samuel Hall, 1795.

Mosca, Matthew John. "The House and Its Restoration." *The Magazine Antiques: Mount Vernon,* February 1989.

Mount Vernon Ladies Association. *Annual Report.* Mount Vernon: Mount Vernon Ladies Association, 1956.

——— . *Annual Report.* Mount Vernon: Mount Vernon Ladies Association, 1957.

Muller, John. *A Treatise Containing the Practical Part of Fortification in Four Parts for the Use of the Royal Academy of Artillery at Woolwich.* London: Printed for A. Millar in the Strand, 1764.

——— . *A Treatise of Artillery . . . to Which Is Prefixed, an Introduction, with a Theory of Powder Applied to Fire-Arms.* London: John Millan, Whitehall, 1768.

Newman, Gerald. *The Rise of English Nationalism: A Cultural History, 1740–1830.* New rev. ed. Hampshire: Palgrave Macmillan, 1997.

Newman, Simon P. "Principles or Men? George Washington and the Political Culture of National Leadership, 1776–1801." *Journal of the Early Republic* 7 (1992): 477–507.

Niemcewicz, Julian Ursyn. *Under Their Vine and Fig Tree: Travels through America in 1797–1799, 1805, with Some Further Account of Life in New Jersey.* Translated by Metchie J. E. Budka. Elizabeth NJ: Grassman, 1965.

Noll, Mark A. *America's God: From Jonathan Edwards to Abraham Lincoln.* New York: Oxford University Press, 2002.

Ogden, Uzal. *A Sermon Delivered at Roxbury, in Morris County, March 19, 1781: At the Funeral of Mrs. Hackett, Relict of Colonel John Hackett.* Chatham: Shepard Kollock, 1781.

——— . *A Sermon on Practical Religion.* Chatham: Shepard Kollock, 1782.

——— . *A Sermon on Practical Religion: Delivered at Newark, New Jersey, August 15, 1779.* Chatham: Shepard Kollock, 1779.

Osgood, David. *A Discourse Delivered February 19, 1795: The Day Set Apart by the President for a General Thanksgiving through the United States.* Boston: Samuel Hall, 1795.

Pacheco, Josephine F., ed. *To Secure the Blessings of Liberty: Rights in American History.* New York: University Press of America, 1993.

Paine, Thomas. *The Age of Reason: Being an Investigation of True and Fabulous Theology.* London: Barlow, 1794.

——— . *The American Crisis.* Philadelphia: 1776.

——— . *Common Sense.* Philadelphia: 1776.

——— . *Rights of Man.* Mineola NY: Dover Publications, 1999.

Palladio, Andrea. *The Four Books of Architecture*. 1570. Reprint, Boston: MIT Press, 2002.

Palmer, Dave R. *George Washington: First in War*. Mount Vernon: Mount Vernon Ladies Association, 2000.

———. *George Washington's Military Genius*. Washington DC: Regnery History, 2012.

Pargellis, Stanley L., ed. *Military Affairs in North America, 1748–1765*. New York: Archon Books, 1969.

Park, Helen. *A List of Architectural Books Available in America before the Revolution*. Rev. ed. Los Angeles: Hennessey & Ingalls, 1973.

Pasley, Jeffrey L. *The Tyranny of Printers: Newspaper Politics in the Early American Republic*. Charlottesville: University of Virginia Press, 2001.

Phelps, Glenn A. *George Washington and American Constitutionalism*. American Political Thought. Lawrence: University Press of Kansas, 1993.

Pincus, Steve. *1688: The First Modern Revolution*. New Haven CT: Yale University Press, 2009.

Pocock, J. G. A. *The Ancient Constitution and the Feudal Law: A Study of English Historical Thought in the Seventeenth Century: A Reissue with a Retrospect*. Cambridge: Cambridge University Press, 1987.

———. "States, Republics, and Empires: The American Founding in Early Modern Perspective." In *Conceptual Change and the Constitution*, edited by Terrence Ball and J. G. A. Pocock, 55–77. Lawrence: University Press of Kansas, 1988.

Price, Richard. *Observations on the Nature of Civil Liberty, the Principles of Government, and the Justice and Policy of the War with America: To Which Is Added, an Appendix Containing a State of the National Debt, an Estimate of the Money Drawn from the Public by the Taxes, and Account of the National Income and Expenditure Since the Last War*. London: T. Cadell, 1776.

Rakove, Jack N. *The Beginnings of National Politics: An Interpretive History of the Continental Congress*. New York: Alfred A. Knopf, 1979.

Ramsay, Chevalier. *The Travels of Cyrus: To Which Is Annexed, a Discourse upon the Theology and Mythology of the Pagans*. 7th ed. London: James Bettenham, 1745.

Randall, Willard Sterne. *George Washington: A Life*. New York: Holt Paperbacks, 1998.

Reed, William Bradford. *Life and Correspondence of Joseph Reed*. 1847. 2 vols. Reprint, Boston: Adamant Media, 2001.

Richards, William. *Reflections on French Atheism and on English Christianity*. Lynn: Printed by William Turner, 1794.

Rozbicki, Michal J. *Culture and Liberty in the Age of the American Revolution*. Charlottesville: University of Virginia Press, 2011.

Sandoz, Ellis, ed. *Political Sermons of the American Founding Era, 1730–1805*. 2nd ed. 2 vols. Indianapolis: Liberty Fund, 1998.

Schama, Simon. *Citizens: A Chronicle of the French Revolution*. New York: Random House, 1989.

———. *Embarrassment of Riches—Interpretation of Dutch Culture in the Golden Age*. New York: Alfred A. Knopf, 1987.

Schwartz, Barry. *George Washington: The Making of an American Symbol*. Ithaca: Cornell University Press, 1990.

Shalev, Eran. *Rome Reborn on Western Shores: Historical Imagination and the Creation of the American Republic*. Charlottesville: University of Virginia Press, 2009.

Sharp, James Roger. *American Politics in the Early Republic: The New Nation in Crisis*. New Haven CT: Yale University Press, 1993.

Sharpe, Kevin. *Reading Revolutions: The Politics of Reading in Early Modern England*. New Haven CT: Yale University Press, 2000.

Sheffling, Charles, and Cynthia Shattuck. *The Oxford Guide to the Book of Common Prayer: A Worldwide Survey*. New York: Oxford University Press, 2006.

Slaughter, Thomas P. *The Whiskey Rebellion: Frontier Epilogue to the Revolution*. New York: Oxford University Press, 1988.

Sloan, Herbert E. *Principle and Interest: Thomas Jefferson and the Problem of Debt*. Charlottesville: University Press of Virginia, 2001.

Smith, Richard Norton. *Patriarch: George Washington and the New American Nation*. Boston: Houghton Mifflin, 1993.

Smith, William. *A Sermon on the Present Situation of American Affairs, Preached at Christ-Church, June 23, 1775, at the Request of the Officers of the Third Battalion of the City of Philadelphia, and District of Southwark*. Philadelphia: James Humphries, 1775.

———. *A Sermon, on Temporal and Spiritual Salvation: Delivered in Christ-Church, Philadelphia, before the Pennsylvania Society of the Cincinnati*. Philadelphia: Thomas Dobson, 1790.

Smollett, Tobias George. *A Complete History of England, from the Descent of Julius Caesar to the Treaty of Aix la Chapelle, 1748, Containing the Transactions of One Thousand Eight Hundred and Three Years*. 11 vols. London: For J. Rivington and J. Fletcher, at the Oxford Theatre, 1757–65.

Sparks, Jared. *The Life of George Washington*. Boston: F. Andrews, 1839.

———. *Washington Writings: Being His Correspondence, Addresses, Messages, and Other Papers, Official and Private*. 12 vols. Boston: 1827–37.

Sparks, Jared, and Herbert B. Adams. *The Life and Writings of Jared Sparks, Comprising Selections from His Journals and Correspondence.* Vol. 1. Boston: Houghton Mifflin, 1893.

Stein, Susan. *The Worlds of Thomas Jefferson at Monticello.* New York: Harry N. Abrams, 1993.

Stillman, Samuel. *Thoughts on the French Revolution: A Sermon, Delivered November 20, 1794: Being the Day of Annual Thanksgiving.* Boston: Manning and Loring, 1795.

Strout, Cushing. *The New Heavens and New Earth: Political Religion in America.* New York: Harper & Row, 1974.

Summerson, John. *Inigo Jones.* New Haven CT: Paul Mellon Centre BA, Yale University Press, 2000.

Swan, Abraham. *The British Architect, or, the Builder's Treasury of Staircases.* London: n.p., 1745.

Sweet, Leonard I., ed. *Communication and Change in Religious History.* Grand Rapids: Eerdmans, 1993.

Sydnor, Charles. *Gentlemen Freeholders: Political Practices in Washington's Virginia.* Chapel Hill: University of North Carolina Press, 1952.

Syrett, Harold C., ed. *The Papers of Alexander Hamilton.* 27 vols. New York: Columbia University Press, 1961–79.

Thompson, Mary V. *"In the Hands of a Good Providence": Religion in the Life of George Washington.* Charlottesville: University of Virginia Press, 2008.

Toland, John, ed. *The Oceana of James Harrington and His Other Works.* London: Printed and to be sold by Booksellers of London and Westminster, 1700.

Unger, Harlow Giles. *The Unexpected George Washington: His Private Life.* Hoboken: John Wiley and Sons, 2006.

Upton, Dell. "Vernacular Architecture in Eighteenth-Century Virginia." *Winterthur Portfolio* 17 (Summer–Autumn 1982): 197.

Waldstreicher, David. *In the Midst of Perpetual Fetes: The Making of American Nationalism, 1776–1820.* Chapel Hill: University of North Carolina Press, 1997.

Walsh, Lorena S. *Motives of Honor, Pleasure, and Profit: Plantation Management in the Colonial Chesapeake, 1607–1763.* Chapel Hill: University of North Carolina Press, 2010.

Washington, George. *Diaries.* Edited by Donald Jackson and Dorothy Twohig. Charlottesville: University Press of Virginia, 1976.

———. *Diaries, 1748–1799.* Edited by John C. Fitzpatrick. 4 vols. New York: Houghton Mifflin, 1925.

————. *The Diaries of George Washington.* Edited by Donald Jackson and Dorothy Twohig. 6 vols. Charlottesville: University Press of Virginia, 1976–79.

————. *The Diaries of George Washington: An Abridgement.* Edited by Dorothy Twohig. Charlottesville: University Press of Virginia, 1999.

————. *George Washington's Rules of Civility.* Translated by John T. Phillips. Leesburg VA: Goose Creek Productions, 2005.

————. *George Washington's Rules of Civility and Decent Behaviour in Company and Conversation.* Edited by Dr. J. M Toner. Washington DC: W. H. Morrison, 1888.

————. *The Journal of Major George Washington, Sent by the Hon. Robert Dinwiddie, Esq., His Majesty's Lieutenant-Governor, and Commander in Chief of Virginia, to the Commandant of the French Forces in Ohio.* Williamsburg: William Hunter, 1754.

————. *The Papers of George Washington.* Colonial Series. Edited by W. W. Abbot, Dorothy Twohig, and Philander Chase. 10 vols. Charlottesville: University of Virginia Press, 1993–95.

————. *The Papers of George Washington.* Confederation Series. Edited by W. W. Abbot. 6 vols. Charlottesville: University of Virginia Press, 1992–97.

————. *The Papers of George Washington.* Digital ed. Edited by Theodore J. Crackel. Charlottesville: University of Virginia Press, Rotunda, 2008.

————. *The Papers of George Washington.* Presidential Series. Edited by W. W. Abbot and Dorothy Twohig. 11 vols. Charlottesville: University of Virginia Press, 1985–.

————. *The Papers of George Washington.* Retirement Series. Edited by Dorothy Twohig. 7 vols. Charlottesville: University of Virginia Press, 1985–97.

————. *The Papers of George Washington.* Revolutionary War Series. Edited by W. W. Abbot, Dorothy Twohig, Philander D. Chase, Theodore J. Crackel, and Edward G. Lengel. 20 vols. Charlottesville: University of Virginia Press, 1985–.

————. *Quotations of George Washington.* Bedford MA: Applewood Books, 2003.

————. *The Writings of George Washington from the Original Manuscript Sources, 1745–1799.* Edited by John C. Fitzpatrick. Washington DC: Government Printing Office, 1931–44.

Waterman, Thomas Tiletson. *Mansions of Virginia, 1706–1776.* Chapel Hill: University of North Carolina Press, 1946.

Webb, Thomas. *A Military Treatise on the Appointments of the Army. Containing Many Useful Hints, Not Touched upon before by Any Author: and Proposing Some New Regulations in the Army, Which Will Be Particularly Useful in Carrying on the War in North-America; Together with a Short Treatise on Military Honors.* Philadelphia: W. Dunlap, 1759.

Weintraub, Stanley. *General Washington's Christmas Farewell: A Mount Vernon Homecoming, 1783*. New York: Free Press, 2003.

Whiffen, Marcus. *The Eighteenth-Century Houses of Williamsburg*. Rev. ed. Williamsburg Architectural Studies. Williamsburg: Colonial Williamsburg Foundation, 1984.

Wiencek, Henry. *An Imperfect God: George Washington, His Slaves, and the Creation of America*. New York: Farrar, Straus and Giroux, 2003.

Wills, Garry. *Cincinnatus: George Washington and the Enlightenment*. Garden City NY: Doubleday, 1984.

Wilson, Kathleen. "Empire, Trade, and Popular Politics in Mid-Hanoverian England: The Case of Admiral Vernon." *Past and Present* no. 121 (1988): 74–109.

———. *The Sense of the People: Politics, Culture, and Imperialism in England, 1715–1785*. 1st pbk. ed. Cambridge: Cambridge University Press, 1998.

Wood, Gordon. *The Americanization of Benjamin Franklin*. New York: Penguin Press, 2004.

———. *The Creation of the American Republic, 1776–1787*. Chapel Hill: University of North Carolina Press, 1998.

———. "Interests and Disinterestedness in the Making of the Constitution." In *Beyond Confederation: Origins of the Constitution and American National Identity*, edited by Richard Beeman, Stephen Botein, and Edward C. Carter II, 69–109. Chapel Hill: University of North Carolina Press, 1987.

———. *The Radicalism of the American Revolution*. New York: Random House, 1991, 1992.

Wright, Louis B. *The First Gentlemen of Virginia: Intellectual Qualities of the Early Colonial Ruling Class*. Charlottesville: University of Virginia Press, 1964.

Young, William. *Manoeuvres, or Practical Observations on the Art of War*. London: Printed for J. Millan, 1771.

INDEX

GW = George Washington

Act of Toleration of 1689, 90

Adams, Abigail, 202

Adams, John: diary of, 15, 84; and
GW, compared, 5–6, 62, 97, 200,
227; on GW's intellect, 1–2, 9; on
Hume's *History of England*, 85; and
marginalia, 60; nominates GW as
commander of revolutionary army,
101; presidential inauguration of,
181; on reading, importance of, 84–
85; and rhetoric of the American
Revolution, 126–27; and threat of
war with France, 184–88; and U.S.
Constitution ratification, 155

Adams, Samuel, 99

Addison, Alexander, 185, 270n13

Adolphus, Gustavus, 38

The Adventures of Peregrine Pickle
(Smollett), 237n13

Age of Reason (Paine), 179

Albemarle, Duke of, 37

Alexander the Great, 38

Alexandria Academy, 195–96

The American Crisis (Paine), 119, 135

American Magazine, 155

The American Museum (Carey), 155

American Philosophical Society, 49

American Revolution: black soldiers in,
108, 189; defeat at New York, 114–19;
GW as commander-in-chief, 99–137;
GW's collection of political tracts
and periodicals on, 133–36; GW's
collection of sermons on, 127–33;
GW's strategy development, 124–26,
256n33; rhetoric of, 126–27; role of
religion in, 257n51; siege of Boston,
112–14; victory at Princeton, 123;
victory at Trenton, 119–22, 123–24

Annals of Agriculture, 144–45

Annapolis Convention, 152

Annual Register for 1781, 136

Annual Register for 1782, 136

Anson, Lord, 67–68

Anti-federalists, 156–57, 167

*An Appeal to the Justice and Interests of
the People of Great Britain* (Lee), 135

*An Appendix to the Representation
(Printed in the Year 1769) of the
Injustice and Dangerous Tendency of
Tolerating Slavery* (Sharp), 132, 190

atheism, 179

Attorney's Pocket Book (Meriton), 88

59–97, 245n9; revolutionary and military, 11–12, 70–73, 99–137, 225; while in Virginia Regiment, 35–39, 240n46; youthful, 22–24, 246n17

Washington, George Augustine, 182, 269n2

Washington, Lawrence, 21–22, 24, 68, 84, 207–8, 212, 224

Washington, Lund, 8, 144, 210, 273n27

Washington, Martha: books belonging to in GW's library, 14, 62–63; character of, 71–72; children of, 71, 221; education of, 237n3; entertaining at Mount Vernon, 168; and foreshadowing of GW's death, 271n29; during GW's retirement at Mount Vernon, 199, 212; marriage to GW, 71–73, 79; press attacks on, 168; raising her grandchildren, 158, 221–22; redecorating Mount Vernon, 209; Robert Cary and Company as agent of, 216; slaves owned by, 191–92

Washington, Mary Ball, 20–22, 65–67, 68, 236n3, 269n2

Wayne, Anthony, 173

Webb, George, 88

Webb, Thomas, 104

Webster, Noah, 148, 155

Wedderburn, Alexander, 51, 53

Weems, Mason Locke, 4, 19, 22, 246n12

Wesley, John, 132

Whately, Thomas, 52

What Think Ye of the Congress Now (Chandler), 134

whiskey excise tax, 162, 173

Whiskey Rebellion, 173–75, 177

Whitefield, George, 89

Wilson, James, 174

Wilson, Woodrow, 4

Wolcott, Oliver, 183

Wolfe, James, 70

Woods, Joseph, 191

Woodward, William, 4

Wythe, George, 46, 218, 275n40

Young, Arthur, 144–45, 190

Young, William, 105, 115–16